GOOD GRIEF

A COLLECTION OF STORIES AS ONE WOMAN JOURNEYS FROM HEARTBREAK TO HEALING THROUGH HONESTY AND HUMOR

BOBBIE LIPPMAN

DANCING MOON PRESS
NEWPORT, OREGON

Good Grief: A collection of stories as one woman journeys from heartbreak to healing through honesty and humor
copyright © Bobbie Lippman, 2016
All rights reserved

Publisher's Note: Without limiting the rights under copyright reserved above, no part of this publication may be reproduced, stored in, or introduced into a retrieval system, or transmitted in any form, or by any means (electronic, mechanical, photocopying, recording, or otherwise) without the prior written permission of the author except in the case of brief quotations or sample images embedded in critical articles or reviews. The scanning, uploading, and distribution of any part of this book via the Internet, or via any other means, without the permission of the author is illegal and punishable by law. Please purchase only authorized editions and do not participate in or encourage electronic piracy of copyrightable materials. Your support of the author's rights is appreciated. For permission, address your inquiry to: bobbisbeat@aol.com

All proceeds from this book to the ROTARY FOUNDATION of ROTARY INTERNATIONAL

Paperback ISBN: 978-1-937493-97-4
Ebook ISBN: 978-1-937493-98-1
Library of Congress Control Number: 2016944251

Lippman, Bobbie
Good Grief: A collection of stories as one woman journeys from heartbreak to healing through honesty and humor
1. Grieving; 2. Grieving-humor; 3. Grieving-short stories; 4. Healing from Grief; 5. Death, Grief, Breavement. I. TITLE

Book editing, design & production: *Carla Perry, Dancing Moon Press*
Cover design & production: *Sarah Gayle, Sarah Gayle Art*
Cover photo of the Yaquina Bay Bridge: *Gina Nielsen*
Author photo: *by Colin Park*
Manufactured in the United States of America

DANCING MOON PRESS

P.O. Box 832, Newport, OR 97365
541-574-7708
www.dancingmoonpress.com
info@dancingmoonpress.com

FIRST EDITION

Dedication

This book is dedicated to my husband, Burt, the love of my life. He nagged me for years to put my writings into book form, but tackling such a daunting task was never on my bucket list. It took his sudden death and the devastating effect it had on me to put my grief into words in a weekly human-interest column that began in 1985 for the Newport, Oregon, *News-Times*.

Mail started pouring in from readers near and far who had also lost a loved one and the common thread of their words was, "Thank you for writing about your grief. I no longer feel so alone." It began to dawn on me that this book needed to happen, that my open, raw honesty might help others in their own grief journey. I know Burt is watching, smiling, and saying, "You go, Babe!"

Acknowledgements

With deep appreciation I wish to thank the following:

PAT LEWIS, who asked me to lunch that fateful day and so I was right there to hold my husband Burt in my arms as he took his last breath.

JULIE ALMQUIST of Portland, Oregon, a graphic designer who planted the seed that this book needed to happen.

My daughter, ROCKI MARTEL LONGARINI whose wise words helped me through meltdowns and taught me to laugh again.

GINA NIELSEN, my close friend and invaluable personal assistant.

MICHELE LONGO EDER who wrote *Salt In Our Blood*, about the loss of her son at sea. Michele convinced me this book could and should happen.

PEGGY GAINES of Tucson, Arizona, my writer friend of 30 years who has relentlessly pushed me to keep on writing.

KATH SCHONAU, RN, my dear friend who stayed by my side as emergency room staff tried so hard to resuscitate my husband Burt.

LOUISE WAARVICK, confidant and trusted friend of many years.

JOHN HAINES, M.D., my ophthalmologist and friend, without whose help and constant encouragement, I could not have gotten through these past twelve years of fighting macular degeneration.

LORNA DAVIS and NEWPORT CHAMBER OF COMMERCE.

STEVE CARD, my long time friend and editor, Newport (Oregon) *News-Times*.

All the FEMALE FRIENDS who showed up the week after Burt's death with their loving support, hugs, coffee, and cinnamon rolls.

The coast-to-coast READERS of my raw words of grief who wrote to thank me for putting into words exactly how they were feeling over the loss of a loved one.

ROTARY CLUB of Newport.

Emergency staff of SAMARITAN PACIFIC COMMUNITIES HOSPITAL.

And CARLA PERRY of Dancing Moon Press. Without her professional help and gentle guidance, this book would still be a vague dream.

> **All proceeds from the sale of this book will be donated to the ROTARY FOUNDATION of ROTARY INTERNATIONAL to advance its goals of world understanding, goodwill, and peace through the improvement of health, the support of education, and the alleviation of poverty.**

Contents

Introduction 11
An Open Letter To My Readers 13
Good Grief 16
Burt Lippman--Newport's Mensch 20
Widow's Walk 23
It Hurts As Much As It's Worth 27
Story Of The Coffee Cup 30
"I've Got You, Babe" 33
Attitude Of Gratitude 35
Endings And Beginnings 39
From Midwife To Mid-Life 43
Memories 45
When Angels Show Up To Help 48
Flappers, Dreams, And Stepping Out 51
From Mucking To Mowing 54
When It's Time To Say Goodbye 57
A Few Life Lessons 61
The Power Of Words 64
Making Progress 67
The Locket 70
The Traveling Fruitcake 73
The Dreaded Firsts 76
Two Virginal Coats 79
Marriage Made In Heaven 82
A Turning Time 86
Birthday Pajamas For One And All 89
The Seven-Month Gift 92
Dogs, Dodge, And New Beginnings 95
Bring It On 98
Another Of Life's Mysteries Solved 101
Current Events—Then And Now 106
"A Toast To Life And Love" 109
The Amazing Magical $700 Dress 112
Billboards And Happy Feet 115

Mishmash	118
What Goes Around Comes Around	121
From Bed Hopping To Bubbles	124
Three Steps Forward and a Big Step Back	128
Do You Know Miss-Direction And Siri?	131
Bucky And The Sternwheeler	134
The Home Show and the Bladder Shaker	138
With Age Comes Wisdom-- Or Not	142
Community Legend—Alice	145
License Plate Memories	148
When Time Takes It's Time	151
Quirks That Work	154
Foot In Mouth Disease	157
At Home And Aweigh	160
Reflections Of A Painful Year	163
A Glamping We Will Go	167
Small Goats And Smaller Windows	171
Underground Beeping And Chomping	175
You Betcha	178
Blame It On The Brass	181
Because Of You—Suspension Bridge	184
Catching Up	188
My Remarkable Margaret	191
Nose Rings And Other Things	194
A Week In Chains	197
Jericho	200
Winter	203
Meltdown With A Message	206
Loretta	209
Knocking The 'Stuffing' Out Of Christmas	212
The Consummate Romantic	216
Have You Ever Been In Secure?	219
Computer Dating	222
Don't Hold Back	225

"The Thing"	227
Just In Time	230
Try Anything Once	233
The Power of Words and Hugs	236
Food, Feathers, Fun And Frolic	239
Any Lap Will Do	242
I'm Keeping My Fork	245
Meet Waldo	248
Waldo Report	251
Shredding My Life	254
Sea Change	257
And Now To Heal	260
Everyone Needs a Humptulips	262
Medical Moments	265
'Where My House Go, Mama?'	269
Towanda!	272
All Aboard	275
Female Fortitude	278
That Cheatin' Heart	281
G Strings And Other Embarrassments	284
Burt's Bucks	287
A Remarkable Response	290
When We Danced With Denny	293
Otherwise	296
The Woman Who Could Not Stop Crying	299
Death Is Nothing At All	303
About The Author	305

INTRODUCTION

Burton "Burt" I. Lippman

Burt Lippman made his transition on July 18, 2013 in Newport, Oregon, surrounded by his wife and many caring friends, including fellow Rotarians.

He wrote this obituary himself, leaving it in the care of his beloved wife Bobbie, who has added a few thoughts you might want to know about this incredible man who lit up a room—any room—just by walking in. He specifically left orders that his obituary not read like a resume.

Burt was involved in Bobbie's hospice work for a long time and occasionally helped her with male patients. He knew many hospice nurses and volunteers who used the term "transition" rather than "died," and came to strongly feel that there is no such thing as "death," but rather a transition from this life to the next.

Good Grief

Burton I. Lippman was born in Brooklyn, New York, on March 21, 1927. He loved growing up in Brooklyn in an affectionate Jewish family who taught him strong values that stayed with him his entire life. He graduated from Brooklyn College, earned a CPA degree, and joined the Navy to serve his country. Eventually, he moved to southern California and spent many years as a key executive in the entertainment industry.

What mattered most to Burt was how he treated other people—always with kindness, generosity, integrity, and often with a big hug. Most people got a hug from Burt whether they were ready for it or not. Sometimes even a kiss on the cheek—not always easy for other guys to accept—but Burt was usually bigger, taller, and stronger, and if he liked you, you knew it.

As Burt grew older, he became happier and extremely contented with life—especially life on the Oregon coast. He loved the community, the people, the ocean, the sunsets, even the long rainy winters with a fire in the fireplace, his feet on the coffee table, his wife, and his dog at his side, and often the cat in his lap. Daily he declared he was "one very happy and lucky man." Burt was deeply spiritual and early every morning he went outside to thank God for another day.

Burt is survived by his wife Bobbie, his daughters Meryl and Robin, Bobbie's daughter Rochelle, and their respective husbands Tony, Ron, and Glen. Burt treasured his five grandchildren: Max, Jamie, Zoe, Emily, and Autumn.

A celebration of life was held on August 30, 2013 at the Newport Performing Arts Center. Burt wanted all his friends to show up, raise a toast, have a good time, and say nice things. He loved his life and says to tell you he "had a very, very good ride!" He knew it is a rare and wonderful blessing to have been loved by so many people.

An Open Letter To My Readers

In case you did not see Burt's obituary in Wednesday's *News-Times*, this is to let you know he went Home to be with God on July 18, 2013. Tomorrow we would have celebrated our 523-month-aversary.

When you can't sleep at 3 a.m. and you have been a passionate writer your entire life, you may as well get up and write. Staring at the ceiling is not what I need to do during this terrible time of grief and loss when I don't know what else to do but cry. I am astounded by the amount of emails, cards, and phone calls coming from near and far. Flowers have been left on the front porch and more food than will fit in the fridge, mostly healthy stuff like fruit and yogurt and soup, but someone left killer cinnamon rolls (no note) and that person needs to fess up.

There is a common thread running through the emails, cards and calls—that "a light has gone out because Burt Lippman is no longer here to love, encourage, help, and hug anyone and everyone in his path." Another common thread is, "Please, please do not stop writing!" One reader refers to this column as their Friday Family Fix.

Burt expected to predecease me and during this past year, he tried several times to make me promise to keep writing. Most of you probably don't know our "Friday Routine." Burt never knew the subject of this column ahead of time. It was like a game between us. We would leave the house mid-morning on Fridays, often stopping at the lab where he had to have frequent blood tests because of all the heart medications. Then we would stop at the Chamber of Commerce office and pick up a copy of the Newport *News-Times*. (Our copy arrives in the mail later in the day). Then we would go find a quiet place to park where nobody could disturb us. I would unbuckle my seatbelt, lean back with eyes closed, and listen to Burt as he read the column to me. If he laughed in the right places or got choked up with a serious subject, this told me I had nailed it and gotten it right for the rest of you readers. Then we would go to the weekly Chamber lunch meeting where Burt would hear feedback from folks who had read the paper already. Those Friday moments in the car were so special I often told him if he ever left me, there would be no point to continue writing this column.

For those of you who live with and love your pets, I need to share what is going on with ours. A week before Burt "graduated," we were sure it was time to let Charley go. He's an old dog now and his hind legs are giving out. When Charley spent two whole days sleeping and ignoring his food, I told Burt it was getting close to making a decision. Burt was not raised with pets, and often said my intuition about them was amazing. But a lifetime of living with animals is a lifetime of lessons they teach us and you pet people know exactly what this means. And now, without Burt in the house, both cat and dog are confused and looking for him. Lap Sitter is about ten now and hasn't been a playful cat since we rescued her from the animal shelter six years ago. The other night I was sitting in my lazy girl chair in a quiet house that frankly has gotten pretty messy since last Thursday and I could not care less. Picture a pile of unread newspapers on the floor in front of me. So far, I haven't moved Burt's coffee up either. Lap Sitter suddenly decided to plow under the newspapers and play. Charley was sleeping nearby and got up to see why the cat had disappeared under the papers and was having such fun. When he poked his nose under the newspapers, a paw reached out and smacked him on the nose, something she did only one time before—the day she came from the shelter, just to let curious Charley know she was now boss of the house. The dog was so surprised, that he backed up on those unsteady hind legs and just stared at the pile of moving newspapers in disbelief. She stuck her head out and stared back at him. It was like some kind of a funny performance going on just for my amusement. Then Charley went to his basket of stuffed toys, chose a ratty thing he hasn't played with in ages and dropped it on Lap Sitter's head. Game over. How could I not laugh? And all that happened just when I was sitting there thinking, *Will I ever laugh again?*

    I'm not sure this will end up in print, but it has been therapeutic for me to write. My editor will be surprised to receive this and, knowing him, will probably try to find space in Friday's paper. If so, thank you readers for allowing me to vent, and thanks to all of you who have ordered me to keep on writing.

    Maybe I will.

GOOD GRIEF

These words are being written late on a Saturday night, something I haven't done since I was a kid and wrote my heart out with a pencil and flashlight under the blanket so my parents wouldn't catch me and yell. I kept my journals and notebooks hidden under the mattress.

A tiny handful of people have sent emails suggesting nicely that I quit writing or take a few months off from writing these columns. They mean well, but obviously think what I do is difficult and stressful. NOT! But the majority (and there are more of you than I can count or believe) state these words: "Please keep writing." Can it be the minority have never known an artist who has to draw, a dancer who has to dance, or a musician who cannot bear life without music?

I can think of other passions, and so can you. Some may call what I do "writing." I call it "sharing," and the following words will give you an honest glimpse into this past week of dealing with the loss of my husband and best friend Burt. There are degrees of grief, and no one goes through life without experiencing it in some way. Consider the little kid whose gold fish or hamster dies, and parents who help soothe the child with a burial ceremony in the backyard.

My big lesson so far is I never knew grief could be so incredibly painful. I've lost babies (stillborn), parents, brothers, close friends, and beloved pets, and it never ever hurt this much. I've spent many years as a hospice volunteer with dying people and their grieving loved ones. Only now do I know what someone at their bedside was possibly feeling. This lesson has caused a far deeper shift within me regarding compassion and understanding. Burt gave me this gift, and I will use it in his honor during whatever future is ahead.

I spent several days after Burt's death needing to be alone with my grief. Daughters and friends wanted to come immediately and be with me. I asked them to wait. Everyone has the right to deal with grief doing what they need to do. By Wednesday, I said OK to the group of women with whom I bicycle. They said they needed to be with me, and it felt right to open my home and my heart. They brought coffee, cinnamon rolls, paper plates, napkins, and I didn't have to do a thing. I don't know how many were here, but when the last one left, I felt loved and nurtured by these wonderful women.

It's Thursday—one week after having said my goodbyes to Burt on the floor of the Embarcadero Resort & Marina at 1:10 p.m. Burt was unconscious by then, but still breathing. I held him in my arms and did what I have counseled hospice families to do for their dying loved one—I crawled up close to his ear and gave Burt permission to leave, if he had to, thanked him for loving me all these years and told him I would be safe and taken care of because that had been his main mission in life. I even told him to greet the stillborn baby we lost in 1972.

Some people need ritual and, for me, I had to be in the perfect place at 1:10 p.m., maybe alone, but maybe with just the right person. I needed to go to our old beach, which gave us such joy and fun for our first 14 years on the Oregon Coast. Burt and I walked that beach, hunting for agates, often followed by our miniature goats, and watching our dogs run freely. But first, I made one call, then put on my grubby beach coat and headed north one mile to our old spot on a cold, windy and foggy day. Perfect, because no one was there—except for my neighbor

Nancy who came walking toward me in the fog and took me into her arms. We both cried as we walked, and at 1:10 p.m., we stood silently looking at the ocean and thinking of Burt. Nancy and her family were our only neighbors back then, and we share many happy memories. Thursday was another step in my healing.

On Friday morning, there was a knock on the door and in walked Patti and Chuck Littlehales, two of the first great friends we met in 1983. Patti had an armload of the *News-Times* papers, and Chuck handed over cinnamon rolls. They had come to ask if I planned to carry on "The Friday Routine" (described in the previous column) about how Burt read that day's "Bobbie's Beat" to me while parked where no one would bother us. Of course, Patti and Chuck had read the column, and none of it was news to me because I had written it. But somehow, this ritual felt right. We three sat out on the deck on a gorgeous sunny morning. I leaned back in my chair (feeling as though I should unbuckle a seat belt), closed my eyes, and listened to Patti read the column. It wasn't exactly the ritual Burt and I had done for so many years, but it felt warm and loving. Then they surprised me by reading Dan Glode's special tribute to Burt Lippman, "The Mensch of Newport." Dan's wonderful writing about his long relationship with Burt was astonishing. Did I cry? What do you think? This week was all about allowing friends to help me take a few more baby steps in healing this thing called grief.

It's now midnight, and the dog and cat are confused because I'm at my computer and not in bed where I'm supposed to be. Just think how confused they would be if I was under blankets writing this by hand with a stupid flashlight—especially Lap Sitter, the cat who likes to snuggle next to my cheek at bedtime.

All any of us can do in life, especially when awful things happen, is take one step at a time and allow others to help—when we are ready. I am overjoyed to tell you that my precious daughter Rocki is on her way to me. She has known since age nine that Burt was "the one" for me. In fact, she knew it before I did. I am now ready to let her come.

Stay tuned. The Beat just may go on.

Burt Lippman--Newport's Mensch

(Editorial by Dan Glode in the Newport *News-Times*, 7/26/13)

We were all saddened to hear of Burt Lippman's recent passing. There is a Yiddish term, mensch, which applies to Burt. Roughly translated, it means a very good person and, in fact, a person better than most. The word describes an individual whose integrity and honor are qualities that all admire and emulate. A mensch is a rare person, a cut above. Burt was a mensch in the truest sense.

I saw Burt a lot when I was working as district attorney, as we shared some of the same community activities. After my retirement, and Burt and Bobbie's move to California and ours to Russia, we did not see as much of him. More recently, we spoke briefly at events, and sometimes had a long talk session while buying vegetables at the Saturday Market. It must have been quite a sight, two big, gray-haired guys hugging while having an animated conversation. But, ah, when he hugged you with those big arms, you knew he cared. Many shared that experience over the years. My connection to Burt was a strong one, and my respect for him grew over the years. With all of this in mind, and in preparation for this column, I asked a friend if she could provide details of his more recent activities. In the end, though, I decided that was unnecessary since it would describe what he did and not who he was.

Burt was born in Brooklyn, and while you could take Burt out of Brooklyn, you could not take Brooklyn out of Burt. He had the accent, the gesticulations, the arm touching to make a point, and a sincere smile as large as New York City itself. I was born and raised not too far from where he grew up, and so there was a comfort we shared (not to mention we knew what a pastrami sandwich was supposed to be like).

Burt was a schmoozer. He was dapper. And he made everyone immediately comfortable, no matter who they were or where they came from. He was very intelligent, and had a knack for getting to the bottom line no matter the subject. Combine this with his keen sense of analysis and you can partially understand why he was in such demand by service clubs and community organizations. His help, which he readily gave, was invaluable. He gave his time, rolled up his sleeves, and dug in.

Several times back in the 1990s, he and I found ourselves selling glasses and shirts for the Chamber of Commerce at the Newport Seafood and Wine Festival. Our booth was the first stop for most people who attended the event. No matter how tired he got from being on his feet for hours, and hauling boxes of glasses downstairs, he always greeted everyone with a huge smile and made them feel as if he had personally printed the T-shirt or glass himself—just for them. If you knew him for ten minutes or ten years, Burt made you feel valued. Then there was the time we donned Santa outfits for the YMCA.... I could go on.

In my opinion, the most significant thing about Burt is also the most difficult to write about—his relationship with Bobbie, his wife. She was his heart and soul. She was the brightest diamond in his life, as he was to her. I have known many couples over the years. Most go through life together in a loving and respectful way. Burt and Bobbie transcended this, and it was obvious to all. Their level of devotion, their love for each other, and their deep connection is rare. You could feel the energy and the oneness between them.

I am reminded of the old essay, and later the poem by John Donne called, "For Whom the Bell Tolls." In it, he says:

> No man is an island,
> Entire of itself,
> Every man is a piece of the continent,
> A part of the main.
> If a clod be washed away by the sea,
> Europe is the less.

I believe John Donne was trying to get at the concept of how we are all interconnected and that we are all diminished by the loss of one of us. Newport, and all of us, is diminished by Burt's passing. And yet... and yet we have been so enriched and elevated by his presence. In my mind's eye, I can see the white hair, the white beard, the broad smile, and the twinkle in his eye. I hear his enthusiastic, "How ayah, Dan!"

I miss you Burt, we all do. And Burt... thanks.
—Dan

Dan Glode

Widow's Walk

That word in the headline, the first one beginning with "W" is not me. At least not yet. That word is a foreign word dangling way out far in the universe from some scaffolding. It doesn't apply to me. I can't wrap my brain around the thought that the "W" word is now what I am. In time, I will have to accept the reality of it, but it's too soon.

There is a huge stack of cards on the coffee table, and only two or three people just signed their names and let the message on the card speak for itself. Most messages are in handwriting I can't read, so friends have been reading them to me. The words about Burt are what I call "keepers" because they come from hearts that are also hurting and feeling the loss of my incredible guy. A friend offered to type and print the handwritten letters in a larger font and put them in a file for me to read at a future time. I will share these with our daughters.

There are more emails from readers responding to last week's column than I will ever manage to answer. Many are from people whose names I do not recognize. Here's an example of a message that arrived this morning. I am not using her name, but what she had to say is special.

> I'm so sorry for your loss. I rushed for the paper to see if you were in this week's edition, and you were! Thank you so much for being there. I feel your pain, I know your pain, and I have for just over a year. I understand the shift within and that shift just proves how connected to your loved one you

really are and always will be. I love your column, and I hope you can find it in yourself to have "The Beat" go on. If you don't, OK. But know this—your column of August 2 made all of us in the Sisterhood of Widows proud. You have truly captured the feeling of that tragic event in our lives... and yours. All the best to you and your family.

I've also been hearing from men who have lost their wives, and I can feel their pain in their emailed words. They also had to get used to the "W" word. I think it must be harder for men to continue on without their women. Perhaps God knows this, which is why nursing homes are predominantly filled with aging women and a very small minority of men.

I know without question that Burt could not have gone on without me. He said as much—often. We had many end-of-life conversations, always with Burt advising me what to do after he "left." I would look at him and say, "Who put you in charge and said YOU get to choose? I could get wiped out on my bike by some idiot on the Bay Road who loses control of his truck." Burt would go ashen and get angry when hearing those words... even if I was halfway kidding.

And now, a glimpse into this past week. My daughter Rocki arrived at dawn on Tuesday. You do not want to know the airline nightmare she dealt with; she takes these things in stride. I sat up waiting for her to walk through the front door. The Littlehales had driven to Eugene in the wee hours so Rocki could avoid the hassle of renting a car.

When Rocki got here, we grabbed three hours of sleep, then she hit the ground running, i.e. taking charge of the scary stuff Burt has handled for 44 years and trained her to do for the past 12—just in case.

Good Grief

Rocki helped me through mood swings, unexpected bouts of crying, one panic attack (my first), and she made me laugh a few times. She literally forced me to start eating nutritious food. She spotted the weight loss I tried to hide under baggy sweats. When she pushed food at me, I kept getting the vision of her in a highchair with me pushing a spoon of baby food into her little bird-like mouth, always using the words "new bite." Then she had to head back to her California home.

I need to leave you with a smile, especially those of you asking about our old dog and aging cat who seem to be going through a change of life just as I am. Friends drop by, and Charley gets all excited and goofy, like he did as a puppy. More than once someone said, "Is this the dog you told Burt was ready to go to the vet so he could do the kindly thing?" Obviously, something weird is going on. Our friend Gina Nielsen has been in and out of our home at least twice a week for five years and has never seen Lap Sitter so playful.

Last night, feeling sad with Rocki gone, I needed a quiet evening for listening to music and mulling over events of this past week. I needed soft sounds and a quiet house. The animals thought differently. Charley dug a stuffed critter out of his toy box that still has a working squeaker. He walked around squeaking that thing and if I were normal right now, I would have put that toy away. At the same time, the cat decided to play with a tiny toy bird that chirps like a real bird. Our neighbors, the Stankeys, are cat people and gave us the toy three years ago. Lap Sitter thought it beneath her dignity to play with it—until she heard Charley and his obnoxious squeaky toy. Those two animals put on a stupid, squeaky, chirping concert for me that lasted longer than any of you sane people would have put up with. But in my tenuous condition, it was such unusual and funny behavior I wasn't about to interfere. They soon got tired—or bored—and went to sleep. So did I.

Apparently, for now and for you, and because writing for me is therapy, it looks like The Beat will go on.

It Hurts As Much As It's Worth

The moment I sent last week's column to the newspaper, I realized there was so much left out, such as questions asked by you readers in your emails. You asked if "The Friday Routine" continued. You asked if I did any kind of special ritual at 1:10 p.m. on the second Thursday of Burt's "transition," other than go to the beach as I had to do on that first Thursday. Those who have walked the walk sent advice, most of which makes perfect sense. And one old, but young friend in Chicago named Dana wrote an amazing letter and ended it with this quote by Julian Barnes: "It hurts just as much as it's worth." That quote is so powerful and so right on I have been carrying it around in my shirt pocket every day since then. Go back and read it again and feel the power of those words, especially if you are dealing with the loss of a loved one.

My Thursday ritual. What felt right was to go out to my greenhouse, sit on the old wooden stool, be away from the telephone and just be. Lap Sitter appeared, jumped up on a potting table, walked over my leg, and asked to be held. She never does this as outdoors to a cat means being on guard. She cuddled quietly in my arms for about nine minutes, then jumped down and left—her tail in the shape of a question mark as if to say, "Well you needed to hold something warm, right?"

Regarding "The Friday Routine" of Burt reading my columns aloud to me in the car. On Friday, August 2, my daughter Rocki drove Burt's car and we stopped to pick up a copy of the *News-Times*. Somehow, we ended up in the empty parking lot of the Performing Arts Center. I unbuckled the seat belt, leaned back, closed my eyes, and listened as Rocki read the column called "Good Grief." Like Burt, she did not know the content ahead of time, and I'm afraid she went through quite a few tissues. Her reaction made me cry and I had written the darn thing. Then, together, we went to the Chamber luncheon. Yes, it was difficult walking in, and I would not have done it alone—kind of like falling off a horse and getting back on again? I was incredibly proud to introduce her to so many good friends, and it was one more step in my healing.

Advice from those who have suffered a loss: Do not make any big changes for at least a year. No big decisions.

Judy Bateman called and told me about a book that helped her get through the three years since her husband Gene died. It's called *Healing After Loss*, by Martha Whitmore Hickman, a day-by-day book of meditations. I immediately downloaded it onto my Kindle (for large font I can easily read) and bless you, Judy, for reaching out to me.

So, how am I doing in general? I'm moving forward, with some days better than others. Friends and family are calling to check, but no one is overdoing it. This morning my kid brother Paul called from Omaha to tell me he, his wife Dot, and their missionary daughter Julie (from South Africa) will be here for the Celebration of Burt's Life on August 30 at Newport's Performing Arts Center. This news made me so happy that it caused my sense of humor to kick in. I think Paul sucked in his breath when I admitted to learning a lot about the "Here After." He laughed when I explained how often I wander from one room to another and just stand there wondering, *What in heck am I here after?*

Daughter Robin asks during every phone call if Burt's empty coffee cup is still where he left it. "Yep," I say, "And I will move it when I'm ready, but right now it somehow helps to see it sitting there on the table next to me." Grieving people have the right to do whatever feels comforting or quirky at the time, no matter how bizarre, and no one—absolutely no one—has the right to tell a grieving person to "Get over it already!"

To sum up my progress so far, here is how I visualize myself: picture a spring bulb—like a crocus or a daffodil—just beginning to poke its head above ground. Not the whole thing, just the tippy top. That's me, with great appreciation to all of you who are urging me to "keep writing."

Burt, Bobbie, Dot, and Paul

STORY OF THE COFFEE CUP

If you have been following my grief journey you know I have not been able to move my husband's coffee cup since his death on July 18, 2013. It has remained on the table where he left it that last morning we had together. Most people who lose a loved one, such as a life partner, know how comforting it is to have certain rituals. I heard from a woman who sleeps in her husband's T-shirt because his scent is still in it. A widower writes that he has not been able to remove clothes from his wife's closet. She's been gone for 19 months.

A couple of years ago I wrote a column titled, "My Coffee Cup Epiphany." There was so much reader response, that I sent it to *Chicken Soup for The Soul,* and the story was published in a book called *Married Life.* Here it is in case you missed it.

My Coffee Cup Epiphany:

I recently had a huge epiphany. Maybe my experience will give you some food for thought. I had gone to a meeting of one of my women's groups. We spent part of the evening discussing a book with such a humorous title that it makes most people smile: Why Men Don't Listen – and Women Don't Read Road Maps.

Yes, it's true. Men and women come into this world wired so differently it's a wonder relationships last as long as they do. I think if this book were given as a wedding gift, there would be far fewer divorces.

Speaking of books, I gave a copy of Chicken Soup for the Soul,

Good Grief

Runners to a male friend who is a runner. Since my story of taking part in the Newport (Oregon) Marathon was published in that book, I autographed it for my friend. A few days later, he sent an email thanking me "for the loan of the book." Loan? I emailed back that it was a GIFT and did he not see that I wrote a special message to him on the first page? He emailed back a very nice thank you and added that maybe it was a "guy thing" to not look at the first page. Whatever. So what? No big deal. But men and women are definitely different in dozens of ways.

If you are a woman reading this, maybe you're thinking, Oh yeah, and how come they leave the toilet seat up? If you are a guy reading this, you might be thinking, Sure I don't listen—because she never shuts up! During the discussion with my women's group of the book, Why Men Don't Listen... I decided to share one of my pet peeves about my husband—he never carries his darn coffee cup to the kitchen even though he is going right past the sink on his way to somewhere else. This has bugged me for 40 years and no amount of nagging makes a difference. I did not feel one bit disloyal sharing this with my women friends. Some of them chuckled because they deal with the same thing (or worse).

The very next morning, my weekly radio program was on the air and it was one in which my husband helped me read a funny comedy routine that sounds best with two people. An hour later, the telephone rang. It isn't unusual to get emails and phone calls regarding my stories in Chicken Soup For The Soul, this column, or my human-interest radio program. But that particular call was from a dear lady I've known for 20 years. She lost her husband not long ago (a 60-year marriage) and this is what she said on the phone: "Bobbie, I loved the show you and Burt did together this morning. Don't ever stop appreciating him and what a blessing that you have each other!" Her words smacked me between the eyes. I hung up the phone and sat there staring at our two empty coffee cups.

As usual, my husband had wandered off and, as usual, the only way those cups would make it to the kitchen is if I carried them. But instead of feeling irritated, I started thinking, What if there was only ONE coffee cup to carry? It was a major epiphany and a total turnaround in my perspective over a dumb coffee cup.

Indeed, how blessed I am to have TWO cups to carry to the kitchen. None of us knows how long we will be here. Life can change in a heartbeat. So what if men don't listen and so what if women (well, not all women) don't read road maps? Viva la difference.

Note: if you check your dictionary, you will see more than one meaning for the word "epiphany." The one that applies to me is: "A sudden insight usually initiated by some simple commonplace experience."

May I never again complain about that coffee cup!

And now you know why Burt's coffee cup has stayed on the table where he left it. As I write this it has been exactly one month since he died and today I'm OK (sort of) with taking his cup to the kitchen. Of course, I would give anything—anything—if I could have kept him with me for many more years, but God had other plans for this incredible guy who made such a difference in my life and the lives of so many others.

"I've Got You, Babe"

With so much going on (friends and family arriving from near and far for Burt's Celebration of Life), there wasn't going to be a column this week, but each time I got to the sentence, "Call me by my old familiar name," a story began to take shape.

I don't remember when Burt started calling me "Babe," but it was well over 40 years ago. I doubt it had anything to do with Sonny and Cher singing, "I've Got You Babe," but who cares. To me it was an endearing name, and I started calling him "Babe" in return. That's how we communicated almost 100 percent of the time, privately and publicly. Many couples have pet names for one another. I think the only time we used Burt and Bobbie was when we were speaking about one another to other people.

I've heard from widows and widowers who tell me they "talk" to their partner who is no longer here. I wasn't able to do this because the only time I called Burt by his given name was when I was mad at him or really needed to get his attention.

Since receiving "All Is Well" from Bruce Mate, I am now so comfortable, especially at bedtime, carrying on long (and longing) conversations with my Babe. If you want a visual, picture me looking up at the top of his beloved flagpole, the extra tall one he bought such a short time ago. The solar lights work amazingly well even in our foggy, rainy coastal weather, which means the huge American flag can wave respectfully 24/7. There I stand, sometimes longer than you would believe, talking to the man I almost always called Babe. It never occurred to me that other people might have noticed or thought it funny about us calling one another Babe until 14 years ago when we drove from L.A. to Yosemite for Rocki and Glen's wedding. In our backseat were two people who needed a ride—one was a buddy of Glen's named Gary. I've no idea what Burt and I talked about during that long drive because we never ran out of things to talk about, but what I do know is that this guy Gary must have been paying attention. Two years later, we heard about Gary doing this very funny comedy routine at a party about some couple who carried on a back-and-forth conversation while calling one another "Babe."

I don't know how you are reacting to this tidbit of history, but the term "Babe" makes me smile and maybe one day Gary will show up in my life again and I'll beg him to do his comedy routine.

Those of us who are dealing with grief need all the smiles we can get. Right? Right!

Rocki and her husband Glen on a cruise

Attitude Of Gratitude

I am writing this column today with an enormous attitude of gratitude to all of you who helped (and are still helping me) with my Grief Journey over the loss of my husband. The journey isn't over, but it will change with time and it will go on as long as it needs to—for all of us whose lives were touched by Burt Lippman. I would love to thank each of you with a handwritten note, but you would not be able to read my handwriting. Macular degeneration is a challenge for folks stuck with it, but a computer can kick up type into a larger font and for that, I am grateful. I am also extremely grateful for the things I can do, like daytime driving and spotting a small blob of cat barf on the carpet before my dog Charley finds it. Dogs and cats often do disgusting things but I am grateful that both pets are here to keep me company. Perhaps only pet owners understand the unquestioning devotion animals give us.

So I send a gigantic "thank you" to all of you who helped in so many ways. You know who you are. If I mentioned one name, I would have to include an unbelievable number of names. I hope, in time, to let you all know the important part you played, whether it was dropping off food on our porch, sending lovely letters with your cards, or your kind words showing up in a few hundred emails.

During one of my miserable meltdowns, my daughter reminded me on the phone, "Mom, you are very fortunate to have so many people offering help. Remember this: You have a village!" Those reassuring words are anchored in my mind and heart. How sad it must be for people who lose a loved one and have little or no help in dealing with their grief.

For those of you who could not attend Burt's "A Life Well Lived" celebration last Friday night at the Newport Performing Arts Center, here is a brief overview. I will continue to glow with the sheer joy of it for a long, long time. OK, I lied about not mentioning names because Lorna Davis, director of the Newport Chamber of Commerce, and her magical staff took care of every tiny detail of the "party." Burt would have loved it.

The honest truth is he sensed his time was coming and told me way too frequently what he wanted. He covered more details than I could bear to hear about when he wanted to talk. Yes, I am just as guilty as most people who live in denial about death and like to think we are all going to live forever. But Burt was realistic and open about growing tired. He was adamantly opposed to one more medical procedure. He'd had it with being poked and prodded, and after spending weeks on a catheter, he threatened to pitch the darn thing into the wetlands below our home.

Meanwhile, back to the Performing Arts Center. People just kept on coming—to the extent Newport's finest were on hand for crowd control. Somehow, I think everyone managed to squeeze in and enjoy delicious food and drink—enough and some to spare, as Burt liked to do whenever we entertained. As guests made their way through the lobby of the PAC, guess who got hugged so many times she ended up feeling like a child's teddy bear whose fur has been worn off from so much love?

The program was a perfect blend of humor, videos, music, and six well-chosen speakers who spoke from their hearts. I sat there, fifth row center, in seats we bought back when the Performing Arts Center was in its infancy. Those two seats have little brass nameplates with our names. As I listened to each speaker express him or herself about the impact my husband had on their life, I kept thinking of our grandkids that were here to honor their grandfather. (Autumn is still in Australia on her 15-month honeymoon).

And I thought of all the other people in the crowd listening to words about a life well lived. An underlying message from the speakers was how they all knew Burt believed in "paying it forward"—to step up, give of oneself, and try to make a positive difference in the lives of others. If he had been sitting next to me, he would have squirmed in embarrassment. As for me, I was bursting with pride and gratitude that this fabulous person walked into my life on February 27, 1969 and changed me forever.

I promise those of you who keep asking that this column continue that very soon there will be humor once again to leave you laughing instead of tearful. But for today, please make a little pact with yourself to reach out to someone less fortunate than you are and do a Burt thing: pay it forward.

Final thought. I watched people laugh when they spotted the photo on the back of the printed program—Burt in a business suit with a spoon on his nose. Through the years, we attended many dinner occasions that took themselves way too seriously—we would give each other the "look" and expertly hang a spoon on our noses while keeping a straight face. It takes a bit of practice, but you can do it too. If children are at your table, they will love you for being silly.

Burt Lippman doing the "spoon trick"

This photo graced the back cover of the program for the celebration of Burt Lippman's "life well lived" at the Newport Performing Arts Center
Friday, August 30, 2013

Endings And Beginnings

It's a struggle finding the right words for this first paragraph but I need to explain how the subject of today's column took form. Bear with me for starting off on such a serious note. I promise to lighten up if you keep reading.

On the day my husband made his transition, I was in a state of shock as the dreadful drama moved from the Embarcadero Resort & Marina to the ambulance to the emergency room at Samaritan Pacific Communities Hospital. I watched the medical personnel try so hard to restart Burt's heart, but I knew deep down in my own heart they could not bring him back. As I sat in a chair praying, shaking, watching, and weeping, I overheard the news that a young couple we know was upstairs in the maternity ward welcoming their baby boy into this world.

Before long, a very compassionate doctor told me they could do no more, while these words from the Bible kept playing over and over in my head: "There is the going out and the coming in." I knew there was more to it than that, but the message was clear that life for all of us has beginnings and endings. I have since met baby Benjamin, and I have since learned the entire verse from someone who knows his Bible: "The Lord will keep your going out and your coming in from this time on and for evermore." Psalm 121:8.

I am aware of several other young couples having babies, or close friends meeting new grandbabies—most of these newborns delivered in the traditional hospital way and a few at home by midwives—which brings me full circle to why you are about to read a very funny day brightener. All this, plus the fact my beloved granddaughter, Autumn, is returning from her 15-month adventurous honeymoon in South America and Australia. (I can't imagine where she got her insatiable sense of adventure, can you?)

Many years ago, my daughter Rocki asked me to document Autumn's birth. So, in a mountaintop home near Santa Barbara, I watched as three midwives assisted this amazing new little person into the world. So now, with thoughts of the going out and the coming in and the miracle of new life, I think you women readers will love today's day brightener. As for you guys, maybe not so much. I clearly remember Burt's answer when I asked him if he wanted to join me for Autumn's birth. He said, "You can't be serious!" Here it is:

> **"The Middle Wife"** *by anonymous Second Grade teacher*
>
> I've been teaching now for 15 years. I have two kids myself, but the best birth story I know is the one I saw in my own second grade classroom.
>
> When I was a kid, I loved show and tell, so I always have a few sessions with my students. It helps them get over shyness and usually show and tell is pretty tame. Kids bring in pet turtles, model airplanes, pictures of fish they catch, stuff like that. And I never, ever place any boundaries or limitations on them. If they want to lug it into school and talk about it, they're welcome.
>
> One day this little girl, Erica, a very bright, very outgoing kid, takes her turn and waddles up to the front of the class with a pillow stuffed under her sweater. She holds up a snapshot of an infant. "This is Luke, my baby brother, and I'm going to tell you about his birthday. First, Mom and Dad made him as a

symbol of their love, and then Dad put a seed in my Mom's stomach and Luke grew in there. He ate for nine months through an umbrella cord." Erica is standing there with her hands on the pillow and I'm trying not to laugh and wishing I had my camcorder with me. The kids are watching her in amazement.

"Then, about two Saturdays ago, my mom starts going, 'Oh, Oh, Oh, Oh!' Erica puts a hand behind her back and groans. "She walked around the house for like an hour, going Oh, oh, oh!" (Now this kid is doing a hysterical duck walk and groaning.) "My dad called the middle wife. She delivers babies, but she doesn't have a sign on the car like the Domino's man. They got my mom to lie down in bed like this." (Erica lies down with her back against the wall.) "And then, pop! My mom had this bag of water she kept in there in case he got thirsty, and it just blew up and spilled all over the bed, like psshhheew!

Then the middle wife starts saying 'push, push,' and 'breathe, breathe.' They started counting, but never even got past 10. Then, all of a sudden out comes my brother. He was covered in yucky stuff that they all said it was from Mom's play center, (placenta) so there must be a lot of toys inside there."

Then Erica stood up, took a big theatrical bow, and returned to her seat. I'm sure I applauded the loudest. Ever since then, when it's show-and-tell day, I bring my camcorder just in case another middle wife comes along.

So OK, I promised to start lightening up, but I have always been open and honest with you readers and it would be phony of me to tell you the Grief Journey is over. Far from it—and mail is still coming in from people who have suffered the loss of a loved one and say this column has helped them deal with their grief. For me, sometimes there are a few good days in a row, then

BAM, like a sneaker wave, painful feelings of loss, fear, and loneliness hit and leave me sitting in my lazy girl chair staring at the wall, desperately wishing Burt would walk into the room.

And that's how it goes. Thanks to all seven of you who sent "The Middle Wife." Please do keep the funny stuff coming in.

Burt and granddaughter Autumn

From Midwife To Mid-Life

Reader response is always interesting. Last week's day brightener called "The Middle Wife" drew a great deal of letters from young women, but few from men—maybe because younger women's memories of childbirth are much keener than those of us (ahem) older gals, while men don't care for the subject one whit. At the end of that column, I encouraged readers to keep the funny stuff coming in. We all need laughter, which is so good for the soul. The following day brightener arrived shortly after last Friday's paper rolled off the presses. It came from a 54-year-old who asked that I not use her name. Brace yourselves.

> **Mid-Life. (Author unknown)**
>
> I've seen two shows lately that go on and on about how mid-life is a good time for women. Just last week, Dr. Oz's entire show was about how great menopause will be. Puleeeze.... I have a few thoughts of my own and would like to share them with you.
>
> Whether you are pushing 40, 50, 60 (or maybe just pushing your luck) you will probably relate. Mid-life is when the growth of hair on our legs slows down. This gives us plenty of time to care for our newly acquired mustache and chin hairs. In mid-life, women no longer have upper arms. We have wingspans. We no longer wear sleeveless shirts. We are flying squirrels in drag.
>
> Mid-life is when you stand in front of a mirror and you can see your rear without turning around. Mid-life is when you go for a mammogram and you realize that this is the only time

someone will ask you to appear topless. Mid-life is when you want to grab every firm young lovely in a tube top and scream, "Listen honey, even the Roman Empire fell and those will too!"

Mid-life brings the wisdom that life throws us curves, and we're sitting on our biggest one. Mid-life is when you look at your know-it-all-cell-phone-carrying teenager and think, "For this I have stretch marks?"

In mid-life, our memory starts to go. In fact, the only thing we can retain is water! Mid-life means that our Body by Jake now includes Legs by Rand McNally —more red and blue lines than an accurately scaled map of Wisconsin. Mid-life means you become more reflective. You start pondering the big questions such as, What is life? Why am I here? How much Healthy Choice ice cream can I eat before it's no longer a healthy choice?

But mid-life also brings with it an appreciation of what is important. We realize that bosoms sag, hips expand, and chins double, but our loved ones make the journey worthwhile. Would any of you trade the knowledge that you have now for the body you had way back when? Maybe our bodies simply have to expand to hold all the wisdom and love we've acquired. That's my philosophy and I'm sticking to it.

Life is short. Break the rules. Forgive quickly. Love truly. Laugh uncontrollably. Never regret anything that made you smile!

Thanks to the disgustingly young woman who sent this to me. I don't know her, but I hope she doesn't have to pluck chin hairs...yet. Her day brightener certainly made me smile and I hope it did the same for you.

Memories

Just when I thought it was time to feel OK about using the dreaded "W" word (widow), an email arrived from a woman who lost her beloved husband six years ago and she still can't check the box on various forms that ask you to specify "married, widowed, or single." She checks the "M" box and who are we to judge her? Everyone deals with the loss of a loved one in ways that seem odd to others.

Consider the woman who wrote that she sleeps in her husband's T-shirt because it still carries his scent. If I hadn't done a ton of Burt's laundry on the morning he died, I'd be wearing one of his T-shirts, too. You steady readers know I could not move his coffee cup for a month. He loved that cup because his daughter Robin had it specially made for him, with photos on the cup of loved ones. Guess who has that coffee cup now? It was time to hand it over to Robin, who treasures it because her Dad used it every day.

Since I am always open and honest with you, here are some odd things I do that, for me, feel comforting. Remember that load of laundry I did on that fateful morning? I carefully folded both loads of my husband's clothing and arranged them in stacks on his side of the bed. That way, during those toss and turn sleepless nights following his death, I would tell myself that the mound of his clothing was him. I also took the pillowcases off the pillows he used and kept them near my face because his scent was on them. Speaking of scent, here is maybe the strangest thing I do for comfort and I can't believe I'm confessing this. When Burt was courting me way back in 1969, he sometimes remembered to dab on English Leather cologne because he knew I liked it. Men do seem to make an extra effort when they are in pursuit of a woman and there are plenty of women reading this and nodding their heads in agreement. (I'm picturing the wife who would love to go out for a romantic dinner but her guy is slumped in a chair with a beer watching a football game). After we were married, Burt sort of forgot about English Leather unless I nagged or actually put a little on him before we headed out for the evening. He never bought any for himself but the stuff is still available. Guess who has a bottle of English Leather in the medicine cabinet and spritzes it on the towels in our bathroom? A bit crazy, you think? Maybe, but I don't care. The smell of English Leather brings back warm and fuzzy memories.

On the subject of happy memories, wonderful letters and emails are still coming in—sent either to our home address, or to my email address, or to the special email address set up by Lorna Davis and the Newport Chamber of Commerce for just this purpose. Today I want to share with you a letter written by our longtime friend and critter sitter, Esther Mentzer of Seal Rock. I had totally forgotten about the day a couple of years ago when I decided to invite several "senior ladies" to join me for lunch. None of these ladies knew one another, but each one accepted the invitation with enthusiasm. Here is Esther's letter:

> **Memory of a Wonderful, Thoughtful Gentleman**
>
> Bobbie called to invite me to go to lunch with her and some of her friends at Kum Yon's restaurant. Bobbie said she might need help reading the menu and the bill, so that was my assignment—to be her eyes, if necessary. Our server was a

single mother and she showed us a picture of her young son. While we were eating, Burt came in the restaurant and gave each of us a kiss and a beautiful long stemmed red rose. Since one of Bobbie's guests had not been able to attend the luncheon, Burt had an extra rose. When he paid for all our lunches, he presented our server with the rose. The server came over to our table with tears in her eyes. She said no one had ever done anything like that for her, ever. Burt said goodbye to us and gave us all another kiss, and there we sat—six women smiling and feeling so special because of Burt's thoughtfulness and generosity.

Except for my friend Edna Abbot and Esther, the other women who came that day are now gone, but the memory of Burt walking in with roses is such a special memory. Thank you Esther for sharing and for all the years you stepped up to care for our various dogs, cats, and even our South Beach barnyard full of miniature goats. Most of all, thank you for so many years of being our true and faithful friend.

Hey, dear readers, if you are still thinking of sending that special memory of how Burt touched your life in some way, it's not too late. Just look at how Esther's letter made my heart sing—and I had totally forgotten about that day at Kum Yon's, and the young mother who waited on us and cried because no one had ever given her a rose.

As an added incentive, please know I am sharing these stories with our daughters and loved ones. May the memory of this special man who knew how to make a difference in the lives of others live on in all of us as a reminder to reach out to others.

WHEN ANGELS SHOW UP TO HELP

If you are like most people, you love hearing stories of things you did when you were a little kid. My Aunt Victoria must have known a bit about child psychology. She often told the story of when I was a three-year-old and climbed up on a tall stool in a department store and stood there, hands on hips, defiantly refusing to get down. Aunt Vic, in her wisdom said, "Beverly, don't you dare get down off that stool!" Zip—down I came. Burt always knew of my independent streak and during the past couple of years would counsel me, "If I'm not around, you better learn to ask for help."

The past couple of weeks are loaded with examples (at least nine) of having to ask for help, and today I'm sharing just a few. I hesitate using names because there are just too many angels involved, and not everyone wants their name in print, so I will keep it limited.

This latest saga began on a recent rainy Sunday morning as I was late getting to the Presbyterian Church in Newport. I was raised a Presbyterian and now that I'm alone, I've been finding comfort, love, and a whole lot of warm hugs when I show up. I fired up my car, and in my rush, backed out of the garage—without opening the garage door. A first for me. I was horrified. The door went up but would not come down. Now the big decision—to go, or not to go to church. An inner voice said, *Go. You will accomplish nothing by staying home and worrying about getting that door fixed.* I was sure a new door would cost thousands of dollars.

As soon as the service was over, I headed for home, stopping briefly at JC Market for a few groceries. When I was at the checkout register, our dear friend Ted walked up and said, "You look like you could use a hug." I fought back tears while blubbering about my broken garage door.

"Oh," said Ted, "that happens to lots of people. Why don't I come out and take a look?"

Huh? Now? In the rain? An hour and a socket wrench later (whatever that is), Ted had the garage door fixed and working perfectly again. My car wasn't damaged because the bike rack on the car knocked the garage door off its tracks. It's not easy admitting doing such a dumb thing and I have such gratitude for Ted stepping up to help.

Here's another. Everyone is still reeling from the recent October storms hitting the coast. I rushed to clean out drains to keep the garage from being flooded. Then, during the worst of the storm, I noticed Burt's beloved American Flag being battered by the wind and about to be blown off that tall flagpole he got last year at the Home Show. I threw on my slicker and headed out on the deck to wrestle with that telescoping pole, having no idea how to get the pole and flag to descend. There I stood, soaking wet, hanging on to the deck rail, and mad at Burt for leaving me with all these problems. Suddenly I remembered that our son-in-law Glen has the same pole and flag. I called Glen in L.A., and in spite of the noise of the wind, he told me how to get the flagpole down and save the flag.

Two days later, on a Tuesday, a switch went out that controls half of the electricity in the kitchen. I may or may not get in trouble for disclosing this, but my young friend Gina has fallen "in like" with a very nice guy named Brett. They both declared Tuesday nights a time to come over, cook dinner, and watch a movie with me. As a non-cook, why would I turn down such a kind offer? Our friend Mark chose that night to drop by and fix a door that keeps sticking and maybe take a look at the broken switch. Five minutes later, another young man who had heard I needed help with that switch showed up. Try to picture the craziness going on. Gina's salad was ready on the kitchen counter and, always the consummate Girl Scout, she proceeded to get a blazing fire going in the fireplace. She has been coming here for several years and Burt usually had a fire going. She and Brett decided to carry on this tradition in Burt's honor. My only assignment was finding a working plug for the rice-maker. Meanwhile, Brett was busy preparing his coconut shrimp, while Mark and the other guy were fixing the broken switch.

I stood watching this circus-like scene and could almost hear Burt chuckling, "See what wonderful things happen when you ask for help?" I refuse to accept the fact that these angel helpers (all in their 50s) were here to lend a hand to a helpless older lady. Nope, there was too much fun and laughter going on to even consider that concept.

Life is full of angels and miracles, whether we label them that or not. I am learning to let go of my stubborn Swedish independent streak. The truth is that there have now been several nights when I crawled into bed with a smile on my face instead of tears—and another large lesson learned. It's okay to ask for help and then let go and let God figure out the answers.

Flappers, Dreams, And Stepping Out

I almost said "no" when Julie Hanrahan invited me to join her and Mark at the Columbia Bank table for a recent gala at the Hallmark Inn—a fundraiser for Habitat for Humanity. "It'll be such fun," said Julie, "and the theme is The Great Gatsby, so we'll all get gussied up. Gina and Brett are going, and you can come with them." *It's too soon,* I thought, *and it won't be any fun without Burt.*

I decided to sleep on it and let Julie know the next day. That night I dreamed of Aunt Victoria, who appeared so real in the dream. Perhaps she showed up because I mentioned her and her wisdom in last week's column. Who knows? I stopped questioning such things a long time ago. And I might be over-analyzing this, but Aunt Vic, born in 1898, was definitely a flapper because I've seen photos of her looking like she could have appeared in *The Great Gatsby* movie. Most of us can look back and think of a special mentor who deeply influenced our lives. Such a person was my Aunt Vic. I lived with her in Seattle for a while when I was 17. She was recently widowed and had gone back to work as an RN. I personally believe nurses are more realistic about life and death than most people. She also had a wicked sense of humor, which made me love her all the more.

How well I remember an evening in a home of some relative when I was about seven. If there was anything Vic could not stand, it was a boring occasion. Picture a living room full of stodgy Scandinavians sitting around quietly drinking coffee. I was curled up at my mother's feet when suddenly Aunt Victoria left the room. A kid knows when something is up. She soon reappeared wearing my flannel pajamas, which she could barely hold together across her ample bosom. For what it's worth, she kept on her heavy-duty bra and girdle—the kind worn by most old ladies of her day. (Did I say old? She was in her early 50s then, but when you're a little kid, anyone over 13 is old.) With a straight face, she waltzed around the room like the most fashionable model until everyone started laughing. She did things like that. If I had known then about the Spoon on the Nose trick, I would have taught her how to do it.

Another memorable occasion, this time when I was 17, was when Aunt Victoria decided to host a luncheon for the new pastor of her church. About 20 church ladies were sitting in the living room, balancing trays of food on their laps, everyone acting stiff, proper, and serious. Suddenly, the poor minister lost track of his tray and it hit the floor upside down. I quickly glanced at Aunt Vic to see what she would do. Without missing a beat, she flipped her own tray to the floor and everyone broke up laughing—especially the surprised pastor who was saved from embarrassment. Can you imagine what I learned from this? Sure you can—the importance of making people comfortable no matter the occasion.

Aunt Victoria taught me a great deal about life and love during that time with her. One rainy Seattle night we were sitting by the fire and she said, "You know, Bobbie, when I lost your Uncle Paul, I lost the best friend I ever had." Those words stayed with me during a "friendless" first marriage, but especially during the 44 years of Burt being my best friend.

Getting back to that dream when Aunt Vic showed up (and I

swear she was wearing a flapper outfit), her message was loud and clear: "Get yourself together and go to that party. Life is too short and you know it!"

Did I go? Did I gussie up? Did I enjoy it? What do you think?

Today, as you read this, I have been without my best friend for exactly three months. Burt would have loved the Gatsby party and I am somewhat suspicious that he was the one who sent Aunt Victoria in her outrageous outfit to push me into going. To be honest, it felt like both of them were at the party whooping it up and having a great time.

**Bobbie with Brett and Gina at the "The Great Gatsby"
Habitat for Humanity Gala**

From Mucking To Mowing

When you need help, do you come right out and ask for it, or beat around the bush, or whine pathetically, or try to do whatever needs doing yourself? I've been struggling with this issue, especially now since Burt left me and now I must go it alone. You steady readers know I have a bizarre sense of humor and today I am sharing two instances related to that old saying: "Do not engage mouth until brain is in gear!"

Instance Number 1

Back in the 1980s, Burt and I moved from Los Angeles to South Beach, Oregon, with our cat and two rescued Russian Wolfhounds. We fenced a large chunk of the doublewide lot and called it The Barnyard. Because the original owner had a horse, the property came with a small barn and you do not want to waste a perfectly good barn, so we started accumulating miniature goats. Someone dubbed our place "The Home of Tall Dogs and Short Goats."

How I loved that little barn full of sweet smelling alfalfa and straw. Even the goats smelled nice, like baby powder. I was not dumb enough to have a billy goat—they are the ones that smell terrible. But any barn occupied by critters needs an occasional mucking out. I even enjoyed doing that and Burt would often pitch in and help.

Is this how pitchforks got named pitchforks?
Never mind.

Good Grief

One month, I found myself housebound due to surgery on a detached retina. Our good friends Dave and Linda Miller of local radio station fame called to ask if there was anything they could do. I jokingly said, "Sure, Linda, you can muck out our barn." Believe me, I was kidding. The next day, Burt said it would be good for me to get out of the house, and we'd go for a little drive. We were not gone long but imagine our surprise when we returned and the Miller van was there. So were the Millers and all five kids who were in the barnyard with wheelbarrow, rakes, brooms, and Dave with a pitchfork, getting the job done with the questionable help of goats and dogs. It was a stunning sight and that barn ended up so clean, Burt and I could have moved in and set up housekeeping. Linda had taken me seriously.

Before I get to Instance Number. 2, which is very current, there are so many "angel helpers" in what my daughter Rocki refers to as my village—people who step up to help without me even having to ask. A perfect example are the Littlehales, who insist on driving me for visits with my retina surgeon. We have a good time, although poor Chuck can't get a word in because Patti and I never stop talking.

You know I also have another Charley in my life—our aging standard poodle. Not too long ago, Burt and I thought it was time to make "the big decision" when Charley stopped eating and just slept for two days. His hind legs are giving out, but when Burt died, Charley decided to hang around and keep me canine company. However, he can no longer withstand going to the groomer, and I can't lift him into the car anyhow. Kudos to Charley's long time dog groomer Gloria McCreadie at Amore's in South Beach. Last week, Gloria insisted on coming here to cut Charley's nails and do a bit of hair clipping to tidy him up. A poodle has hair, not fur, and it just keeps growing and growing.

Gloria did this as a friend and refused to let me pay her. Talk about a random act of kindness.

Instance Number 2

In L.A., there's a funny saying about gardeners. Many people need them and often use the term "mow, blow, and go." When we lived there, a guy showed up once a week, mowed the lawn, trimmed the hedges, and used a power thing to blow all the leaves and crud from our yard into the yard next door. Then the neighbor's gardener would arrive and blow all the leaves and crud back into our yard. So much for life in L.A. For three years, a young man has been coming here to keep the place looking nice, but no more. Long story. No need to explain why, but it is just one more thing I have to deal with on my own.

One night, while driving to a meeting with my neighbor Janet Anton, I jokingly mentioned that our grass was almost knee deep. "Oh," said Janet, "I love to mow. I'll come over with our mower and do it!" Huh? What? Not only did Janet show up the next day, but so did her husband Al, in their truck with a power mower, edger, and blower. Just like that long-ago scene in the barnyard, I was stunned to see these good neighbors efficiently getting to work. Of course, I wasn't about to just sit and watch so I joined in to do some serious weed pulling. When Al fired up his power blower, he blew all the pine needles and crud in our driveway into a neat pile, which will now bio-degrade on our property and not end up in our near neighbor's yard.

Yes, I'm learning to ask for help, although so far friends are stepping up faster than I can ask. But I do need to put a clamp on my sense of humor and remember: "Do Not Engage Mouth Until Brain Is In Gear." Unless, of course, I seriously need something done.

When It's Time To Say Goodbye

People with old or ailing animals often ask, "How do you know when it's time to let them go?" I once heard a veterinarian answer, "You just know."

The other morning, our dog Czar let me know it was time. There was no mistaking the look in those big brown eyes that said, 'I'm old, and there is no longer any quality or dignity to my life. It's time.' After a long walk on the beach trying to prolong the decision, I came home knowing there was no choice. To make it easier for Czar, our veterinarian agreed to come to my house on his lunch hour. I spent the morning sitting next to the old dog as he lay on his blanket, his head in my lap.

My thoughts drifted back to the day Czar came into my life. He was owned by people who perhaps shouldn't have had a dog as big as a Russian Wolfhound—or Borzoi--which is the official name of this breed. Czar was never allowed in their house and I was told he spent much of the time standing outside, looking mournfully at the humans through the window.

One day, the family maid said, "I'm tired of washing nose prints off the glass. Either that dog goes, or I do." Apparently, good maids are harder to find than a good dog, and Czar was soon on his way to the animal shelter. It was love at first sight when this tall hound and I discovered each other. He stood up on his hind legs, planted his front paws on my shoulders, and greeted me with a big kiss.

Bobbie Lippman

When I was a little girl, we always had dogs, but usually of the mixed-breed sort. I distinctly remember a series of vodka advertisements showing a pair of tall, elegant, snow-white Russian wolfhounds. I dreamed of someday owning one but honestly believed only the wealthy could afford such a beautiful animal. Finding a dog like Czar at the shelter was indeed a dream come true. After several months of adjusting to each other, I took Czar through a 10-week dog obedience course. When you spend a great deal of time training an animal you seem to bond with them even more closely. On Commencement Night, several friends came to watch, bringing doggy gifts for the new graduate. Czar gave the exercises his enthusiastic all and received the first place trophy.

Not long after that, my brother Dan came for a visit and, after unpacking, sat down in the living room. Five minutes later, Czar carried in a sweater from the guest room, depositing it in my brother's lap. Dan is still wondering if perhaps Czar was trying to say, "You look cold, here's your sweater." Or maybe, "I think you've stayed long enough. You can go home now."

I took Czar everywhere with me. One day while sitting on a grassy bank watching a tennis tournament, a boy circled, then finally approached. He stared at Czar for quite some time and finally asked, "What do you s'pose a dog like that costs anyhow?"

"Oh," I answered absently, "probably about $500."

"Well," said the boy, "you certainly got your money's worth!"

While spending the final hours with Czar, I thought of this thing called grief and remembered the time when I stopped by the vet's office to pick up some medicine for a sick cat. The only others in the waiting room were an elderly man and woman who were standing by some plastic plants in the corner, their backs to me. I sat there, watching, with curiosity.

Good Grief

Just then, the vet came out and said to them, "I'm very sorry I was hoping surgery would help, but your Laddie was just too old. He didn't make it." I will never forget the sight of that elderly couple, walking toward their car, shoulders bent in grief. In the old man's hand was a frayed, red dog collar.

When I started dwelling on all my long walks on the beach with Czar—and how there would be no more—my tears fell down onto his muzzle. His tail wagged feebly, and he looked up at me as if to say, "Please don't cry. Just look at all the good years we've had together."

I sat with Czar, thinking about what animals bring to us. Some are trouble, especially in the early days of training them to fit into our lifestyles. But eventually they almost always give back total loyalty and love. The last hours with this grand old dog went by too fast. Soon, Dr. Brown arrived and moments later, it was done with the quiet dignity of euthanasia. There are people who avoid having pets because it hurts too much to lose them. But unless we expose ourselves to the painful lows in life, how can we ever experience the happy highs?

Before the day was over, friends dropped by. Some came just to hug. Some brought bunches of flowers. And later, another note arrived from the local animal shelter saying a donation had been made in Czar's name so that other animals might live. (If you care about someone who has lost a pet, this is a wonderful idea.) Czar had a long, good life and gave so much. The least I could give to him was a kind and gentle death.

NOTE: This story was published in *Chicken Soup for the Soul*, under the title, "What I Learned From The Dog."

**Bobbie & Czar (age 13)
Last walk on the beach
(photo by Burt Lippman)**

A Few Life Lessons

Last week I thought there would not be a "Bobbie's Beat" column because I was laid flat with a miserable cold. (Is there any other kind?) I haven't been ill in many years, but now I know that grief lowers the immune system and I was wide open to bugs. To be sick and alone is awful, but at least I had Charley and Lap Sitter keeping me company, although pets are hopeless at looking sympathetic or bringing a sick person tea and oranges.

But you regular readers know there is usually a story behind a story. My office is up a flight of stairs and Charley's failing hind legs allow him to go down steps but not up. I tried blocking him from following me up to my office, which caused such separation anxiety he had an "accident" on the downstairs carpet. What to do, what to do? Burt might have figured it out, but he isn't here to problem-solve.

Bingo! A light bulb went on in my head and I devised a wide elastic strap that works as a sling around his belly. Now the two of us slowly climb the stairs, with me holding up his rear weight with the sling. He is presently asleep at my feet and his happiness helped inspire last week's dog column. I have been mildly surprised at the amount of reader response—folks who clearly love dogs and had not read the Czar story before. What makes me smile is these people are not asking how I am doing, but only about old Charley. Here's my stock answer: I am not about to make the euthanasia decision as long as Charley is still enjoying life and can be with me as I write. After every meal, he feels so good he plays with a squeaky toy for about three minutes and then takes a nap. You do not euthanize an old dog who still wants to play.

Speaking of mail from readers, I continue to hear from widows and widowers who claim this column is helping them. I search through their words for advice on how they are dealing with this thing called grief. No one warned me about crashing immune systems and getting sick. No one wrote about weight loss or how most food tastes like sawdust. No one confessed she backed into her garage door without opening it first. No one encouraged me to get out and do things whether I feel like it or not. What I'm doing is one step one day at a time, and trusting my intuition whether to go out or stay home.

This past week, once I started feeling better, I made a last-minute decision to attend the traditional Halloween gathering at Chuck and Patti Littlehales' home. Burt and I have gone to this for years. Their neighborhood streets are legally blocked off because hundreds of children show up in costumes. Going to this festive affair without Burt was one more step in moving forward in life. At the party, I made a new friend who just moved to Newport and is dealing with being a widow. We bonded instantly and I learned more from her about grief and widowhood than from most other sources. I tend to think she is the major reason my intuition said, "Go to that party." I also know full well that Burt would have been ticked at me for staying home and feeling sorry for myself.

Saturday night I was given tickets to the Newport Symphony at the Performing Arts Center and I almost didn't go. Once more, that inner voice told me to get it together, and once more I ended up spending quality time with a widow (much younger than me). I have known this person for a long time and have thought of calling her for advice on how to be a widow, but kept procrastinating. Not only did we enjoy the symphony together, we also did some valuable sharing time on the ride home. An important lesson today is for all of you people out there who are alone and dragging your feet about getting out and discovering what gifts are just waiting to enrich your lives. Trust your intuition. Nothing ventured, nothing gained.

Since today is all about lessons, here's one of my favorites:

Pickup in the rain

One night at 11:30, an older African American woman was standing on the side of an Alabama highway trying to endure a lashing rainstorm. Her car had broken down and she desperately needed a ride. Soaking wet, she decided to flag down the next car. A young white man stopped to help her, generally unheard of in those conflict-filled 1960s. The man helped her get assistance for her car and then put her into a taxicab. She seemed to be in a big hurry but wrote down his name and address and thanked him. Seven days went by and a knock came on the man's door. To his surprise, a giant console color TV was delivered to his home. A special note was attached. It read: "Thank you so much for assisting me on the highway the other night. The rain drenched not only my clothes, but also my spirits. Then you came along. Because of you, I was able to make it to my dying husband's bedside just before he passed away. God bless you for helping me and unselfishly serving others."

Sincerely, Mrs. Nat King Cole.

The Power Of Words

Nobody goes through life without ups and downs, and when you are hit with a huge bummer—a health challenge, loss of a loved one, or other trauma—words from well-meaning people can help or hurt. Words are incredibly powerful, even words left unsaid. There are six words that should never come out of our mouths: "I know just how you feel." Do we really know?

The same goes for when you are excited about tackling a new adventure and people are quick to rain on your parade. When Burt and I decided to escape the Los Angeles fast lane and move to Oregon, way too many "friends" insisted we were nuts. The same negative words bombarded me when I set a goal to bicycle from Canada to Mexico. "You'll get wiped out by a logging truck," people warned. When I chose a hiking-camping adventure in Africa, the words, "watch out for malaria and lions," were not exactly encouraging.

So what triggered this subject today? My husband used to do most of the shopping—groceries, household needs, etc. He loved doing it and would schmooze his way from one end of a store to the other. Now, shopping is my job. The other day a male stranger about my age walked up and said, "How's Burt?" I was dumbstruck by his question and honestly could not speak. I just stared at this man, who obviously knew Burt but is clueless about our community and doesn't read the newspaper. When I finally got out the words that my husband had died, this guy

Good Grief

immediately launched into his story about losing a family member 30 years ago. I wanted to smack him. I wanted him to say something like: 'I'm so sorry. Burt was a great guy and so friendly to everyone. I loved his smile and always felt better whenever I saw him.' Those words have been expressed by countless people who knew Burt, and their words have been an incredible comfort for me. But all this guy had to say was two words: "I'm sorry." My mood in that store was pretty good until this man sent me into such depression I knew the next "Bobbie's Beat" column had to be about the power of words—the ones said and the ones unsaid.

Consider the person who tells you they were just diagnosed with cancer and your first reaction is to start yammering about your own experience with this dreaded disease. Please resist this urge, folks, and either listen or shut up. Last week, I used a term in this column that applied to me: "Do not engage mouth until brain is in gear." I'm trying to forget that insensitive guy in the store. Anger is a foreign feeling for me, but perhaps sharing how his non-words hurt will be of help to you the next time someone needs you to listen. Just when I've been sitting here trying to figure out an upbeat ending to this column, a day brightener showed up from a reader in Chicago. It is absolutely right-on with the subject today, and the punch line left me laughing.

The Pope and the Haircut

A man went to his barber to get a haircut before he left on a trip to Rome. He was telling his barber about the trip when the barber said, "Rome? Why would anyone go there? It's crowded and dirty! So, how are you getting there?"

"We're flying on TWA," the man told him.

"TWA?" exclaimed the barber. "That's a terrible choice! The

planes are old and the flight attendants are ugly. Where are you staying in Rome?"

"Oh, we're at the downtown Marriott."

"What? That dump with its overpriced rooms and poor service? Well, what are you doing when you get there?" the barber griped.

"Going to the Vatican and we hope to see the Pope."

"Yeah? Well good luck. A million people want to see the Pope. You'll never even get close."

A month later, the man was back for another haircut. The barber asked about the trip to Rome. "Oh, it was wonderful. We were on a brand new plane and it was so overcrowded we got bumped to first class where a beautiful young stewardess waited on us hand and foot. And the hotel was fantastic! They had just finished remodeling and were overbooked, so they gave us the presidential suite at no extra charge!"

"Well, I know you didn't get to see the Pope," the surly barber grumbled.

"Oh, but we did!" the man exclaimed. "We toured the Vatican and were chosen to personally meet the Pope! I actually knelt down as he spoke a few words to me!"

"Really?" the barber said, impressed despite himself. "What did he say?"

"He said, 'Where'd you get that lousy haircut?'"

That's it, dear readers. Thanks for your mountain of mail full of encouraging and helpful words during this difficult Grief Journey. It's impossible to personally answer all of you, for which I apologize, but just knowing you're out there, interested and caring, is the reason this column wrote itself today.

MAKING PROGRESS

Confession time. After sending last week's column off to my editor at the *News-Times*, I found myself thinking it was time to pack it in and quit writing. I had written words about the importance of words, especially words said or unsaid to someone who is in a fragile place after suffering a major loss. I had written about being angry (unusual for me) at an insensitive jerk in a local store. In retrospect, I wondered if I should have given him the benefit of the doubt. Maybe he was having a bad day, maybe he really needed to talk about his own loss from so many years ago. Maybe he thought I was tired of hearing the words, "I'm so sorry Burt died." (He would be wrong about that last one).

Then that column hit print, followed by an amazing and unprecedented positive response from readers. I've never kept count before but this week I needed to due to flagging confidence in my own words. It may be unusual for a columnist of a small town newspaper to get sixty "I totally relate and understand" reader responses. So guess what, I'm not quitting.

And as far as anger regarding that guy in the grocery store, I'm over it.

Join me now as I segue into the good stuff that happened since last week. My friend of 30 years, Edna Abbott, is living in a Lincoln Beach care home called Sunshine House. Twice I've lined up friends to drive me, and twice it didn't work out. Third time's the charm and yesterday, thanks to being chauffeured by the Littlehales, it was sheer joy to reconnect with Edna, meet her caregivers, Ana and Christina, and come away knowing how happy, safe, and content my friend is in her new life.

Last night, I accepted a dinner invite from Pat Lewis and Lavern Weber, made possible because Marylou and Bruce Mate were my necessary drivers. It was such fun spending an evening with good friends with whom Burt and I share a long history. I could almost feel Burt looking down, watching, smiling, and happy to see me laughing. I will forever be indebted to Pat Lewis for asking me to lunch that fateful day when cardiac arrest caused Burt to suddenly fall to the floor after a Rotary meeting at the Embarcadero Resort & Marina. God does work in wondrous ways.

I recently decided it was time to start letting go of Burt's things, particularly clothing. People have been writing to me about this issue, and it seems everyone goes about the task when they feel up to it. I approached the job from a strictly selfish viewpoint—it is just too depressing every time I opened a drawer or walked into the closet we shared. I started by getting rid of a ton of unused medical supplies, then socks, clean undershirts and never worn underwear. I turned it over to Kath Schonau of Aging Wisely With Heartfelt Hands who knows where these things will benefit people who have a real need, especially now with winter here. This morning I had an "AHA moment" when my young friend Gina Nielsen reminded me that Burt is continuing to help others who will benefit from all this stuff. I had not stopped to look at it that way. Now the dreaded job will be easier and I will no longer think of it as awful and depressing.

In a way, I guess this column continues to be about words and attitude and getting on with life without your loved one. I know Burt would approve of my progress although he would probably think I've wallowed around feeling sad and depressed way too long. Since I try to end these columns with something to smile about, a day brightener that just arrived from local reader Art Bradley fits the bill. It's a long list of bumper stickers for the elderly. Here are three that made me laugh out loud:

> "I'm retired. I was tired yesterday, and I'm tired again today."
>
> "Campbell's new large type alphabet soup for seniors."
>
> "I asked my wife if old men wear boxers or briefs. She said, Depends."

That's it for today, with gratitude to all you folks who responded so positively to last week's column. Oh, one last thing. I can't resist sharing just a part of one email, but am changing names:

> Dear Bobbie. Yes, we are out here and loving your columns. Keep up the good work. In the few years since my husband Tom died, I've encountered only one person who asked, "How is Tom. I haven't seen him in awhile?" My thoughts rapidly cycled from laughter to tears to a factual response. Just know that your network is out here waiting for you every Friday.

The Locket

Today's column is dedicated to a compassionate nurse whose act of kindness during a time of such shock and stress resulted in showing me, once again, that life is full of surprises and there are always new things to be learned.

A few weeks after Burt died, I needed to get out of the house and just walk. I could have walked in my own neighborhood, or on the beach, but I ended up driving to the north end of town where I wandered around aimlessly as if trying to walk away from my grief. I had no plans or intention of walking into Diamonds By The Sea, but there I stood in the middle of the store having no clue what led me there. Owner Kathy Heater stepped out from the back room, took one look at me, and held out her arms. I've known Kathy for 30 years. She and Burt redesigned my wedding ring for our 20th anniversary and I have several treasures from her store.

Kathy and I shared tears and girl-talk for quite awhile. Somehow, the conversation led to an incident in the emergency room at the hospital that fateful July day and I heard myself telling Kathy about someone who asked if I wanted a few locks of my husband's white curly hair. When I nodded yes, this wonderful woman quickly produced a pair of scissors and two small Ziploc medical bags. Those days and weeks are a foggy blur, but I know our girls and a couple of close friends ended up with Burt's curls.

After telling Kathy Heater this story, she suggested I

consider a locket. "The history of the locket goes back a long way," she said, "and the original purpose of a locket was, and still is, for a lock of a loved one's hair."

This may not be news to you, but it was to me, and I left Diamonds By The Sea thinking and wondering if perhaps Burt had steered me there. Here is where the story takes a dramatic turn. That very night, my friend Gina Nielsen showed up with soup—the only thing I felt like eating. She handed over a small gift bag and asked me to open it.

"This belonged to my mom," she said, "and since you're like a mom to me, I want you to have it."

Gina was only 19 when her mother died, which might help explain our special friendship. I opened the little gift box and inside was a locket on a gold chain. "Go ahead and open the locket," she said, "but you don't have to wear it if you don't want to."

Inside the double-sided locket was my favorite photo of Burt and on the other side a lock of his beautiful white hair. I was speechless, touched, and of course tearful. I've written often in this column that everyone deals with grief and loss in whatever way feels right, and the locket began its own little journey. For a couple of weeks it stayed under my pillow, then gradually into the front pocket of tee shirts I wear every day when I'm home. Eventually, I was able to wear the locket inside my clothing, near my heart. I couldn't risk having someone touch or open the locket, which would have caused me a flood of uncontrollable tears. Have I mentioned that grieving people are very fragile and we need to keep this in mind and cut them some slack?

This week, I am wearing the locket the way a locket is meant to be worn, so I guess you might call this progress. Grief is definitely a journey with many variables, and sooner or later we all have to walk the walk.

And now this story takes another turn. Those of us of a certain age know exactly where we were on the day President Kennedy was assassinated. Since this month marks the 50th anniversary of his death, the media has been full of nonstop news that is no longer news of that terrible day in Dallas, Texas. Most of us know every detail of that day but there was a brief mention on the radio recently about an incident unknown to me. Apparently, back at the White House, Jackie and JFK's brother Bobby arranged for a final private viewing. The casket was opened and Jackie snipped off a few locks of her husband's hair.

I can't help but wonder if she ever got around to putting the president's hair in a locket. I guess we'll never know.

Burt and Bobbie Lippman

The Traveling Fruitcake

"Most fruitcakes weigh more than the oven they are cooked in."
—Erma Bombeck.

Since this column took off in the Newport *News-Times* back in the 1980s, I have rarely missed a holiday season without expounding on the subject of fruitcake. I've admitted to one and all that I personally hate all that rubbery fake fruit and the sawdust that holds it together. Then I sit back and wait gleefully for mail to pour in from irate readers (usually women) who pride themselves on their fruitcakes and act as if I have accused them of producing ugly children. My mother was hooked on Erma Bombeck's columns and I think it was Erma who said, "Fruitcakes make dandy doorstops."

A rather new development has been going on between my daughter Rocki and me in the last six months. Allow me to brag a bit, but she happens to have a high-power, challenging job in Los Angeles, which she loves except for the three-hour commute back and forth from her home. I pride myself on not being a helicopter mother, i.e. hovering over her and wanting to know every detail of her life. I wait for her to call me, unless something is really important. Before Burt died, Rocki put in a "commuter call" to me every other Friday during her bumper-to-bumper drive home. I relished those calls. Now she is calling two or three times a week, just to make sure I'm OK in my new life of being alone. I call this "guilt-free communication with your busy kid."

During a recent call, she suddenly said, "When did you put that damn fruitcake in our garage freezer?" (I'm thinking, *It's about time she found it.*) So here's the story of one particular fruitcake that showed up mysteriously in our freezer, wrapped in Christmas paper and dated December 1997.

We knew Rocki and her husband Glen had put it there, but we never gave them the satisfaction reaction. Not admitting anything was part of the game we played with them for years. That frozen chunk of misery has gone back and forth from freezer to freezer whenever we (or they) could get away with it.

In May 2012, when we drove down to California for granddaughter Autumn's wedding, the ancient fruitcake, disguised in freezer wrap, went along in my suitcase. One day, during our stay with Rocki and Glen, we waited until they left the house. Like a couple of stealth burglars, Burt and I snuck out to their garage freezer and hid the 1997 fruitcake way in the back, never to be thought of again until Rocki's phone call.

The rest of the story is so good it makes me smirk with wicked delight. Rocki and Glen entertain a lot and they recently had more company than expected and consequently less dessert to serve these fine folks. Unlike me, Rocki's mother-in-law Marion is an excellent cook and an outstanding baker. Her zucchini banana bread is drop-dead delicious, and she is very generous with sharing. Marion has always made it with a ton of chocolate chips because it was the only way her kids would eat a vegetable. Somewhere in my daughter's brain, she vaguely remembered seeing that wrapped thing in their garage freezer, assumed it was from Marion, and ran to retrieve it to serve to their guests. Do you know how I would have loved seeing her face when she saw that old fruitcake, and do you know how Burt would have enjoyed this story?

Meanwhile, with half-hearted apologies to all you ladies busily baking fruitcakes, the bottom line today is not how much I hate fruitcake, but how much I am enjoying the frequent commuter calls from my daughter. This morning I peeled one of my favorite magnets from the refrigerator door. It's right here on my desk now because I want to leave you with the exact quote: "No matter how old she is, a mother watches her middle-aged kids for signs of improvement."

Hey Rocki, keep them commuter calls coming. I know you have dozens of people on your "call list," but you have certainly helped your mama get through these past months more than you will ever know.

Burt and Bobbie at granddaughter Autumn's wedding in Santa Barbara, 2012

The Dreaded Firsts

There is a book called *Feel the Fear and Do it Anyway*, by Susan Jeffers. Back in the day as a motivational speaker, I would often recommend this book because most people have a fear of something. I would remind the audience that nobody had a mother who hollered as we were going out the door, "Be sure and take some risks today, honey!" When the laughter died down, I would ask them what their mothers did say and the whole room would echo in unison with "BE CAREFUL!"

This past week I've thought about feeling the fear, but for me it's more like feeling the fear and the pain. These ponderings lead me to a recent event—the annual Rotary holiday dinner that Burt and I have attended for years. I had not given it a thought until being invited as a guest. My first reaction was to say no way, especially when I found out the party was at the Embarcadero Resort & Marina where my husband died in my arms six months ago. Then I decided to examine all my feelings about going. It would be a joyful occasion, and I would be with good friends. And sooner or later, I would have to walk into the Embarcadero anyway, so why not get it over with? My heart said, "Go, feel the pain, feel the fear of crying in front of everybody, and do it anyway."

Was it the right decision? Yes. Did I feel waves of sadness during the evening without Burt beside me? Sure. Was I greeted with a ton of love and Rotarian hugs? Of course. Compassion for others is what Rotary is all about, and to be honest, Burt would have wanted me to be there. By the way, I did get teary-eyed a few times but I did not blubber all over the tablecloth.

On the subject of books, there are so many related to grief and loss recommended to me by friends and readers of this column. One of the good things about a Kindle e-book is being able to enlarge the font needed for a vision challenge, but you can also download free sample chapters to see if a particular book is good enough to buy. Many book lovers believe a book has to be really special or why put a lot of time into it?

When I used to read regular printed books, my life was usually so busy I didn't have the luxury of time to plow through a yawner, so I had a personal rule: if a book didn't grab my interest by the page of my age, forget it. With a Kindle, there are no page numbers, but at least I can usually tell from the sample chapters if a book is for me. After sampling at least 20 books on grief, my favorite is definitely *Healing After Loss*, by Martha Hickman, which is in the form of daily meditations and common sense advice on grief and loss. Each entry begins with a quotation, but recently the words were not in quote form, but simply this: "I was beginning to do better. I thought I was doing better, but a few days ago the holidays just hit me." (Widow contemplating her first Christmas alone). Wow. How true, and I just put quote marks around that sentence because somebody wrote those words, not me. What matters is the heart-wrenching truth for anyone who has lost a loved one and there are all those "firsts" we have to deal with and struggle through.

During the next two weeks will be Christmas and my birthday, but the toughest time will be our 44th anniversary. I've no idea how I will spend that day, but I refuse to dwell on it right now. Others have survived these "dreaded firsts" and with God's help so will I.

I'm learning to take just one day at a time. If I start worrying about the next day, week, month, or year, it makes me crazy so I am forced to focus on the present, which is pretty good advice for all of us. In fact, a reader sent in this gem of wisdom: "Each day is a gift. That's why it is called the Present."

Two Virginal Coats

Allow me to get the gloom over with by admitting to you this has been a miserable week and until right now, there wasn't going to be column. For what it's worth, you steady readers know I haven't missed a week since my husband died six months ago today. Writing is therapeutic for me, as are all the encouraging responses from you folks out there cheering me on. I'm certainly not the only one dealing with grief and the holidays, but I might be alone facing a few other things—like knowing each day may be the last day for our old dog Charley, plus fighting to hang on to my vision (macular degeneration), which has been changing in various ways since Burt died. Stress related? Grief related? Who knows? But I am seeing a lot of my ophthalmologist and retina surgeon.

It also felt like it was time to start getting rid of Burt's clothing. He never bought stuff without me along to help make decisions, consequently every item is a memory. You might be thinking, *Well, what's the big hurry? Everyone faces this chore when they feel its time.* For me, just seeing his things in our closet sent me into such sadness that I am forced to start. Then, last week, while staring at a beautiful sweater we got during our traveling days, my whole body went berserk. For the first time in my life, I had what people call a "dizzy spell." I used Burt's blood pressure cuff and was horrified to see the scary spike in my BP. The bottom line is I saw my doctor this morning and am now getting help.

BOBBIE LIPPMAN

Before writing every column, I take what I call "quiet time" to pray and meditate. Here's my personal philosophy: Prayer is when I talk to God. Meditation is when I shut up and let God talk to me. I never know until I clear the cobwebs out of my head what the column subject will be. So, whether or not you're a believer, here is what I got: "Be honest with your feelings, Bobbie. I gave you the gift of honesty. Then throw in a story because I also gave you the gift of storytelling."

There are often surprises, and today is no exception because you get to read about our Two Virginal Coats. By virginal, I mean these coats have never been worn. Tried on, yes, but never worn.

Virginal coat number one: In 1982, Burt and I knew we were leaving Los Angeles to live on the Oregon coast. All we heard about was rain, rain, and more rain. We set off to hit the malls and finally found what we assumed were coats worn by Oregonians—very nice full-length raincoats. We chose a matched pair and in the mirror, we looked like Mr. and Mrs. Sherlock Holmes. After settling down in South Beach, we soon noticed that nobody wore a Sherlock Holmes raincoat. The locals rarely used an umbrella either, and we had arrived with six. I eventually donated my raincoat to the Salvation Army but Burt somehow could not part with his, although he never wore it.

Virginal coat number two: Early in the 21st century, we were living back in L.A., spending time with kids, grandkids, and close friends we had left behind. Such a friend was Judy, a wealthy widow my age. We had been friends for years. Judy, her husband, and their four sons bought the Burt Lancaster house in Bel Air. Judy got me into playing racquetball—on her own private court—and I coerced her into my world of bicycling, plus a woman's group on sexuality, which lasted years past any discussion of sex. A long-time smoker, it wasn't a big surprise

Good Grief

when Judy was diagnosed with advanced lung cancer. I became her advocate and took her to doctor and chemo sessions until she chose to stop treatment but we continued to see each other several times a week. One day, she asked me to accompany her upstairs to what she called her "fur closet." At this stage of her illness, Judy had installed one of those electric stair chairs because she was too weak to climb steps. She even made me ride the chair for the fun of it.

Up in her fur closet, she directed me to take down a long zippered bag. She stood (weakly) at the closet door watching as I removed the coat from the bag. I had never seen this gorgeous, full-length black leather hand-tooled coat with fox trim before, but we certainly saw Judy at fancy occasions when she wore one of her many furs. "It was a gift from Mike," she said (not the real name of an old wealthy lover). "Bobbie, any idiot can see the coat is for a very tall woman. I guess Mike never noticed I'm only 5-foot-4, but I want you to have the coat and do with it as you please." I may be tall, but I never wore the coat, not in L.A. and certainly not after we moved back to the Oregon coast. Burt's raincoat and Judy's incredible leather coat have been hanging side by side all these years, keeping each other company. Now that I'm closet cleaning, the appropriate decision has been made: the two virginal coats are about to start their new lives in the costume department of the Newport Performing Arts Center.

My fantasy is someday to attend a show starring the coats—perhaps Sherlock Holmes and an extremely tall actress, size 14.

Marriage Made In Heaven

Today's column was inspired by two reasons. First, a ton of advice from others dealing with the loss of a loved one: "Focus on the happy memories, Bobbie. Don't get bogged down dwelling on what you no longer have." So here goes.

Once upon a time, there were two people who were afraid to love again. They had both married young and later divorced. When their marriages failed, the two people, who did not know each other, went around saying "Never again! Divorce is too painful."

And then—one February in 1969—they met in a Beverly Hills business office. The attraction was great, but not as great as the fear of commitment. Many weeks went by before the man and woman began to cautiously date. The woman, who had been single for some time, lived with her nine-year-old daughter. The little girl felt strongly that it was time her mother found someone.

One day, when the daughter and mother were doing dishes, the girl said, "You know, Mom, you're not getting any younger. I think this Burt Lippman you're dating is the one, so please don't blow it." Then the girl added, "I love him, you know."

The mother was surprised that a child would say such a thing, but she started to lose her fear and slowly began to trust her feelings again. The man felt the same way. The little girl loved the man because he was nice enough (or smart enough?) to include her on almost all dates with the mother.

Eight months after the couple met, they were asked by some

friends to fly in a small plane to Las Vegas—just for dinner. The man and woman, who had never been in a small plane before, accepted. On a Saturday afternoon, halfway to Las Vegas at 9,000 feet, the Beechcraft Bonanza flew into a cluster of black clouds. Suddenly, hailstones began pounding the little plane, making a sound very much like the staccato noise of a machine gun. The man and woman turned to look at each other with frightened faces. The man said, "I think we're going to die, and since we're going to die anyhow, will you marry me?"

The woman, who was also certain they were going to die, felt she had nothing to lose, tightened her seatbelt and said, "YES!"

At that very moment—just like in an MGM movie—the little airplane flew out of the hailstorm into blue sky and bright sunshine. The man and woman looked out the window and then at each other, almost expecting to hear a loud voice from heaven saying "Gotcha!"

The pilot and his wife in the front seats said, "Congratulations! We heard the whole thing. You two are officially engaged and we'll celebrate in Las Vegas." When the man and woman realized they were now in a committed relationship, there were new decisions to be made. Somehow, it seemed logical to them that if you get engaged up in the sky at 9,000 feet, why not get married at 10,000 feet? They'd just have to rent a larger plane.

About this time, a relative who heard of the airplane wedding plans registered a complaint. This relative had long been locked into thinking that weddings must always be done in "the traditional way." The couple patiently explained that traditional weddings are obviously no guarantee for living happily ever after, and grownups should do whatever they feel right about doing. The relative shut up.

Finding someone willing to officiate might have been

difficult except for a minister friend who said he would be honored to do it, in spite of the fact he had never flown in a small airplane. Although the minister loved the couple very much, he admitted to being apprehensive. He was heard to say while climbing into the plane clutching his Bible, "Oh well, with God, all things are possible."

The woman's daughter was overjoyed with the news of the approaching wedding. A month later, on a beautiful December Saturday afternoon, the pilot, his wife, a co-pilot, the minister, the couple, and the little girl boarded a six-passenger twin-engine Aero Commander. The plane was decorated with flowers. At 10,000 feet MSL (Mean Sea Level) the engines were slowed as the plane circled over the ocean. Music from *Romeo and Juliet* played, and the girl, who was maid of honor, sat happily in her mother's lap. The minister, with quaking hands, performed the ceremony, finally pronouncing the couple husband and wife.

When a bottle of champagne—stashed under a seat as a surprise—was uncorked, the champagne shot out of the bottle like a geyser. It was then the passengers realized champagne at 10,000 feet in a non-pressurized cabin will not behave. Most of the bubbly landed on the windows, the flowers, and the minister. The little girl, who was crying because her mother was finally happily married, burst into uncontrollable giggles.

Now, whenever this story is told, there are those who seem surprised to hear about a wedding taking place high in the sky, but inevitably, the remark is heard, "Well, it certainly sounds like a marriage made in heaven."

Reason No. 2. Today is our 44th anniversary. Yes, I have tears as I write this, but I am also filled with gratitude for our adventurous and extremely happy marriage.

Burt and Bobbie wedding

A Turning Time

Are you the guy in the plaid shirt who gave me a wordless unexpected hug in the Seal Rock Post Office parking lot? Are you the woman in the motorized wheelchair who grabbed my hand as we passed one another in Fred Meyers and told me to "Please keep writing"? Are you one of the readers who took time to email me words of caring encouragement? You all know who you are, but you really need to know that you helped me get through the past months (barely) without my soul mate, Burt. I knew the holidays might be difficult, but I did not know the depth of the pain, or that being with happy, loving families could send me into tears and depression.

Because of you readers and the love of family and friends, there is a column this week. I came so close to bagging it but after deep reflective thinking and prayer, I feel it's important to share some of the things I've been learning during this Grief Journey, things that may be of help to others who have suffered the loss of a loved one or may do so in the future. Grief leaves you wide open to getting sick (I'm on my second miserable cold). Grief can cause you to question life itself and even wonder what's the point of going on. Yes, I have had such thoughts, which are pretty darn scary. Grief can make some people turn to alcohol or drugs to escape the pain. (Not my way of dealing.) Grief can cause loss of appetite, or make a person turn to food for relief. (I'm down to what I weighed in high school). There are so many variables.

As the holidays draw to a close (finally), I'm beginning to see a tiny light at the end of what feels like a very long dark tunnel. When one is standing on the bottom rung of a ladder there is only one direction to go. Or I guess one could just let go and fall off. My birthday, a major one, is on New Year's Day. I can choose to think of the number as hopeless or hopeful. My daughter Rocki will be here and I will gratefully let her take charge of this gelatin-like mess that was once her vibrant mother. I welcome the role reversal. There are decisions to make and options to be discussed. There are ashes to be scattered over the ocean, which we will do together because it is time. For me, 2014 will be a "turning time"—a time to take a realistic look at my new identity in the coming year. Maybe even add a thing or two on my old Bucket List. Right now I have no idea what that new me will be like—but then who of us does know?

Back in the day when I did human-interest radio programs for the blind (and sighted people, too) there were often requests for a short piece of written wisdom a listener had sent in. Every time I read it over the air, people wrote in for a copy. Somehow, it seems appropriate to share one with you today:

You Learn. (Author unknown)
After a while, you learn the subtle difference
Between holding a hand and chaining a soul
And you learn that love doesn't mean leaning
And company doesn't mean security
And you begin to learn that kisses aren't contracts
And presents aren't promises
And you begin to accept your defeats
With your head up and your eyes open
With the grace of a woman, not the grief of a child

And you learn to build all your roads on today
Because tomorrow's ground is too uncertain for plans
And futures have a way of falling down in mid-flight
After a while, you learn...
That even sunshine burns if you get too much
So you plant your garden and decorate your own soul
Instead of waiting for someone to bring you flowers
And you learn that you really can endure...
That you really are strong
And you really do have worth...
And you learn and you learn...
With every goodbye you learn.

With deep gratitude to all of you who have reached out to me in some way. Because of you, The Beat just may go on.

Birthday Pajamas For One And All

Here is the downside of being a New Year's baby. Your dad never quite forgives you for not being a tax deduction. You don't get a party because the whole world is already busy with their own parties, so you attend those parties, but at midnight, you are the perennial little pouting kid in the corner whining, "But it's MY birthday!" Nobody cares.

I do clearly remember the one and only party on the day of my birthday—a Sweet 16 party attended by my girlfriends who were referred to by my parents as "The Silly Seven." If you count me, that makes eight silly teenagers for an afternoon birthday party of punch and cookies. The girls chipped in and got me a parakeet with cage and keet treats. I was thrilled, but my parents were not. They believed birds belonged in the wild, not in the house. I kept Pretty Boy in my bedroom and trained him to talk (sort of). But teenagers are easily distracted, and one Sunday I left his cage door open. Sundays after church services were family dinner days. Picture a dozen Scandinavians gathered around the dining room table, heads bowed to say grace, when suddenly a bird comes flapping through the house (looking for me, of course).

Pretty Boy not only landed on the rim of the gravy boat, but proceeded to wade jauntily across my grandmother's prized (but overly thick) gravy, leaving a trail of bird tracks and ruined appetites. If swearing had been allowed in our home, I hate to think what would have come out of the mouths of my father and brothers.

Fast forward to my recent 2014 birthday. There could be no better present than the arrival of my daughter Rocki. My friends, Brett Quick and Gina Nielsen, volunteered to drive me to the Eugene airport. They arrived bright and early on that beautiful, sunshiny New Year's Day and they did not arrive empty handed. Gina gave me a huge supply of my favorite candles and a heartfelt card that made me cry. And Brett walked in with an enormous bouquet of birthday balloons, held in place with a hefty box of candy as ballast. I never, ever received helium-filled birthday balloons before.

Now allow me to share with you what Rocki gave me for my birthday. You steady readers know I'm not the only nut in the family. Rocki gifted me with snuggly leopard print pajamas. But in the bag was a matching pair for her, AND—brace yourself—matching PJs for Charley and Lap Sitter, who were sitting nearby having no clue what was about to happen in their otherwise ordinary lives. Rocki set up her camera on a tripod, but first we put on our new jammies. Then we had to outfit the two unsuspecting animals, who are both so elderly they did not have the energy to protest. I cannot remember a time when such laughter rang through this house, and it got even funnier as we tried over and over to capture a good photo.

I would pose, trying to hang onto the dog and cat while Rocki set the timer on the camera. She had seven seconds to join our little group and look cool. We quickly realized that her running toward us caused Lap Sitter and Charley to freak out and try to escape. Each photo op had something wrong, but photo number eight caught the four of us more or less looking at the camera.

Good Grief

Yesterday, back to the Eugene airport, this time with Chuck Littlehales as our driver. I had some concern about going into a funk after saying goodbye to my daughter, but so far, all I have to do is look at the photos we took and all those balloons hugging the ceiling in our kitchen. I did have a brief fantasy of going out on the deck, climbing up on a railing clutching the balloons and taking off over the ocean just for the heck of it. However, since I've eaten that entire box of chocolates and am no longer my high school weight, there is no way those balloons could get me airborne. Happy New Year, everyone. May we all find reasons to laugh and be silly.

Bobbie and daughter Rocki, with Charley and Lap Sitter, in their snuggly leopard print pajamas

The Seven-Month Gift

Another journey has ended. As I write this, there is a presence missing that is no longer curled up at my feet. A few weeks ago, I had to stop the struggle of helping our old dog Charley up the stairs to be with me here in my office so I could write. It was just too difficult for both of us. Hauling an 80-pound dog and an (ahem) older person is not a smart or safe combination. So I used a baby gate to block him from trying to climb the stairs with hind legs that no longer worked. By the way, at no time did he ever whimper or tell me he was in pain, but his confusion while separated from me was pathetic and heartbreaking.

Seven months ago, Burt and I were sure it was the end of the line for Charley and Burt had a young man dig a grave in a corner of our property. Suddenly, Burt died and Charley rallied. Do dogs sense these things? Did this old dog realize I could not bear two losses so close together? Did he know I would need his company during the long and painful grief process of losing my husband? As the months went by, Charley stuck unusually close to me. It was hard for him to get off the floor on those old hips, but he continued following me to the bathroom as he had always done. A bit unnerving, but I was well used to him standing there, head on my knee, waiting to be scratched in all his favorite places.

Dogs have been part of my entire life. Mixed breeds, purebreds, all kinds, all sizes, all different—but none as different as Charley. As a standard poodle puppy, he resembled a curly, active, into-everything, running, tumbling Hershey bar. Some of you dog lovers with "real dogs" such as Labs and German Shepherds, yes, even Corgis, may be thinking "Why a poodle?" It's all the fault of writer John Steinbeck, of whom I'm a huge fan. Here's the back-story of why I eventually wanted to be owned by a standard poodle.

In 1962, a book by John Steinbeck hit the market, called *Travels with Charley*. It's a non-fiction book about the year Steinbeck got into his rickety old camper truck with his dog, Charley, a standard poodle. Steinbeck's goal was to travel America's back roads and meet regular down-to-earth folks. It's a fun book, but his description of Charley is priceless. Steinbeck described Charley's front teeth as being so crooked that it gave the dog the ability to (get this) pronounce his "Fs." Charley would sit in the passenger seat watching the roads go by, and when he had to go, he would say "Fff-t." I know it's a stretch, but hey, I didn't write the book, Steinbeck did, and I can still actually hear his dog Charley saying "Fff-t" when he had to hop out of the truck and "visit a bush." Being one with a wanderlust spirit, I dreamed of doing the same thing (no, not the bush, the travels) but it was only a dream. One does have to deal with the realities of life. So for the next 40 years, I dreamed of having a "Charley dog." Finally, in 2001, after our last dog went to Doberman Heaven, we got Charley.

It was like living with a canine comedian. Charley watched television—his favorite shows were *Animal Planet* and *The Dog Whisperer*. He would park himself in front of the television and stay there, even during commercials. And he knew when a commercial had a dog in it. We didn't know how he knew, but he would come running from wherever he was and bark at the TV. We all hated the Alpo commercial with the stupid voice that yells "BACON! BACON! BACON!"

When I got dressed, he watched, and he could tell if I was about to garden or leave the house. If he saw me putting on my "grubs," his tail would wag, but if I put on my "big lady clothes," his tail dropped and his body language said, "Why are you leaving me?"

Last week, at bedtime, when I took him down the three steps off our back deck to do his "business," he fell. It was a horrifying sight seeing him on his back like a turtle, unable to get on his feet. Thankfully, I had the elastic strap in my pocket and somehow got him back in the house, knowing it was time to do the kindly, humane thing for this grand old dog. The next day, Dr. Eric Brown and Kim, his assistant, came out to the house and two dear friends were here to support me as I said my goodbyes to Charley, grateful to let him go, peacefully and painlessly, surrounded by love in his familiar home. My friends helped bury him in the space prepared last June. I like to think of the past seven months as Charley's gift to me. I will miss him greatly.

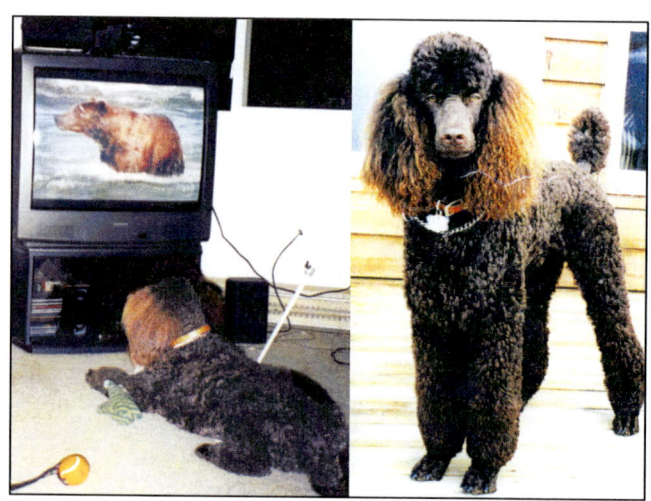

Charley, a standard poodle who "owned" writer Bobbie Lippman, watching *Animal Planet*, one of his favorite TV shows

Dogs, Dodge, And New Beginnings

I continue to wade through emails and cards from widows, widowers, and dog lovers, and my hope today is to offer encouragement to all you readers of this column who have suffered a loss (or are about to), whether that loss is a person or a pet. Not that I'm putting people and pets on the same level, but grief is grief and I've had a big dose of it during the past seven months. My goal today is to share some of the events that have brought me to the place where I am now as I write this column.

From the day my husband Burt died last July, right on through what I call "the horrible holidays," I was a depressed mess. You know this because I have not held back any details of my Grief Journey. Everything changed on New Year's Day when my daughter Rocki arrived and forced me to celebrate my birthday with that hysterical pajama party with us, plus dog and cat, all dressed in matching leopard print PJs. I honestly didn't think I would ever laugh that hard again.

From that day forward, life started looking brighter in spite of knowing time was running out for our old dog, Charley. Last week there was no choice but to let him go with the humane and peaceful process of euthanasia. Of course, it was a sad day, but all of us who choose to live with pets know they never last as long as we do. Cards, emails, and phone calls started coming from folks who understand and care. One such call was from my friend Kath Schonau who checks often to see how I'm doing. Her call was maybe the fifteenth about Charley, and I felt like changing the subject by asking about her life.

"Well," she said, "I'm driving down to Eureka tomorrow morning to spend the weekend with Hannah (her daughter who is interning related to getting her physical therapy license)." Suddenly Kath asked, "Why don't you come along? The redwoods would be good for you."

My mind went ballistic with all the reasons why I could not possibly leave the comfort zone of home. Kath simply said, "Just think about it." My heart was racing and an inner voice kept saying, "Go! This is the healthiest thing you could possibly do for yourself." The idea felt almost as wild and crazy as going on that pack trip with Doc Steve Brown seven years ago. I called friends who not only insisted I go away for the weekend, but said they would take care of Lap Sitter, the house, the mail, and the newspapers. A friend with horses happened to call and used a favorite Western expression, "It's about time you got out of Dodge!" Without Charley to worry about, there went my last excuse for being a hermit.

Early the next morning, in beautiful sunshiny weather, Kath picked me up and we drove down the coast on Highway 101, our coffee cups parked side by side in the cup holder and great music playing. I had not enjoyed that beautiful drive in years and it brought back memories of when I rode a bicycle from Canada to Mexico with a mother-of-six gal pal on a bucket list trip to accomplish before turning 50. We dubbed ourselves "The Many-Pause Milers" because we stopped a lot to smell the flowers.

When one too many young reporters caught up with us to ask, "Why are you doing this?" my very funny friend Roz Memel answered, "Listen, buster, if you had six kids you'd want to get out of the house too!" (That line made it into the *Los Angeles Times*).

The Eureka weekend was magical, the weather perfect, the redwoods healing, and the companionship of Kath and Hannah was the best possible medicine. We stayed in the home of a physical therapist mentor for Hannah where there were three cats wandering around so I had no chance to miss Lap Sitter. When I returned home, I wondered if our cat would ignore me for a while or be all over me. Cats are unpredictable and it's a good thing I was wearing sturdy jeans because she was so happy to see me she literally climbed up my leg and into my arms. On second thought, maybe she was just hungry.

So the message today, folks, is the importance of living in the present, to make the most out of each day because today is all we have. Yesterday is gone and tomorrow isn't here yet. Forgive me if this sounds preachy, but I feel it's important to share that deep and painful grief does not last forever and to also thank you for all the prayers that helped get me to this place today. Allow me to leave you with a quote from *Healing After Loss*, the book of meditations by Martha W. Hickman I read every night: "I have entered a new country. I will be patient with myself."

BRING IT ON

A few months after my husband Burt died last July, an old friend who had been widowed for several years said, "There will come a day, Bobbie, when you will begin to feel a new sense of freedom." At the time, those words were shocking and I couldn't imagine feeling anything but grief stricken for the rest of my life. Anything else felt somehow disloyal to my husband's memory and the wonderful life we had together.

Now, during the past four weeks, I realize my friend was right. My steps are lighter. I'm smiling again, getting out, being with old friends, making new ones. I honestly feel Burt watching and saying, "You go, girl." Maybe even Charley, from wherever old dogs go, is happy that I'm now able to "take off," although I'm not sure where or when that will happen. But the fact I am only responsible now for my cat Lap Sitter must be the new-found freedom my widowed friend was talking about.

Today's column was triggered by seeing a commercial about the Sportsman Show going on in Portland. This flashed me back to the 1960s when I felt a newfound freedom after finally extricating myself from an early and very painful marriage. My daughter Rocki was five years old and we both still talk about the years we lived happily in a Santa Monica wreck of a rented beach house ($200 a month, such a deal). I worked in Beverly Hills and she was a latchkey kid, which may have helped her learn to be the independent and self-sufficient woman she is today.

So what does this have to do with the Portland Sportsman

Good Grief

Show? Hang on, you're about to find out. In 1964, Rocki and I could do as we pleased (with no one yelling at us), so I took her to the Sportsman Show in Los Angeles. In the middle of the large auditorium was a stocked pond full of trout and kids could fish 20 minutes for 50 cents. While I watched Rocki casting her line out to the middle of the pond with a dozen other kids, I absently signed up for a free sports fishing trip.

Within 20 minutes, my little munchkin caught three trout. On our way home, I stopped for gas with Rocki sitting next to me proudly clutching her bag of fish. Not being thrilled about fish cleaning, I turned on the charm and asked the gas station guy if he would do it. "Lady," he grumped, "I don't clean no fish. This here's a gas station!"

In case you're wondering, back then in L.A.—just like Oregon—there were real live people who pumped your gas and cleaned your windshield. Just then, from behind a nearby pump, enjoying a cigarette, stepped this good-looking cop who asked the grumpy guy, "What's the problem?" While Rocki watched with bug-eyed amazement, this nice policeman took out a knife, used the water hose, and quickly cleaned all three trout. As we headed home, I heard my daughter say, "Daddy says cops are no good. I think Daddy is wrong."

Not only were those fish a great meal for us, but when the phone rang with the news that we had won a sports fishing trip to Mexico, we couldn't believe it. So, did we go? You bet. We drove down to San Diego, hopped on an 85-foot fishing boat, and joined 20 other people who all knew the ropes about fishing for albacore tuna. We were clueless, but eager to learn.

Here's the part I don't like remembering, but wonder if Rocki does—or if she even remembers any of this story that I had totally forgotten until now. We were given a delicious dinner and a bunk below decks. The skipper suggested we get some sleep while the boat chugged down to Mexican waters and he said that everyone would be told when it was time to fish. At 4 a.m., there was the loud shout of "FISH UP!" and we raced to the upper deck, only to be hit with a big dose of seasickness. Eventually, after hanging over the rails barfing, we felt somewhat better. A very nice guy helped me start fishing while Rocki played cheerleader. Did I get lucky? Yes, and I don't mean with that guy. We drove home with one very good-size albacore tuna (cleaned by the skipper) and ended up with a BBQ feast in our front yard with the help of several friends.

I'm sort of tempted to go to the Sportsman Show in Portland but they probably don't have a tank full of trout, and I no longer have a five-year-old, so I guess life will have to hand me new adventures.

I say bring it on!

Bobbie and granddaughter Autumn

Another Of Life's Mysteries Solved

Valentine's Day—another dreaded "first" for those of us who have suffered a loss. My husband Burt was an incurable romantic and made a big deal out of every special occasion and many that were important only to us, such as always celebrating our "month-aversary." His greeting cards to me were carefully chosen and never just signed with his name. They all included a loving note in his exquisite penmanship. Consequently, I have saved every single greeting card all these years. OK, so that makes me an incurable romantic, too. I was tempted to start looking at those cards but knew I would only end up crying and feeling sad. This is why the word "choice" was invented. We all have choices, and mine (at least for this year) was choosing to not end up wallowing in a puddle of tears.

So I'm shifting gears to share with you a recent happening that continues to break me up—in laughter. I call this story "The Great Furnace Mystery," and there are nine or 10 friends reading this right now who will shake their heads in disbelief.

The mystery started about the time the recent and unusual bitter cold snap hit the Northwest, along with several inches of snow here on the coast. I prefer a cool house, but icicles hanging from one's nose is ridiculous. So I started running the furnace more often than usual. When it came on, you could hear this strange noise, like punching your fist into a partially inflated paper bag. Of course, I worried that something was wrong with our heating system, but before getting a professional out here, I recruited friends who made the mistake of showing up for various other reasons. After walking around listening and frowning, none of them had a clue as to what the weird noise was or where it was coming from. It wasn't consistent and seemed to move about like a playful ghost. As two of my guy friends left the house, they suggested I should probably call a heating company. Well, being a stubborn Scandinavian, I like to take my time with such major decisions—so I opted to stop using the furnace, put on layers of sweats, and curl up under blankets in my lazy girl chair, thinking and pondering and determined to figure it out myself.

That's when my eyes focused on the bunch of helium balloons my friend Brett gave me for my January 1 birthday. Those balloons have lost much of their helium and look pretty pathetic all clustered in a clump on the sofa, but they make me smile and I'm still too emotionally fragile to get rid of anything that makes me smile. However, something was different about those balloons (still tied together) on the sofa. One of the original eight was missing. I crawled out from under my blankets, turned off the TV, turned on the thermostat, and listened for the mysterious "whoosh" sound. Yep, there it was, this time from over my head. I raced upstairs and peered up at the air vents in the ceiling. What to my wondering eyes should appear but the delinquent balloon, happily hugging a large vent like they were old friends. I burst out laughing. His (his?) string was still hanging, so I took him downstairs and tied him back with the others, putting an end to his drifting around upstairs from vent to vent, which he obviously had been doing.

The freezing weather has ended for now and when I do turn the furnace on it behaves in its old normal way. I was so tempted to call all those people who tried to solve the mysterious noise, but figured it would be more fun to let them read about it in this week's column.

Happy Valentine's Day folks, and in case you are wondering, the birthday balloons are still on the sofa. I'll give them up when I'm good and ready.

Seafood & Wine—Then and Now

This is not a commercial for the Seafood & Wine Festival, which is happening on the Oregon Coast this weekend. My words won't make a bit of difference to the thousands of people who annually converge on this community every February. But for you readers, this column will include a funny story and a tidbit or two you may find interesting.

New-timers probably assume the Seafood & Wine Festival has always been as it is now—huge (over 20,000 attendees in each of the past few years), noisy, and a big deal for the tons of tourists who travel miles to get here. Not so. Us old-timers probably remember the bare-bones beginnings—that the idea was hatched as a way to bring tourist dollars to the Coast during February when it is not exactly bathing suit weather. Yes, it started out small back in 1977, as many new ideas tend to be, but like Topsy, it just grew and grew and would not be possible without the help of hundreds of local volunteers—currently 300-plus.

Of course, my husband Burt and I were quick to pitch in and help. We felt strongly (as I still do) that if you live in a community and have the energy, for heaven's sake get involved in your community. While I signed up for specific volunteer jobs, like selling tickets at the door (no online sales back then), or working in the Chamber of Commerce booth, Burt was a maverick volunteer and I privately teased him for being such an excellent "floater." He enjoyed standing on an upper level with Police Chief Jim Rivers, keeping an eye on the crowds. Or else Burt would wander through the throngs of people, standing tall, looking tough, and quick to help break up a skirmish when folks had too much wine or even looked like they wanted to cause trouble.

There is a famous, or infamous, story about Burt that many people know, but in case you don't, here it is. There is never enough room inside the tent for everybody (Fire Department rules, you know). Fact: tent capacity now is 4,700 bodies at a time, which means many of the visiting hordes have to wait in line outside, sometimes in the rain. As the story goes, some bad-tempered male finally made it into the tent, saw Burt who was probably wearing an official jacket or badge, and loudly complained to my husband that not only was the line outside too long, but a seagull dumped a load of you-know-what on his hat. Without missing a beat, Burt handed the guy a $5 bill saying, "Congratulations! Our Chamber of Commerce has a policy of giving any tourist $5 if a seagull does doo-doo on a hat." The guy happily hurried away in shocked disbelief to tell his buddies about the fantastic policy of the Newport Chamber of Commerce.

I can't top that story, but one year I started volunteering as a "sweeper." This means you walk around inside (where it's warm) with a broom and a long-handled dustpan. This also means your eyes are on the floor, mostly because wine festival attendees have the stupid habit of dropping (often deliberately) their wine glasses on the floor. The crash of glass also sends up a roar of hilarity from the crowd like this is some kind of major achievement. As a sweeper, you'd better hustle to get that broken glass to a trash bin. That first year, I noticed that people who drink too much do not keep track of their money. I was

Good Grief

continually finding dollar bills on the floor and no one in the crowd acting as if they were looking for lost cash. As a happy sweeper for at least three years, I ended up finding and donating well over $100 to good causes.

So no, this column today is not a commercial, just my usual sharing of what's going on—or has gone on in the past. A few months ago, I was so happy to hear that at the first meeting of the Seafood & Wine Festival Committee a unanimous decision was made to add the letters "XL" to the SF&W publicity as a tag line tribute to Burt. Everyone agreed he believed in living life large. Wow! To his daughters and those of us who loved him, this is just one more example of keeping his memory alive. But wait, it gets better. Last Friday at the Chamber of Commerce luncheon, the program was all about this weekend's festival. I distinctly heard Director Lorna Davis say to the crowd, "Oh, by the way, if a seagull does doo-doo on a tourist, the Chamber will award that lucky tourist TEN BUCKS!"

I'm pretty sure there was laughter coming from heaven and it sounded just like Burt.

Current Events—Then And Now

Okay, class, this is your naggy columnist wanting to know if you have been keeping up on current events—such as the 2014 Winter Olympics, which just finished in Russia. I watched a bit of it, but not even close to the number of sports I used to watch with Burt. Somehow, it wasn't all that appealing this year, but my favorite event is figure skating, especially the females on flying feet in their pristine white skates.

Watching the figure skating is masochistic of me because every four years I end up with an old (very old) déjà vu painful feeling of disappointment. As a kid, I loved ice-skating on frozen Nebraska lakes and ponds (always on borrowed skates or my older brother's hand-me-downs). The Christmas I was 12, the only thing I asked for was skates, just like the ones my idol Sonja Henie wore in newsreels (no TV coverage back then). Sonja was the famous Olympic skater of that time who also ended up in a few movies. I was obsessed with her ability to leap and jump and fly through the air on those white skates, and I was very specific that those skates were the only present I wanted.

When a large box appeared under the tree, I was beyond excited and on Christmas morning, my hands were shaking as I opened that box and carefully lifted the tissue paper. Did I get ice skates? Yes. Were they the answer to my youthful dream of looking as glamorous as Sonja? No. The skates were black hockey skates, not even high-top ones. I almost cried and had to fake a

Good Grief

smile while saying thank you to my parents. I think my mom said something like, "Black is practical." Like I cared. You'd think after all these years I'd get over it, but I obviously haven't.

Moving right along to a more current event—the annual Newport Seafood & Wine Festival right here on the beautiful Oregon Coast—in sunshiny weather for a change. I debated attending because it meant another of the dreaded firsts—doing something without my husband Burt. But I'm finding out the importance (for me) of plowing ahead, feeling the feelings, and doing it anyway. I chose to go on opening night, the favorite time for locals, and it was a good decision. There were so many friendly familiar faces I felt like a teddy bear whose fur has been rubbed off from so much hugging.

However, there was one brief moment when I wandered off (deliberately) to stand alone against a post and just watch the people walking past. Suddenly I spotted a tall, good-looking white haired guy in a brown leather jacket hurrying along in the crowd. Instinctively I started to run after him before realizing it wasn't Burt. It was a moment of sad longing, but it was only a moment, and for all of us whose loved ones have "gone ahead," I'm told it is common to have these moments.

Last week I wrote about the Seafood & Wine Festival and half the fun of writing this column is getting mail from readers. The first to arrive was from Wyma Rogers: "I used to be a sweeper with Don Davis on Sunday afternoons. I recall Burt walking around among the crowd. Maybe he wasn't in charge, but he always looked like he was, and it was a welcome sight." Most of the emails were from readers who were fixated on the seagull story. I'm not repeating that story, class, because you are supposed to keep up with such important details. Several locals wanted me to know that they had also experienced the splat of an overhead bird, usually on their car's windshield. One reader wanted to know if I was carrying on my husband's tradition of handing over $5, then added "ha ha." I guess that means he was kidding. Here is my favorite tidbit from reader Sandy Shelton of Sebastopol, California. "Very funny story, Bobbie. When I was in Mexico recently, swimming with a friend, she told me a seagull had plopped a load on her head. Being a good sport, she just ducked her head in the water and washed it off. A bit later, we were enjoying margaritas on the beach and still laughing when I felt something wet land on my shoulder. I hurried off to take a shower, then rejoined my friend and told her about your seagull story, which started us laughing all over again. We both wished there was someone around like Burt to reward us for being so special."

I have the same wish, Sandy – for a lot of reasons.

"A Toast To Life And Love"

There is a Lucite jewelry box on a dresser in our bedroom—the kind with little drawers that used to easily slide in and out. I bought the jewelry box back in the 1970s when I had a collection of costume jewelry, most of which has been donated to "Be Jeweled," the annual fundraiser for Food Share. My life has been simplified to keeping just a few pieces with sentimental value.

The other day, I opened one of those drawers to see what was left, then could not get the drawer to fit back in the slot. Today, my friend Angie Rozell was here, and I asked if she could help. As I watched Angie wiggle the drawer into place, I noticed a $10 bill that has been in that drawer for more than 30 years. Seeing that money triggered a story to share with you today.

Once upon a time, I dreamed of being published in major newspapers all across America. If a column in the Newport *News-Times* drew a lot of "snail mail" from readers (way before email), I would do a re-write, flesh it out a little, and zap it off to newspapers with a circulation of over 100,000. I didn't know this was called self-syndicating. All I felt was elation when stories were accepted and a check showed up. The first time this happened was in 1977, when a large sum arrived from the *Los Angeles Times*. I was so thrilled and grateful for my "God-given gift of writing" that I started a policy of giving every penny of writing revenue away to those less fortunate—a practice I've continued to do.

Back to today's story and the $10 bill. As my parents were aging, I made frequent trips to Omaha and these visits always included a mother-daughter go-to-lunch day. By 1985, my mother had lost her vision to macular degeneration but not her upbeat spirit, and off we went to a restaurant for lunch. I will never forget that day. First, she shocked me by asking if we could have a glass of wine—not an acceptable thing to do by anyone in my evangelical family. I ordered the wine, not noticing that she was digging around in the pocket of her jacket. When the wine came, this is what happened: With eyes that could no longer see, she raised her glass in my direction, clinked mine with an impish grin on her face and said, "A toast to life and love." I nearly lost it, and in fact, I did when she pushed a $10 bill across the table and added, "This is the allowance we could never afford to give you when you were growing up. Use it for something special." I had tears then, and I have tears now reliving that day with my mom.

Dad and I also had a day together, which included driving by the old house where they raised my brothers and me. Like a rare moment from my childhood, we also stopped for butterscotch malts.

While waiting to board my plane several days later, I started writing the next column for this newspaper. Here are my first words: "This is being written in the Omaha, Nebraska, airport with a huge attitude of gratitude. Why? Because I still have my precious parents and we have just spent an incredible week together." There wasn't a whole lot of detail, except toasting that glass of wine with my mother, the $10 "overdue allowance," and the butterscotch malt with my dad, but when the mail came pouring in from readers, I knew if people liked it in Newport, they might like it in Miami. Little did I know. I did a fast rewrite, only this time I included my brothers and their football obsession. I wrote about the Nebraska state slogan being "Go Big Red," the state tree being a goalpost, the state bird being a football with wings, and the third largest population in Nebraska being in Lincoln on a Saturday afternoon in the fall.

That story became a full page spread in the *Oregonian*—in color. It included a large drawing of two hands toasting wine glasses. One of the hands shows old veins, the other hand does not. The headline is "A Toast to Life and Love." The story also sold to so many major newspapers I lost count—a writer's dream come true. Of course, my parents were proud when it was published in the *Omaha World Herald* (which continued to buy everything I sent) and my not-always-patient father had to read my stories to Mom several times.

Life is full of changes, as we all know. My parents are gone, and so is my beloved husband Burt. Nebraska is still obsessed with football, and I'm down to one brother who, with his wife Dot, will be here for a visit in May. In the meantime, I need to follow through with my mother's request—to do something special with that $10 bill. I'm sure I'll think of something.

Bobbie with her mother during a special mother/daughter lunch. Omaha, Nebraska, November 1985

The Amazing Magical $700 Dress

I just ran across a photo of "the dress." I've shared this story before, but never with a photo—until now. Believe me, every once in awhile women who read that column ask, "Do you still have that incredible dress?" So here's the scoop in case you are new to this column.

Most folks of a certain age know about the actress Loni Anderson, formerly married to show biz people including Burt Reynolds. I've never met Loni Anderson but for a long time one of her dresses hung in my closet. Here's how it happened.

In the late 1970s, when we lived in Los Angeles and I was back in Nebraska helping my aging parents, my husband and several friends went to a Hollywood celebrity auction in Beverly Hills. Movie and television stars donated things to be auctioned for a worthy cause—such as tuxedos, jewelry, even sports cars.

If you have ever seen Loni Anderson, you know she is not only blonde and talented, but also has a drop-dead figure. In fact, she could almost give Dolly Parton a run for her money in the upstairs department, if you know what I mean. The auctioneer, with microphone in hand, held up a long dress and told the audience it was donated by Loni Anderson. "Just look at this beautiful evening dress," he declared dramatically. "This dress originally cost $700 and was worn only once by Loni Anderson on a television show. Who will start the bidding at $35?"

Silence. Nobody bid, so Karen, a friend of mine, said, "Hey,

Good Grief

Burt, why don't you open the bidding? That dress might (ha ha) fit Bobbie." Being the good generous guy he is, my husband bid $35. Nobody raised and he ended up with Loni Anderson's dress.

I arrived at LAX the next morning tired from what had been a stressful trip. All I wanted was to relax and unwind. All Burt wanted to do was yammer on and on about a very special dress waiting for me at home. I felt absolutely no enthusiasm, especially after hearing that this was Loni Anderson's dress. To be truthful, I was furious and certain that any dress belonging to her would look like a joke on me. It was depressing just thinking about it. When we got home, my husband insisted—I mean, REALLY insisted—that I try it on. He sat down in the living room to wait. (Men can be so clueless). I walked into our bedroom and there on the bed, encased in see-through plastic, was THE DRESS. I tried to ignore it but finally my female curiosity got the better of me. After all, it's not every day you get to see a $700 dress up close. After circling the bed a few times, I pulled off the plastic and there it was, a full-length symphony of cascading champagne- colored chiffon. Empire style—or OM-PEER as the French say— with elegant hand-beading and semi-precious stones on the bodice. A truly breathtaking dress. I figured the only way to shut up (stifle?) my husband was to put the darn thing on and prove to Burt that he had made a very big mistake. To my amazement, the dress fit perfectly.

I wore it to five black-tie occasions, always wondering what would happen if I ran into Loni Anderson in the ladies room. What would she say? What would I say? Fortunately—or maybe unfortunately—that never happened. What did happen was, after wearing the dress several times, I took it to dry cleaners that specialized in fancy dresses. The lady looked it over and said they would have to be extremely careful with all that hand beading. When she told me how much it would cost to clean, I nearly choked. Uh huh, $35! How ironic is that?

I retrieved the dress, mumbled thanks to the lady, and said I needed to confer with my husband, which of course, wasn't true. What I did was take the dress to our regular cleaners where they said they would do their best. Well, not one single bead fell off and the charge for dry cleaning was $10. Remember folks, this was the late 1970s, and things were a whole lot cheaper.

Then we moved to the Oregon Coast and started attending fancy parties where the dress was worn twice by me and once by a Newport friend whose body is ALSO a far cry from Loni Anderson's body. Eventually, I donated the dress to a local charity bash where the auctioneer got the audience so excited that the dress ended up with a lady doctor who practices medicine in Central Oregon. She bid an exorbitant amount of money and, as far as I know, she still has that dress.

What I've figured out is this: for $700 you get a dress that automatically knows how to adjust itself to ANYBODY'S body. Thank you, Loni Anderson, wherever you are.

Burt and Bobbie Lippman, with Bobbie wearing "The Dress"

BILLBOARDS AND HAPPY FEET

I am big on truth, and the truth is I was WAY far away from my desk last week, like maybe a thousand miles, but I also know it is stupid to advertise you are going on vacation, even though friends happily moved into my home to take care of Lap Sitter, the mail, newspapers, houseplants, etc.

On the subject of truth, you steady readers have followed along on my Grief Journey as I dealt openly and honestly with the miserable sadness over losing my husband Burt. Going on a real vacation was the farthest thing from my mind—until my friend Kath Schonau called.

Kath, a seasoned traveler, said her whole family was headed for a "baby fix" (first grandchild) in San Diego. She managed to convince me it was time to go to Los Angeles and visit my family and friends. She offered to make all my travel arrangements from Portland to Burbank, said she and husband Don Taylor would get me to and from Portland, and a 10-day vacation would be good for me. I was terrified. Yes, I have traveled the world, alone and with others including Burt, but that was before the challenge of macular degeneration. I do just fine in familiar surroundings, but if you can't read small print or signs pointing to restrooms, you might feel like a fish out of water—and like a fish, Kath would not let me off the hook. She can be very persuasive.

I just got home, and my mind is spinning with so much to share with you, so to avoid this column being crammed with what I call "the whole kitchen sink," I have chosen just a couple of highlights. Every day was filled with activities, parties, old and young friends, family and, of course, granddaughter Autumn, whom I haven't seen since we drove down to Santa Barbara for her wedding two years ago.

My new adventure started as I sat alone at PDX waiting to board Alaska Airlines. A stranger asked where I was headed. "Los Angeles," I answered. "Oh," she said, "be sure to watch for the billboards."

"Huh?" I asked.

She proceeded to inform me there is a nationwide campaign going on of religious billboards and no, she did not know who started it.

"For example?" I asked, my curious nature gearing up. She rattled off three before she hurried away to get coffee. I quickly jotted them down in my little notebook:

1) "DON'T MAKE ME COME DOWN THERE!" GOD.

2) "KEEP TAKING MY NAME IN VAIN AND I WILL MAKE RUSH HOUR LAST LONGER." GOD.

3) "DO YOU HAVE ANY IDEA WHERE YOU ARE GOING?" GOD.

What an interesting way to kick off my 10-day adventure.

I honestly hope today's column will inspire some of you widows and widowers out there who have responded with stories of your own Grief Journeys and various ways you have found to move forward in life. If you are open to new experiences, which I am, here is just one oddball thing I did, and I am still relishing the memory. My long-time cycling friend Roz insisted on treating me to a place called Happy Feet, one of many similar establishments that have sprung up in Los Angeles since I left years ago. The minute you walk in the door of Happy Feet, you are transported to Asian-style peace and quiet. You hear the tinkling sound of a water fountain and soft music. Only the girl at the front desk speaks English. Roz and I were escorted by two lovely Asian girls to a rather dark, curtained-off cubicle with two side-by-side beds. (I counted a dozen others in the place.) I have had massages in my life, but never with my clothes on. Roz had told me to wear loose clothing, i.e. comfy jeans and a shirt with sleeves that could be rolled up. While your feet are immersed in warm water, you recline on your stomach, and then your shoulders, back, arms, legs, and all knotted muscles are massaged. You think it can't get any better—until the girl with magical hands motions for you to turn over and works on your bare feet until you feel as if you never want it to end. I have not been that relaxed in months, and we left there on extremely Happy Feet. Would I go again? In a heartbeat. Would you believe all this pampering for only 25 bucks for a solid hour?

Although friends drove me all over L.A. and Santa Barbara, I did not spot one billboard message from God. But I did spend a lot of time with Autumn, who is now settling down to regular married life after her 15-month honeymoon. She and husband Abe plan to get a few chickens, so I am winding this up with a really dumb joke I heard on my way home:

What do you call a chicken coop with four doors?

Answer: A chicken sedan. If it took you a minute to "get it," don't feel badly. By the time I heard it, my mind was on such overload from 10 days of vacation merry-go-round I didn't figure out the joke for quite awhile.

Stay tuned. There is so much more to share with you.

Mishmash

Today's column is a mishmash, which is what life has been since returning from Los Angeles. The dictionary definition of mishmash is a hodgepodge jumble. That about sums it up because in this community you can keep bopping from one event to another, which seems to apply to me at this stage of life with so few restrictions. Even Lap Sitter doesn't seem to care if I come or go, as long as someone is here to feed, pet, and provide a lap.

Did you get the dumb joke in last week's column? Did you see last week's column? If not, here is the joke again: What do you call a chicken coop with four doors? Answer: A chicken sedan. The emails from Baby Boomers started arriving early saying they did not understand the joke. Then my granddaughter, Autumn, wrote, "I love chickens, and I love chicken jokes!"

Say what? I wrote back (actually I'm getting pretty darn good at texting) and asked her to explain, which she immediately did. "Coupe's have two doors and sedans have four doors. Am I missing something else?" I texted back, "No, and you are the brightest bulb in my chandelier!" Just clean fun, folks, and the Boomers now know they can learn something from younger people. The generational skirmish certainly brightened the day for this writer.

The next item on my dance card was attending the monthly meeting of my women's group, called the GLAMS, where we listened to guest speaker Barbara Roberts share some of the highlights of her journey toward becoming the first woman governor of Oregon. GLAMS stands for Gathering With Laughter and Meaningful Sisterhood, now in its fourth year. GLAMS is open to women who wish to grow, learn, listen, and laugh. No fundraising—just fun raising. Barbara was clearly one of our best programs yet. She is funny, inspiring, honest, and real. I have memories of watching with admiration from afar years ago as she found her way into the political world dominated mostly by men. Boy oh boy, as women we have come a long way, baby!

Next on my dance card was the annual fundraiser for our local lighthouses. This kid-friendly family affair was held last Saturday night at the Newport Performing Arts Center. My hope is to carry on Burt's legacy of supporting as many worthwhile local causes as I possibly can, as long as I can. Laughs For Lighthouses was well attended by children and adults. Alex Zerbe, the zany entertainer (who has appeared on America's Got Talent) put on an excellent show geared toward children, and enjoyed by grownups—without one single dull moment.

At intermission, I found a place to perch in the lobby in order to people watch. This habit often leads to column material, and I wasn't disappointed. While the crowd milled around enjoying pizza, Pepsi, and popcorn, I found myself in conversation with Karmen Vanderbeck of Newport. Suddenly a handsome little boy glided up to Karmen and asked for a dollar, which she quickly handed to her eight-year-old grandson Jacob, while also introducing me before he glided off into the crowd. So why the term "glided?" Keep reading. I got to chatting with Jacob's dad, Lance, grandpa John and, of course, Karmen. Jake's shoes are called "Heelies"—shoes with little wheels imbedded in the soles, which explain his ability to glide smoothly over the lobby floor of the PAC. Asking questions is the best way to find out stuff like the name of these shoes on wheels, price, etc. I now know there are parental rules for kids who own "Heelies." School rules, too. I was informed the wheels can be taken off but left on for certain occasions and must be used responsibly. I found out Grandpa John gave the Heelies to Jacob last Christmas.

As I returned to my seat for the second half, I thought of Burt. It doesn't take much to be hit with memories of Burt. He would have been fascinated seeing Jacob gliding around on Heelies. Burt was great at roller-skating, and we used to go often during our early married life. I once signed up for a charity fundraiser that took place in a Los Angeles rink, and the goal was to skate for 25 miles. Burt got many people in his company to sponsor me and I believe we raised at least $4,000 for leukemia research. Of course, 25 miles of skating in a circle in a roller rink can leave you feeling like a hamster in an exercise wheel. But hey, it was a good cause and a lot of fun.

And now to leave you with another dumb joke that should not to be a challenge for any of my readers:

Is chicken soup good for your health?

Answer: Not if you're the chicken.

WHAT GOES AROUND COMES AROUND

During my recent visit to Los Angeles, an old friend asked if I ever looked myself up on Google. "Huh?" I said. "It never occurred to me, why?"

"Well," he said, "you might be surprised."

So of course, I typed my name into Google and was shocked to see one of my stories re-written by someone I do not know. This is OK with me, but the irony is that I recently found an expensive harmonica my husband Burt bought for himself several years ago but never learned to play. My kid brother Paul, and his wife Dot, are coming here next month, and my intention was (still is) to gift Paul with Burt's harmonica. Our entire family enjoyed music and sing-alongs—my brothers and me on guitars, and Dad on his beloved harmonica. Through the years, Burt learned all the songs and joined in singing with my family. Here is the story that appears on Google, dated June 27, 2010:

> "What goes around comes around" is the title of an essay from the Newport News-Times of Newport, Ore., which is a small town on the Central Oregon coast. Bobbie Lippman is the writer, and she happens to be the cousin of MY cousin's former neighbor in Manteca, Calif. Got that straight? Good. "Bobbie's Beat" is worth re-telling, especially this touching story, which began in the summer of 1942 in Omaha, Neb. when Bobbie was six years old. She and her dad were driving home with a load of tomatoes they had picked for canning

when they noticed an outdoor stage performance going on. They pulled up just as a lady in a flowered dress sang the last strains of "White Cliffs of Dover," and the emcee, a man wearing bib overalls, urged the audience to "give the lady a hand." Then the emcee asked if there was anyone else who wanted to entertain the assembled crowd. Bobbie's dad said to her, "Go on up there, honey, and sing 'I've Been Working On The Railroad.'" Bobbie's dad had been a railroad man for Union Pacific all his working life. "I've Been Working On The Railroad" was practically a national anthem in Bobbie's home and she knew the song well. She did not hesitate to obey her daddy and stepped up on the stage. The emcee lowered the microphone and she belted out the song. At the end, there was applause and thanks from the emcee in the blue overalls. Bobbie's greatest pleasure was seeing her handsome dad smiling and clapping for her.

Then there is a leap in time to a winter day in Omaha in 1991. The place is a nursing home where Bobbie's parents are living. Her father, who drove his car into his 88th year, had an accident, serious enough that he was wheelchair bound and needed 24-hour-a-day care. Bobbie was visiting her parents and saw Janet, the activities director putting up a sign that said "JOIN US FOR MUSIC DAY: 2 P.M." Bobbie asked if her parents ever took part in any of the special events. Janet replied that her father had shown signs of depression and disinterest in most everything since moving into the nursing home. They never took part in anything she organized. Bobbie told Janet that her dad had been quite good on the harmonica in days long past. Janet urged her to bring her dad and his harmonica to the MUSIC DAY that afternoon. Bobbie put the old harmonica on her dad's lap and rolled him into the dining room where Music Day was to take place. Her mother came along as well. Bobbie's dad tried to refuse going to Music Day but Bobbie gave him no choice—a bit like that day in 1942 when he told Bobbie to get up on that stage and sing "I've

Been Working On The Railroad" and she obeyed him. By the time Bobbie and her parents got to the dining room, Janet was leading at least 45 folks in singing "Amazing Grace." Her dad did not join in the singing, but her mother did. At the end of a few songs, Bobbie flashed Janet a conspiratorial look. Janet spoke up. "Say, Mr. Jensen, I hear you are pretty good on the harmonica." Bobbie's dad looked at Janet like he did not comprehend what she had said. Bobbie handed her father his harmonica and told him to play "I've Been Working On The Railroad," and like an obedient child, her dad put the harmonica to his lips and played the familiar railroad song. Bobbie said, "What goes around, comes around," about her father playing his harmonica just as 6-year-old Bobbie had obediently sung when her father told her "to go up on the stage, honey." In Bobbie's own words: "When the song was over and everyone applauded, I blinked back tears while watching a new look of pride and strength come over my father. He seemed to sit up straighter in the wheelchair, and he was grinning from ear to ear. Life had come full circle. He had instilled confidence in me as a little girl and now this was my chance to make a difference for him. It was truly a precious moment I would remember forever. Dad died the following year, but the good memories linger on of a loving father, his harmonica, and the strains of that old song, 'I've Been Working on the Railroad.'"

Yes, it was surprising to see my story on Google, written in third person by a stranger. But it was a better surprise finding Burt's harmonica in a box of tambourines. Happy un-birthday, Paul. See you soon.

From Bed Hopping To Bubbles

As I sit here staring at a blank computer screen, waiting to be inspired by my writing muse, here are some questions writers get asked: Where do you get your ideas, how hard is it to pick a subject, do you suffer from writer's block?

When I taught creative writing at Oregon Coast Community College, there were plenty of questions from students. Back then, I often had writer's block, but not anymore. My non-writer husband, Burt, once asked me to tell him what goes on in my brain when it's deadline time. Here is how I tried to explain it: "Picture a file cabinet in my head," I told him, "and whatever story is right up front (in that file cabinet) is the story begging to be written."

"Oh," said he, seemingly satisfied with my answer.

Back to today's subject. There are what I call the Los Angeles People, the Seattle People, and the Village People—not to be confused with the wildly crazy singing group well known back in the 1970s for their rousing rendition of "YMCA." My personal Village People are the folks here in this community. The Los Angeles People are composed of a large group of old friends and young family members whom I recently visited. They are in my brain's file cabinet, but not in the front file at the moment, which brings me to the Seattle People.

This latest adventure began with a recent phone call from Marylou Mate, a long-time friend, as is her husband, Bruce. If I had gone anywhere in the world with the Mates, Bruce would most likely be referred to as doctor or professor because he is famous worldwide for his knowledge of oceanography and marine life, especially whales—their migration habits, breeding and birthing grounds, etc. To me, he is just Bruce. To his grandchildren he is Papa. To my great surprise, the Mates thought it would be dandy for me to go along with them to Seattle, to (a) celebrate the 12th birthday of grandson Emmett, and (b) help cheer for their daughter Michelle, who was running a full marathon on Whidbey Island. Until now, I did not know the Mate's extended family and I could not help but question why on earth I was being included.

I'm beginning to realize now in my new widow world that friends and family can be pretty persuasive in getting me out of my comfort zone. When Marylou rapidly ran "the schedule" by me, it was mindboggling, but my inner voice said, *Go, this might be an adventure.* We would drive to Seattle, stay with Michelle, her husband Chuck, and kids ages 8, 12 and 14. The kids would give up their beds and switch to sleeping bags. At some point, we would trek to Whidbey Island for the marathon (a fundraiser for lymphoma and leukemia). On Whidbey, we would all be crashing at the home of friends of friends and get up at dawn for the marathon, after which we would return to Seattle by ferry and crawl back into our assigned beds.

I could not keep any of this straight in my head, but I've learned to reach for the brass ring on this merry-go-round called life because it may never come around again. I almost said "no" until Marylou threw in the ferry ride AND the fact we would be returning to Oregon by train. I have been a train nut my entire life and this added tidbit was irresistible.

If you astute readers are wondering why we drove up and

took a train home it's entirely too complicated. Just chalk it up to the fact Bruce Mate loves classic cars almost as much as he does his family and whales, and he needed to deliver a car to someone in Seattle.

I'm not at all sure what the point is of today's column. Maybe it's to encourage you folks who have suffered a major loss, and I hope you will eventually let go of the pain and start living again. I know in my heart that Burt is cheering me on. I could feel his encouragement to get a weeklong glimpse into the lives of the Mates that most people in the world never see. The interaction between them and their family is special, and I felt privileged to be part of it. By the time we got on the train, I was clearly out of energy. I'd like to think the Mates were tired, too, but they are so used to traveling the world and so good at stuffing stuff in a backpack and taking travel in stride. (I think they leave soon for Slovenia, where Bruce will present something on the subject of something whale related).

When we got back to their home, Marylou bailed out of the car to hurry off to choir practice. Bruce hopped out and grabbed a bucket and two long sticks. "Oh no," said Marylou. "Bobbie is too tired!" He ignored her (as Burt often ignored me) and put the mystery bucket and sticks in the car. Then he drove me home. The Mates have what I call "a lively inner child," and I think Bruce wanted to end this trip with one final burst of fun.

Out came the bucket of soapy suds and the sticks (with attached strings) while I stood open mouthed as Bruce put on a glorious and colorful bubble show for me, right there in my driveway. Fortunately, I was alert enough to take pictures.

I'm not answering the phone for at least a week... but on second thought, I've never been to Slovenia. Just kidding, Marylou.

Note: If you don't know about the famous Bruce Mate, just type his name on Google. Watch his short video on Vimeo: *Bruce Mate—Advice to Students*. You will love it!

**Bobbie, with the help of Bruce Mate, pets a seal pup.
Baja Gray Whale Expedition**

Bruce Mate and bubble

Three Steps Forward and a Big Step Back

The following poem seems to say what I am feeling:

> The sun was warm but the wind was chill
> You know how it is with an April day
> When the sun is out and the wind is still
> You're one month on in the middle of May
> But if you so much as dare to speak
> A cloud comes over the sunlit arch
> A wind comes off a frozen peak
> And you're two months back in the middle of March.
>
> —*Robert Frost*

This column is especially for you folks (men and women) dealing with grief over the loss of a loved one—and you are many because I hear from you. And I hear your pain.

I learned a big lesson on Easter Sunday when I was suddenly blindsided with almost unbearable sadness and longing for my husband Burt. Those of you following this column, particularly the columns about the fun I've recently had traveling, might assume "she's over it." Not so. The Grief Journey is not all full-speed ahead after the initial shock wears off and the months roll by. I can only describe it as three steps forward and just when

Good Grief

you think you are doing OK, something will trigger a memory of your loved one, and you are thrown back into your grief. For some it might be a song, or a sunset, or a spring flower poking up. I'm still not sure what happened on Easter, a day in the Christian calendar that is supposed to be full of joy, but the entire week continued to be filled with sadness no matter how hard I tried to pull out of it. All you can do is feel the feelings. To deny the pain only pushes it back, and it will surely rise up again when you are least expecting it.

You folks who write to me about how my honesty has helped need to know that your letters have helped me, too. Here is one from someone I have yet to meet, and she has given her permission to use her words and name:

> Bobbie,
>
> I am sure you get mail thanking you for writing about your precious husband and your walk now without him. This is my first Easter Sunday without my husband. We were married 50 years. Married as teenagers and stayed in love and had a fun adventurous time together. His love for God, family, and laughter made him everyone's friend. Not long ago, a friend told me to start reading your column for encouragement. I did, and it made me realize I am not as alone as I think I am in my unbearable grief. So, I just wanted to thank you for sharing your feelings, even though you can't possibly realize how many people's lives you have touched.
>
> —*Sally Baker, South Beach*

As I write this today, the sun is shining and the terrible longing for Burt is lifting. I tried to write a fun and flippant column for Friday's newspaper, but my conscience would not let me get away with it, certainly not after hearing from Sally Baker.

These words today on the subject of grief are especially for dear friends who lost their son not long ago, and also for Burt's daughter Robin, who is about to lose Ronee, her best friend from childhood. Robin's grief path is ahead of her (actually, she is already on it), and I am trying to help her walk the walk as best I can. For my friends who lost their son, I can't even relate to their pain. Parents are supposed to go first, not our children.

I will finish this with words from the author of the book, *Healing After Loss*, which has been my nightly reading companion for nine months: "I am strong. I am saddened, sometimes tired, discouraged. But I've made it so far and will not be overcome."

Do You Know Miss-Direction And Siri?

If you are under 50 (or maybe 60), you are probably not noticing how our world has changed, specifically electronically. My parents and grandparents would be stunned. I myself continue to be blown away, but I do remember feeling badly for my dad because he could not get the hang of using a remote control, so he would struggle out of his chair, walk over to the TV and change channels the old-fashioned way.

The other day in the grocery store a woman next to me was talking to her husband on her cell phone, asking him what he wanted for dinner that night. She caught me eavesdropping, put her hand over the phone and stage-whispered, "He hates shopping, but he likes to go with me and watch the people. He's over in the furniture department relaxing on one of those nice sofas."

If you look around it seems everyone is plugged into something, and it's worse (or more obvious) if you get out of Dodge and spend time in bigger cities, as I have recently done.

Los Angeles and Seattle were pretty much the same, but Eureka, California, is more like Newport. In Seattle, I watched groups of teenagers walking together, but all of them were texting on their cell phones. Makes you wonder if anyone is actually still able to talk to another person face-to-face.

A few years ago, my husband Burt got a new car, and it was his first experience with GPS. We drove that car down to L.A. for granddaughter Autumn's wedding. For most people, Los Angeles is a straight shot on I-5, but Burt insisted on programming the GPS lady—whose voice became so annoying I dubbed her "Miss-Direction." She was helpful in directing us around various places in Santa Barbara, but heaven help us if we changed our minds and turned left instead of right. I half expected Miss-Direction to yell at us. I couldn't wait to get home and not have to listen to her yammer the word "RE-calculating."

A few weeks ago when I was in Los Angeles, my friend Roz Memel was driving and we got into a discussion about the lyrics of a certain song. Roz, being a lyricist herself, whipped out her smartphone, punched a button and asked a lady named Siri to recite the lyrics. Everyone seems to have a personal relationship with Miss-Direction and Siri. I still use a dumb phone and all it does is make and receive phone calls. Can you imagine that? The dumb phone does not work here at home due to poor cell reception. This is no problem because I seem to be in the growing minority of people who still have a landline.

Yes, the world is changing faster than many of us can keep up. Even personal computers (desktop types like the one I'm using now) are being replaced by laptops, tablets, smart(er) phones, and who knows what else computer nerds are working on. I just received a really weird thing in an email and I cannot bring myself to call it a day brightener. It's more scary than funny in my opinion, but you get to decide for yourself. Keep in mind that it was sent to me by a minister friend who is one of three clergy-persons in a big city mega church. Brace yourselves.

Good Grief

CHURCH SERVICES OF THE FUTURE PASTOR: "Praise the Lord!"

CONGREGATION: "Hallelujah!"

PASTOR: "Can we please turn on our tablet, PC, iPad, cell phone, and Kindle Bibles to 1 Cor. 13:13. And please switch on your Bluetooth to download the sermon." (Pause) "Now, Let us pray, committing this week into God's hands. Open your Apps, BBM, Twitter, or Facebook and chat with God..." (Silence) "As we take our Sunday tithes and offering, please have your credit and debit cards ready. You can log on to the church WiFi using the password Lord909887." (Ushers circulate mobile card swipe machines among the worshipers. Those who prefer to make electronic fund transfers are directed to computers and laptops at the rear of the church. Those who prefer to use iPads flip them open. Those who prefer telephone banking take out their cell phones to transfer their contributions to the church account. The holy atmosphere of the church becomes truly electrified as all the cell phones, iPads, PCs, and laptops beep and flicker!)

Final blessing and closing announcements—"This week's ministry cell meetings will be held on the various Facebook group pages where the usual group chatting takes place. Please log in and don't miss out. Thursday's Bible study will be held live on Skype at 1900 hours CDT. You can follow your Pastor on Twitter this weekend for counseling and prayers. God bless you and have a wonderful week!"

I keep thinking how mystified (even horrified?) my conservative Midwest parents would be if they were still of this world and read about the Church of the Future. Maybe I need to lighten up and just accept Miss-Direction and Siri as helpful new friends. Actually, with our world changing so fast, even those two gals might be replaced tomorrow.

Bucky And The Sternwheeler

This column is for two women who will never read it. They do not know one another and I do not know them, but here is what they have in common: they are not local readers (in fact they live four states apart), both are widowed, both receive this column from family members, and both no longer wish to know about my life, particularly details of my Grief Journey.

When the first email arrived, I was surprised. When the second one showed up, I was not only surprised, but sad. It seems these two ladies are unhappy with my moving forward from what I call my "pity party." It's too bad they won't be reading this because today because I get to share with you a fantastic remedy for anyone hiding out at home feeling lonely and miserable. There's an old saying, "Life is what you make it," and no hunky knight on a stallion is going to ride up and make magical things happen for you or for me.

If you follow this column, you know I had an unexpected meltdown on Easter Sunday, a very big step back into sadness and grief. It lasted about six days, but on day three, a small notice caught my eye in the *News-Times*. The words "Willamette Sternwheeler," "carousel," and "day trip" jumped out at me, as did the words "60+ Club." I called the number and made a reservation. Then I sat back and questioned my sanity. I figured I wouldn't know anyone else going on that trip. But I showed up on time, clutching my coffee mug for security, and climbed into

Good Grief

the slick 12-passenger van with eight other people I now consider new friends. Our driver, Peggy O'Callaghan, Newport Senior Center activities director, made sure we all exchanged names, had our seatbelts fastened, and were ready for a good time.

First stop was the Wednesday Farmers' Market in Salem where there were so many lunch choices we had a hard time deciding. From there to Riverside Park and the 42 hand-carved, hand-painted beautiful carousel horses. Those of us who chose to mount up, certainly did. I have never met a carousel that did not beckon me to hop on. I deliberately chose a mean-looking bucking bronco (named Bucky) because he brought back memories of having been bucked off a live one when I was a kid. Next was an event that has been on my bucket list for years, but I could never talk my husband into it—the Willamette Sternwheeler.

As we chugged up and down the Willamette River, the captain pointed out historical sites and obligingly encouraged us to take over the helm. I wasn't about to miss the chance, and it was a hoot putting on a hat and looking the part of a riverboat captain.

The entire day was so much fun. A running joke in the group was about keeping an eye out for ice cream, but we'd had no success. Peggy took a vote on what route to take back to Newport and no one seemed to care, so I voted for Highway 18 since I had not driven it in years. Although the clock was now pushing toward dinnertime, most of us were still obsessed with having ice cream. For a nutrition nut like me, this was way out of character, but what the heck. We slid to a stop in Depoe Bay, piled out of the van, and descended on the poor guy who was about to close shop for the day. Several of us got a huge scoop of Tillamook ice cream. Some of us felt guilty and I, for one, skipped dinner that night, but I went to bed smiling and extremely happy about discovering Club 60+.

Will I go again on one of their many and varied excursions? You bet I will. And if you are someone sitting at home reading this and interested in making new friends, having new adventures while leaving the driving to someone else, pick up the phone, call the Newport Senior Center and find out what Club 60+ has on their planning board. I'll see you in the van, but at the end of the day, I will probably pass on having ice cream for dinner. Or maybe not. Since today's column is focused on seniors 60 and up, I have to leave you with a day brightener that recently broke me up.

> Jacob, age 92, and Rebecca, age 89, living in Miami, are excited about their decision to get married. They go for a stroll to discuss the wedding, and on the way, they pass a drugstore. Jacob suggests they go in. Jacob: "Are you the owner?"
>
> Pharmacist: "Yes."
>
> Jacob: "We're about to get married. Do you sell heart medication?"
>
> Pharmacist: "Of course, we do."
>
> Jacob: "How about medicine for circulation?"
>
> Pharmacist: "All kinds."
>
> Jacob: "Medicine for rheumatism?"
>
> Pharmacist: "Definitely."
>
> Jacob: "How about suppositories?"
>
> Pharmacist: "You bet!"
>
> Jacob: "Medicine for memory problems, arthritis, and Alzheimer's?"
>
> Pharmacist: "Yes, a large variety. The works."

Jacob: "What about vitamins, sleeping pills?"

Pharmacist: "Absolutely."

Jacob: "Everything for heartburn and indigestion?"

Pharmacist: "We sure do."

Jacob: "You sell wheelchairs and walkers and canes?"

Pharmacist: "All speeds and sizes."

Jacob: "Adult diapers?"

Pharmacist: "Sure."

Jacob: "We'd like to use this store as our bridal registry."

Bobbie tries her hand at the helm of the Willamette Sternwheeler

The Home Show and the Bladder Shaker

Did you go to the recent Home and Garden Show at the Newport Rec Center? That place, under the able direction of Jim Protiva, Parks and Recreation director, is amazing. It not only lends itself to keeping fit, but it's also a perfect venue for various events.

At the Home Show, I ran into friends Cheri Aldridge and Kath Schonau. The three of us just happened to stop and chat in front of an exhibit of three high-tech exercise machines that we decided to try out. The salesman directed us to stand this way, then that way, and insisted we also sit and experience the shaking and the quaking. A silly photo was taken, and after we got off the machines, I dubbed them the "the bladder shakers" and headed for the nearest restroom—which leads me to a day brightener that last ran in 2011.

For All The Men In Our Lives Who Ask, "What Took You So Long?"

When you have to visit a public bathroom, you usually find a line of women so you smile politely and take your place. Once it's your turn, you check for feet under the stall doors. Every stall is occupied.

Finally, a door opens and you dash in, nearly knocking down the woman leaving the stall. You get in to find the door won't latch. It doesn't matter, the wait has been so long you are about to wet your pants! The dispenser for the modern "seat covers" (invented by someone's mom, no doubt) is empty. You would hang your purse on the door hook, if there was one, but there isn't, so you quickly drape it around your neck (Mom would turn over in her grave if you put it on the FLOOR!), yank down your pants, and assume "the stance."

In this position, your aging, toneless (gosh, I should have gone to the gym!) thigh muscles begin to shake. You'd love to sit down, but you certainly hadn't taken time to wipe the seat or lay toilet paper on it, so you hold "the stance."

To take your mind off your trembling thighs, you reach for what you discover to be the empty toilet paper dispenser. In your mind, you can hear your mother's voice saying, "Honey, if you had tried to clean the seat, you would have KNOWN there was no toilet paper!" Your thighs shake more. You remember the tiny tissue that you blew your nose on yesterday, the one that's still in your purse. (Oh yeah, the purse around your neck.) That will have to do. You crumple it in the puffiest way possible. It's still smaller than your thumbnail.

Someone pushes your door open because the latch doesn't work. The door hits your purse, which is hanging around your neck in front of your chest, and you and your purse topple backward against the tank of the toilet. "Occupied!" you scream, as you reach for the door, dropping your precious, tiny, crumpled tissue in a puddle on the floor, lose your footing altogether, and slide down directly onto the toilet seat. It is wet of course.

You bolt up, knowing all too well that it's too late. Your bare bottom has made contact with every imaginable germ and life form on the uncovered seat because YOU never laid down toilet paper -not that there was any, even if you had taken time to try. You know your mother would be utterly appalled if she knew because you're certain her bare bottom never touched a public toilet seat because frankly, dear, "You just don't KNOW what kind of diseases you could get."

By this time, the automatic sensor on the back of the toilet is so confused that it flushes, propelling a stream of water like a fire hose against the inside of the bowl that sprays a fine mist of water that covers your butt and runs down your legs and into your shoes. The flush somehow sucks everything down with such force that you grab onto the empty toilet paper dispenser for fear of being dragged in too.

At this point, you give up. You're soaked by the spewing water and the wet toilet seat. You're e-x-h-a-u-s-t-e-d. You try to wipe with a gum wrapper you found in your pocket and then slink out inconspicuously to the sinks. You can't figure out how to operate the faucets with the automatic sensors, so you wipe your hands with spit and a dry paper towel and walk past the line of women still waiting.

You are no longer able to smile politely to them. A kind soul at the very end of the line points out a piece of toilet paper trailing from your shoe. (Where was that when you needed it?) You yank the paper from your shoe, plunk it in the woman's hand, and tell her warmly, "Here, you just might need this."

As you exit, you spot your hubby, who has long since entered, used, and left the men's restroom. Annoyed, he asks, "What took you so long and why is your purse hanging around your neck?"

This is dedicated to women everywhere who deal with public restrooms (Rest? You've got to be kidding!). It finally explains to the men why it really does take us so long. It also answers their other commonly asked questions about why women go to the restroom in pairs. It's so the other gal can hold the door, hang onto your purse, and hand you Kleenex under the door.

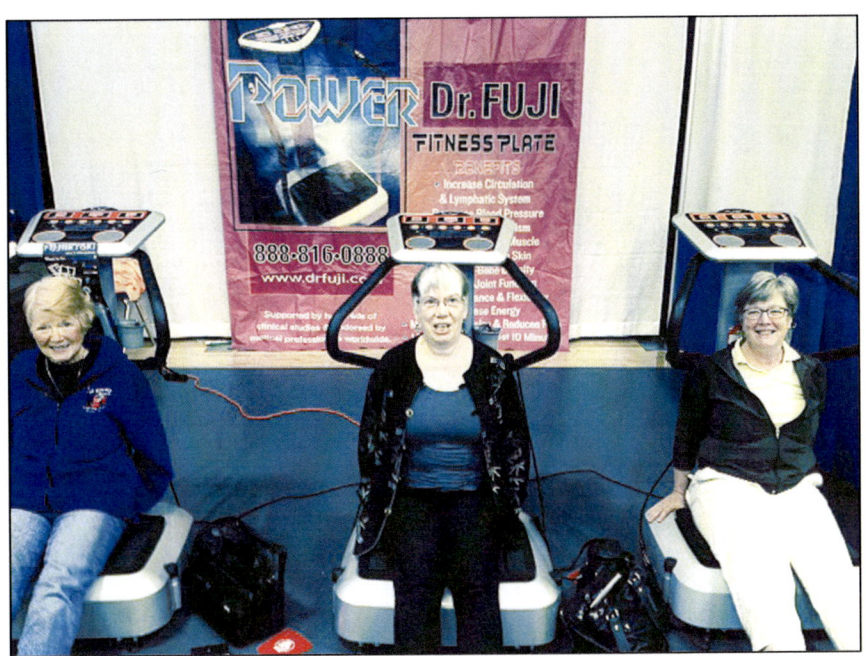

Bobbie (left), Cheri Aldridge, and Kath Schonau try out "the bladder shakers" at the Home and Garden Show, Newport Recreation Center

WITH AGE COMES WISDOM-- OR NOT

"Running is an unnatural act—except from enemies and to the bathroom."   *(Author unknown)*

I know you will quit reading if you think this column is just about marathons and running. Only a small percentage of people relate to that subject, so trust me and keep reading, although this past weekend a few thousand souls descended on this community for the running of the annual Newport Marathon. This is good for local business in many ways, but it also stimulated my brain to think outside the box for tidbits you might find interesting or downright funny.

Tidbit #1 — Not long ago, I traveled with Bruce and Marylou Mate to help cheer for their daughter Michelle, who was running a marathon on Whidbey Island, Washington. As we passed the building where runners sign in, collect their numbers and various goodies, Bruce suddenly stopped the car and bailed out. He came back clutching his cell phone full of photos he had taken at a booth full of T-shirts for runners. Here are a few of the best T-shirt slogans:
The Older I Get the Faster I Was.
Who Moved the Finish Line?
Didn't Your Mother Warn You About Fast Women?
It's A Hill. Get Over It!

Good Grief

My Mascara Runs Faster Than You Do.
See Dick Run—See Jane Run Faster.
Dear God, Please Let There Be Someone Behind Me To Read This.

Tidbit #2 — A couple of years ago, I decided to get in shape for the Newport Marathon. In my younger days, I once set a goal to run half a dozen 10Ks (a 10K amounts to 6.2 miles of running). An added perk is you get a cute T-shirt. My husband Burt always supported my crazy ideas, in fact, he never failed to be at the finish line (with a stopwatch) wearing an original T-shirt he had made for himself: "10K Athletic Supporter." I know your mouth just fell open, but that's an example of his humor. As preparation for the Newport full marathon, I also decided to sign up for a half marathon in Lincoln City. That's Lincoln City, Oregon! You had to do this online, via computer. Neither Burt nor I were good at computer-ing, so we sat down together and very carefully filled out the form, including using a credit card for the $35 entry fee. We held our collective breaths and hit the "send" button. Up came a screen saying, "Congratulations and welcome to the Lincoln, Nebraska Half Marathon." What the...? We tried getting our money back, even made a phone call, but it was too complicated. When Burt realized the half marathon was sponsored by the Nebraska State Guard, he let them have the money as a donation. What a guy!

Tidbit #3 —My kid brother Paul and his wife Dot are in town for a few days of fun and adventure with big sister Bobbie, but mainly to take ownership of Burt's car, a request my husband made a year before he died. I will have to get used to not seeing that car in our garage, but it's time for me to honor Burt's wishes. I was 13 when Paul was born, and for some strange reason, Paul and I have always had a competitive thing between us—from roller-skating, to tobogganing, to bicycling. Then one year, back in my running days, Paul challenged me to come to Omaha and run a 10K with him—just us in a private run. Paul is a math nut (like Burt). In fact, he teaches math at a Christian school. Paul methodically mapped out exactly 6.2 miles for us to run in Omaha. This was not to be a race, but rather a fun run for a brother and sister to enjoy together. We were both in good shape and there is a saying among runners: "If you can't talk to someone while running, you need to get in better condition." Most memorable about running with Paul on that beautiful autumn day in Omaha is that it was the first—and only time—he shared his Vietnam experiences with me.

Now they are here, and we are making new memories. Paul and I won't be running (we are both much older and wiser now), but if we were, there is a T-shirt I would wear for sure: "I Run Like a Girl—Try To Keep Up."

Bobbie Lippman—"a few years ago"—with her kid brother Paul

COMMUNITY LEGEND—ALICE

This is dedicated to someone who not only contributed so much to this community for many years, but who has changed our lives in a major way. Burt would want me to write about Alice Silverman, from our own personal perspective because she was incredibly instrumental in launching us into our new life in Newport. Come along with me as I share the story that began back in 1983 when we escaped the Los Angeles fast lane and moved to South Beach. My husband loved telling of how our lives changed during our first week here, always adding the fact we had not even unpacked our boxes of stuff yet.

As you read this, Alice Silverman, who will soon be 96 years old, will either be reading it herself, or her caregiver daughter, Rose Marie Dotta, will be reading the words to her. I paid Alice a visit recently and it seems we held hands the entire time. Alice is very special to me, as she was to my husband and many "old(er) timers" whose lives were also touched by this gracious lady. Perhaps she has forgotten many of our experiences together, but to me it feels like it was just yesterday.

When we first arrived here, Burt was still with his former Hollywood company. He was nine years to retirement and everyone (both business and personal) was shocked that we were leaving. Burt's company made an offer he couldn't refuse. Which meant five days in Hollywood and weekends at our South Beach home—a grueling commute. But life on the beach with me and our assortment of animals was worth it (he said). We had been subscribing to the *News-Times* for two years, ever since I had discovered Newport during a Highway 101 bicycle trek from Canada to Mexico. I honestly felt God calling us to live here and firmly believed that eventually we would be able to break ties with southern California. It wasn't easy, but you know the expression, "With God all things are possible."

During the very first week in our new home, I spotted a notice in the paper regarding an open meeting for the local animal shelter. While at the meeting, I bought two tickets for a fashion show fundraiser being held at the Best Western Inn the following Saturday night. Together, Burt and I found the hotel, the ballroom, and two seats in the back of the room. Seated at the table was a gentleman who told us the show was organized by his wife Pat and someone named Alice Silverman. At this point, we did not know Pat, Alice, or anyone else in the community, but hey, at least we met Erling Grimstad. When the fashion show ended, Erling introduced us to his wife and 5-foot-2-inch Alice, who said, "I'm having a party next Saturday night at the Embarcadero Resort & Marina, it's black tie and I would love for you to come." Not being exactly the shy and bashful types, we said yes, but on the way back to South Beach, Burt looked at me and said (his exact words) "Who the hell is Alice Silverman?" I had no idea, but a week later, we put on the finery and managed to locate the Embarcadero ballroom. There was Alice in a beautiful long gown, four-inch heels, and a warm smile of greeting. We were caught up in a whirl of introductions and passed around that ballroom from group to group as if we were a box of bonbons. After the party, we were blown away by how fast we were swept up into this community when we thought we were moving to a quiet Oregon Coast town where all I wanted to do was walk the beach, be a writer, and get my husband to slow down and smell the seaweed. Thanks to Alice Silverman, our lives quickly shot fast forward. She loved giving parties (at her own expense), frequent dinners in her home, and Fourth of July barbecues watching fireworks on her Bayfront deck.

I need to throw in a bit of back-story here in case you don't know Alice and assume she spent her life in party mode. Not so. During the Big War, Alice was an airplane welder. If you're old enough, try to picture her as Rosie the Riveter. Somewhere along the line, her life changed when she married a Texas ship builder named Ben Silverman, but Alice's heart was always right here in Newport. After Ben died, a movement was on to build the Newport Performing Arts Center. If you have been there, you surely noticed the large letters saying "Alice Silverman Theatre" and a lovely oil painting of her in the lobby. She got us involved in fundraising for the PAC, which segued into helping support many other worthwhile community causes. When I tried to explain Alice Silverman to old friends in L.A., I often referred to her as "The Pearl Mesta of Newport." (Only you readers of a certain age would know about Pearl Mesta.)

Someone, someday (not me) should write a book about Alice, her free spirit, her six kids, and her generous heart.

Alice Silverman (center) with Burt and Bobbie Lippman

License Plate Memories

Almost every column generates mail from readers, but there is always an extra response if I touch on how I'm dealing with the loss of my husband Burt. There are so many folks who have lost a loved one and I feel honored when they share their Grief Journeys with me. I just heard from a woman whose son died 10 years ago and a few family members think it's time for her to "get over it." They think it's odd that she keeps so many photos of him around, or that she cries so easily. Her words make me want to go find those people and whack them over the head. We all deal with grief in whatever ways give us comfort, and nobody has the right to criticize our sometimes bizarre behaviors. (Some of mine are too crazy to put into writing—although maybe I will.)

Last week, my brother Paul and his wife were here to spend five precious days with me, but the main purpose was to take ownership of Burt's car with the license plate—BURTXL (the XL stands for extra large). Saying goodbye to Paul and Dot was tough enough, but no longer having my husband's car in the garage sent me into an unexpected bout of the blues. I could not bear to see them drive away, so I sat in my lazy girl chair and had a good cry. (Crying is an okay and healthy thing whether you are a woman OR a man). When the sadness lingered for several days, I suddenly remembered a long ago column that was such fun to write. I decided dig it out of my archives and run it again. Just re-reading that thing got me over the blues. Here it is.

Good Grief

ADAYNLA (originally published Nov. 20, 1985)

This is being written in a hotel room high above "beautiful downtown Burbank." If you squint, you can almost make out the line of people waiting to get into the Johnny Carson show at NBC. My first column in the *News-Times* was about what it felt like moving to Oregon from California. Now it's fun to catch some impressions the other way around. Although this is not my first time back in L.A., I am far more aware of the differences. Burt is busy working, so why don't you hop in the rental car and come along with me. There's plenty of room.

Heading out from the hotel, the first thing you notice is that people of all ages are walking around in shorts and flip-flops. Most are wearing headphones. Some are on skateboards or roller blades. Everyone has a tan and a lot have hair bleached white by the sun. You wonder if these people ever go to work. The temperature is almost 90 and the air isn't moving—barely a breeze. But it moved recently when the Santa Ana winds kicked up and caused some serious brush fires.

Today, however, is hot and smoggy, so let's swing onto the freeway and head for Santa Monica where we can breathe. You begin to think everyone in L.A. has a personalized license plate. Ahead is one that says YBNORML (Californians are allowed seven letters, Oregon, six.) On our left is a sports car with a plate that says MOMSTOY—a young man is driving. On our right, a VW Rabbit zips by with HOP2IT on the plates. Quick, here's my writing pad. Let's get these written down.

Oh, oh, traffic has come to a complete stop on the San Diego Freeway. Up ahead an accident has three lanes closed, and it's taken 30 minutes to go two miles. May as well relax and look around. Amazing how many type-A types are talking on their phones. Nice to know that some people are working—or are they calling their girlfriends? Hmm, there's an interesting plate: IMARUNR. So why doesn't he just get out of the car and run to work? Meanwhile dudes on motorcycles are whizzing by, not at all inconvenienced by the snarl.

We finally arrive in Santa Monica. Old ladies in flowered dresses are sitting on benches holding colorful parasols over their heads. Teenagers with green and purple spiky hair are headed for the beach lugging enormous transistor radios. We wonder why they aren't in school. A lot of people are wearing sunglasses—not on their faces but on top of their heads, like ornaments. We linger for lunch at an outdoor café, and you are just as fascinated as I am listening to people speaking in languages other than English.

It's time to head back to the hotel before rush hour traffic. At the freeway onramp, we think about the peace and quiet of home. At that moment, a car races by and cuts us off. The license plate says IENVEU. Now, how did that guy know we're from Newport, Oregon?

My husband's personalized license plates are about to arrive in Nebraska. I did not want to keep them. Paul says he will put them on their garage wall and think of his "big brother Burt" and the terrific times we had together for 45 years. Saying goodbye to that car with the personal plates was just another difficult, but necessary step in my journey.

Bobbie says goodbye to Burt's car bearing the license plate BURTXL

When Time Takes It's Time

This week has been an emotional roller coaster. I knew last Friday's column would cause a spike in reader response because I admitted to a meltdown over the recent absence of my husband's car in the garage. It's not the car I miss. After all, it's now being enjoyed thoroughly by my kid brother and his wife in Nebraska. What I hate is seeing that empty space where Burt's car used to be.

A widow told me how hard it was selling her husband's convertible. Being local folks, they cherished the Oregon days when they could drive around with the top down. She knows, like me, there is nothing to do but accept the feelings and just keep putting one foot in front of the other. Everyone says "time heals" and I say, "Okay, time, do your thing already." This week I've been on the phone a lot trying to help Burt's daughter Robin, whose best friend died after a long fight with cancer. No longer being able to share every aspect of your life with a best friend of 37 years is not less painful than losing the love of your life.

One of my youngest readers (age 24) is wise beyond her years. She follows this column and occasionally sends an inspirational quote or short piece of writing. Here is one of her gems (author unknown): "Life begins at the end of your comfort zone." The other night as I was waiting for the sleep fairy to finally show up, I heard the chime of an incoming email. Here is the latest from my young friend:

"Losing You," by Lang Leav

I used to think I couldn't go a day without your smile. Without telling you things and hearing your voice back. Then, that day arrived and it was so damn hard, but the next was harder. I knew with a sinking feeling it was going to get worse, and I wasn't going to be okay for a very long time because losing someone isn't an occasion or an event. It doesn't just happen once. It happens over and over again. I lose you every time I pick up your favorite coffee mug, whenever that one song plays on the radio, or when I discover your old T-shirt at the bottom of my laundry pile. I lose you every time I think of kissing you, holding you, or wanting you. I go to bed at night and lose you when I wish I could tell you about my day. And in the morning, when I wake and reach for the empty space across the sheets, I begin to lose you all over again."

Well, for all of us dealing with a loss, those words are hard to read without tearing up—but those words made me take action the next morning rather than just wallow around in my lazy girl chair. I called a friend who is also a movie buff and we went to see a film called *The Fault In Our Stars*. I have always followed reviews of movies and books, and there has been much hype about this book and now the just-released movie. Both are a huge hit in what is called the Y.A. (young adult) market. The book has been a best seller for weeks. It's the story of two teenagers who meet in a cancer support group. Both these young people are total eye candy, but not in the Hollywood glitzy way. You know they are actors, but the movie is so honest, believable, and mesmerizing. The film pulls you in, heart first. My friend was concerned the story would be depressing for me. It wasn't. What surprised me (happily) was a big chunk of the movie took place in Amsterdam. As the camera followed the young couple (who make the journey through a fictional "Make A Wish" program), I scooted forward in the seat, determined to not miss a moment.

During our traveling years, Burt and I spent several glorious days in Amsterdam. Instead of sadness, I found myself caught up in happy memories of when we explored that amazing city together on foot, bicycles, and canal boats. We visited all the museums (especially the Van Gogh) and spent a long time in the Anne Frank house, climbing up all those steps just as the young couple does in the movie (while struggling with a portable oxygen tank).

What I came away with, for those of us dealing with the loss of a loved one, is the importance of focusing on the happy times, the good memories, the times we laughed and loved and shared. We all know people who spend their entire lives not having a soul mate, or a best friend, or knowing what it is like to truly, deeply love someone. They are the ones who have a reason to feel sad—not those of us who have been incredibly blessed.

Here is one more gem from my young reader: "You are not starting over—you are just continuing on."

Quirks That Work

Do you remember that old magazine called *True Confessions*? For all I know, it's still out there on newsstands, right next to the *National Enquirer*. Today I'm confessing to a couple of oddball quirks, and I do hope the paper runs a photo since pictures are much more interesting than words.

Quirk No. 1: Some folks might label me anti-social, but those are the people who think it's perfectly OK to pay you a visit without calling first. (A close friend just told me she and her husband had gone to bed early last night to read when unexpected company showed up). How annoying! But she certainly inspired a column idea. I figure drop-in people were raised that way, but I have never understood it and I wouldn't think of pounding on someone's door without checking to see if my visit is convenient or even welcome. This is why I keep a very visible vacuum cleaner near the front door. I'm not a clean freak, but I'm not a slob either. Like others, I treasure my privacy. If an unexpected person shows up (depending on who it is) I either tell them I'm in the middle of cleaning or invite them in. If the house is messy, obviously they can tell when they walk past the vacuum cleaner that I'm about to rearrange the dust balls. Case closed.

Quirk No. 2: I recently put an almost life-size stuffed Doberman by the front door, complete with doggy dish full of cat treats since I am presently dog-less for the first time in my life.

Good Grief

Burt gave me the stuffed dog years ago and I'm not ready to give it up. Recent visitors think the "Dobie with Dish" is funny. So do I, which is why I put this scenario by the door, knowing full well a fake Doberman is not going to scare away unwanted visitors. My husband and I had Dobermans for many years in South Beach. They were total pussycats but they certainly did not look harmless since Dr. Steve Brown had given the dogs ear jobs. Stand up ears on a Dobie makes most people step back with respect, waiting for you to say "It's OK. They are friendly."

However, we did put a sign near the entry gate that read, "We can make it to the fence in 3 seconds—can you?" Whenever visitors rang the bell at the gate, the dogs would race down the steps barking their brains out. We felt a little guilty if the visitors were clutching religious tracts. They would hurry off to the neighbors before we even got down the stairs.

I miss having a dog. I miss chocolate poodle Charley for his cuddly company, but mostly because, even in his advanced age, he barked loudly when anyone approached our front door. It feels strange being dog-less, but a dog is far more responsibility than a cat—and not having a dog is liberating. I can take off on trips without having to make complicated arrangements.

Fortunately, friends are willing to take care of Lap Sitter and the house. I do have a certain amount of anxiety that the phone is going to ring one day with a friend saying, "Bobbie, there is this amazing dog available that needs a good home and would be perfect for you." It could happen. When your life is in a transition time and you are open to new experiences anything can happen.

To leave you with a smile, here is a day brightener, sent by Linda Kilbride of Newport:

Can cold water clean dishes?

This is for all the germ conscious folks that worry about using cold water to clean. John went to visit his 90-year-old grandfather in a very secluded, rural area of Saskatchewan. After spending a great time chatting the night away, John's grandfather prepared breakfast of bacon, eggs, and toast. However, John noticed a film-like substance on his plate, and questioned his grandfather. "Are these plates clean?"

His grandfather replied, "They're as clean as cold water can get 'um. Just you go ahead and finish your meal, Sonny!"

For lunch, the old man made hamburgers. Again, John was concerned about the plates as his appeared to have tiny specks around the edge that looked like dried egg and asked, "Are you sure these plates are clean?" Without looking up, the old man said, "I told you before, Sonny, those dishes are as clean as cold water can get them. Now don't you fret, I don't want to hear another word about it!"

Later that afternoon, John was on his way to a nearby town and as he was leaving, his grandfather's dog started to growl and wouldn't let him pass. John yelled and said, "Grandfather, your dog won't let me get to my car."

Without diverting his attention from the football game he was watching on TV, the old man shouted, "Coldwater, go lay down now, yah hear me!"

Foot In Mouth Disease

In case you missed last week's column, the subject was dogs and the fact that I am presently dog-less for the first time ever. I admitted to having anxiety that the phone might ring with some well-meaning person offering me a dog. It was a tongue-in-cheek comment, but now may be more like foot-in-mouth.

No sooner did the *News-Times* arrive in the hands of readers when my telephone rang with a local voice saying there is a young Great Dane available for a good home. I nearly choked, especially when told the dog's name is Rocky. If memory serves, that's the name of my daughter—actually her nickname. Her full name is Rochelle Jolene, which was way too much name for a tiny newborn, so in a fit of hormone overload, I called her Rocki.

However, this brings back a very clear memory of standing in a grocery line holding my three-week-old munchkin (in pink) when a little old lady stopped by my side and said, "Such a beautiful baby. What's her name?" When I answered "Rocki," the woman glared at me with frowning disapproval, muttered "Humph!" and stalked off.

Back to the person on the phone. I'm keeping the caller anonymous because my brain went ballistic listening to her go on and on about Great Danes. I'm still not exactly sure of the details. Since that call, I have been walking around like a nutcase over how bizarre this whole thing is, knowing full well the story would end up as column fodder. Certainly proves the power of the press, doesn't it—or maybe the wisdom of having an unlisted phone number?

Travel back in time with me to the early 1970s and the day I took my husband to his first dog show. He wasn't raised with dogs, but when we met, I was owned by three Borzois otherwise known as Russian Wolfhounds. As the saying goes, love me, love my dogs. Burt obviously accepted the whole package, which included my daughter, the tall, leggy dogs, the cats, and Rocki's assortment of hamsters, gerbils, pet rats, and salamanders. Now, in looking back, he did seem a bit bewildered, but eventually he got over it. More or less.

I had been involved in showing dogs for years and I wanted him to experience the Santa Barbara Dog Show, one of the most prestigious in the country. I also wanted Burt to meet my Borzoi friends who were showing dogs that day. The Santa Barbara Dog Show is a festive circuslike affair, with colorful pennants flying over the fairgrounds, dozens of vendor booths, motor homes, and every imaginable type of purebred dog at the end of someone's leash or in wire pens.

We quickly zeroed in on a large ring in which Borzois were circling at top speed with breathless handlers trying to capture the judge's attention and win that coveted blue ribbon. I kept poking my husband, pointing out old friends he would be meeting after the judging, but Burt's attention was on a ring behind us where a different breed was being shown.

"Oh wow!" he exclaimed. "What kind of dogs are those?"

I looked. "Those are Great Danes," I told him, and no way could I drag his attention back to the Borzoi ring, so I gave up.

Of course, later he was very gracious with my doggy friends. He thoroughly enjoyed his first dog show, but he kept talking about those Great Danes. The next morning I was on the phone networking with dog people. This led me to a Malibu breeder and Burt's very own first-in-a-lifetime puppy. Ta da! Surprise! My husband was smitten with the pup from the get go. Brutus quickly grew into what Burt considered a Real Dog, a man's dog—150 pounds of dog. Great Danes are huge; they don't come in any other size. Brutus was—like Burt—a gentle giant. My husband drove convertibles during our years in L.A. and somewhere I have a photo of the two of them headed down our long driveway—Burt at the wheel with the top down and Brutus sitting tall and majestic in the back seat.

One annoying drawback with a dog that size is a constantly wagging long tail that wipes out all houseplants at tail level. Brutus lived to age 10, which is pretty good for a giant breed. On the day we had to say goodbye to this grand old dog, Burt's tears were a clue he had joined in the legions of dog lovers who sooner or later have to part with a beloved canine companion.

So here it is 43 years later, and I find myself thinking about a Great Dane named Rocky. There is much soul searching to be done. Adopting a dog of any kind is life changing. If I end up saying yes, one thing is for certain: there go the houseplants.

At Home And Aweigh

Today's column, due to all your emails, has to be, by necessity, a three-parter. I sincerely appreciate the readers who write to me, and I also sincerely apologize for not answering—it is simply impossible to keep up and there's no way to delegate the job to someone else because it would not have my personal touch. I don't have the energy of a 30-year-old and I am also fighting macular degeneration, so there's that, too. Enough with the excuses already.

Part One: For those of you waiting with baited breath (which is more pleasant than dog breath), the jury is still out on that offer I got regarding a young Great Dane needing a home. While shopping at Fred Meyer, a person I don't know said she recognized me from the picture in the paper. She got in my face demanding, "So why aren't you taking that dog?" Sometimes I do think fast on my feet and answered, "Because he would not fit in my little car!" She did not see that as a problem and suggested I simply buy a bigger car. Back in our Doberman days, Burt got me a Suburban. It felt like driving a bus. Dave Miller, our local friend with all the radio stations, informed me I was driving a $35,000 rolling doghouse.

Out of more than three dozen emails from readers weighing in about the Great Dane, only one person said I should think about it. Amazingly, all the rest more or less used the words "Go for it, you need a dog." I do? Seriously?

Part Two: Right now, at the peak of summer, folks are either

Good Grief

staying home or traveling. Were you here for the July 4 activities? For me it was important to attend the annual concert last Saturday, a toe-tapping, patriotic musical gift to the public by the incredible Newport Symphony Orchestra. I had to make myself go because, for me, it was another of the dreaded "firsts." By that I mean for all of us who have lost a loved one there are the "firsts" to either get through or avoid in order to somehow escape the pain of the first holiday, the first birthday, the first anything without that person you loved so deeply. One year ago, this concert was the last community event Burt and I attended together.

A traditional highlight in the program is when a uniformed member of the armed services comes out and announces, one by one, each major branch of the service. Active members and veterans are asked to stand as the orchestra plays the appropriate music—i.e. the Marine Corp hymn, etc. As a proud Navy veteran, Burt always stood when the band played "Anchors Aweigh." I have this visual of looking up at him last year. He was standing tall, straight, and proud beside me in spite of the chronic pain in his back. I choked up then, and I knew the tears would come this time for sure, but I was blessed to be with good friends who helped get me through it, and I know next year will be easier. My friend Marian Brown knows me well and has walked the grief walk herself. She sent a note ahead of time saying, "Just remember, tears are OK."

Part Three: One of the many lessons I've learned this year without my husband is to focus on the good times we had together—45 years of good times, fun, and laughter. I guess for some it's easier to wallow around in sorrow, but I would much rather laugh than cry. Burt and I enjoyed traveling, as many of you are doing right now, and I have dredged up two funny things for you.

While on a tour bus in Costa Rica, we were being driven through a most unusual neighborhood—interesting because every house was surrounded by walls and razor wire, the kind used to keep inmates in prisons. The driver said the people treasure their TV sets and don't want them stolen. Then we passed an ordinary looking home (also with walls and razor wire). The bus driver announced, "Would you believe that house has five kitchens?" We all looked at one another in amazement. Who on earth needs five kitchens? The driver waited for silence, then said, "Yep, Mr. and Mrs. Kitchen and their three kids, ha-ha-ha."

It's not just bus drivers and tour guides with a sense of humor, but also captains of cruise ships. On our second trip with the same cruise line, we were invited to a pre-dinner party hosted by the ship's captain. I think the guy was Swedish, with a head of white hair, neatly trimmed beard, and a twinkle in his eyes like Santa Claus. In fact, he looked a lot like Burt. Here's the story he told to all of us listening with rapt attention:

> A woman on a cruise had way too much to drink and needed to be escorted to her cabin by a hunky cruise director and a hunky drummer, one on each side to hold her up. During the walk down the hallway, she says to the cruise guy, "You're passionate!" He is flattered, and they keep going. Then she says the same thing to the drummer. They get to the far end of the hallway and the drummer asks, "Madam, where is your cabin?" She looks at them both like they're nuts and says, "I kept telling you, 'You're passionate!'"

Reflections Of A Painful Year

"Everyone can master a grief but he who has it."
—*William Shakespeare*

One year ago today, a light went out in my world—and possibly yours, too. By the grace of God, I was at the Embarcadero Resort & Marina last July 18 as my husband Burt walked out of his Rotary meeting and was struck down by cardiac arrest. I was there on the floor beside my soul mate, best friend, and protector of 45 years, holding him in my arms and whispering in his ear that I would be OK if it was his time to leave. I even told him to greet the baby we lost so many years ago. He was unconscious but still breathing, and I believe he could hear my words. I will forever be grateful to Pat Lewis who asked me to lunch that day. I am not a go-to-lunch person, but an inner voice had said, "Do it!"

I am grateful that Burt was surrounded by fellow Rotarians. I vaguely remember many cell phones calling 9-1-1. I'm grateful to everyone at Samaritan Pacific Communities Hospital who continued to work on my husband long after I knew their efforts were of no use. I am grateful to the wonderful women friends who encircled me that day with love and support, and the two Rotarians, Ted Smith and Police Chief Mark Miranda, who took our cars back home. If I named all the people who stepped up to help this past year, there would not be space in this newspaper.

My "Bobbie's Beat" column has appeared in the *News-Times* every single week since that fateful day a year ago. You readers have walked the Grief Journey with me, step by painful step. When I chose to hole up in our home and grieve alone, many of you left food, flowers, and cards on the doorstep, and you respected my privacy. Grief comes in many colors, and none of us gets to judge or criticize how anyone else deals with it.

Writing this column has been therapeutic for me, just as your emails and letters have also helped during this entire year. I am certainly not the only one who suffered the loss of an amazing man known as Burt Lippman. It has been a sad time for our daughters, family members, and friends.

Perhaps you read the column about how I could not move Burt's favorite coffee cup for an entire month. There it sat, on the table between us where he left it that fateful morning. It was a personalized cup, made for him by his daughter Robin. She found comfort in the fact he not only loved that cup, but that it stayed in place for so long.

I have been open and honest regarding behavior quirks that have given me comfort. I've heard from readers all over the country (and beyond)—folks who lost a loved one and say they no longer feel odd or alone for how they are traveling their Grief Journey. One widower said he could not bear to remove his wife's clothing for 19 months following her death. A mother, who lost her teenage daughter, could not change one thing in her daughter's room. At first she kept the bedroom door closed, then little by little was able to leave it open.

In this column, I wrote about piling pillows and stacks of Burt's jeans on his side of the bed, so that during long bouts of insomnia I could pretend the mound was him, still sleeping there beside me. You read about our old dog, Charley. A month before

Good Grief

Burt died we were sure it was the end of the road for our dog, and we had a grave dug on our property. When Burt died, Charley rallied and I know he stuck around for another seven months to keep me company.

But I did not write about what happened my first night alone without Burt.

Around 3 a.m. I was aware Charley was not on his pillow at the foot of our bed. I got up to look for him, wandering all over the house, calling his name. I finally found Charley curled up in a tight ball on the floor as close as he could get to Burt's side of the bed. I'm sure you dog people will write me saying, "Charley knew Burt had left. Dogs do mourn, you know."

There have been many lessons for me this past year. One major thing those of us grieving want all of you non-grievers to know—please continue to say the name of our loved one when you talk to us. Do not avoid using the name of the one who has gone on ahead. The sound of that name and those memories mean everything to us. And please continue to share the good memories you have; the good deeds that person did for you.

Somehow, now, after a year without Burt, I sense a shift in my life. None of us knows what tomorrow holds. Today is all we have. If my thoughts go too far into the future, I get terrified, so I pull back to stay in the present. The important thing is that life is for the living and I intend to make the most of the time I have left. My husband would expect no less from me.

Bobbie Lippman and her kid brother Paul get ready for a ride on his Harley, marking another item off of Bobbie's bucket list.

A Glamping We Will Go

The other day, a woman told me about being widowed for 15 years and how the memories of her husband make her sad all the time. I feel badly for her, but I refuse to do that. I've had a year of sadness and I am now trying hard to switch brain gears and focus on the good times, especially the funny stuff. Heaven knows if you live with someone for a long time there is bound to be a bit of everything.

When Burt and I got married, he pronounced me "social director." His exact words were, "I have never been an adventurer or risk-taker like you, but I am willing to try almost anything —once!"

Oh boy, oh boy, I thought myself and immediately signed us up to go river rafting on the Stanislaus River with an official company that furnishes everything and takes 16 people at a time. River rafting was all the rage and I wanted to start Burt out slow and not drag him onto a river like the one in the movie "Deliverance."

But here is the funniest part of the story and I dare you not to laugh. When my husband came home from work, I informed him we were booked on our first adventure. He looked at me warily and asked, "So what are we doing?"

I could hardly contain myself and informed him with great glee, "We are going to go shoot the rapids!" He turned rather pale, stared at me, and finally said, "Bobbie, I wasn't raised with guns as you were, and I could never kill anything." Huh? It took me a few moments to realize he thought I'd said RABBITS! And it took more than a few moments to convince him it was a relatively safe river, and all we had to do was show up.

I call today's subject "glamping" (glamorous camping) because this past week, three different friends set off on their annual camping trips. None of them were doing what I think of as roughing it. One was headed for a nice cabin with friends (and a bathroom), and the other two were packing their big luxurious tent and making sure the electric motor worked for pumping up their extra thick air mattress. Add to this my daughter Rocki's recent announcement about their slick new Airstream and how they were headed to the mountains in comfort with their two Rhodesian Ridgebacks.

Camping Tips

When using a public campground, a tuba placed on your picnic table will keep the campsites on either side vacant.

A hot rock placed in your sleeping bag will keep your feet warm. A hot enchilada works almost as well, but the cheese sticks between your toes.

Acupuncture was invented by a camper who found a porcupine in his sleeping bag.

Lint from your navel makes a handy fire starter. Warning: remove lint from navel before applying the match.

The guitar of the noisy teenager at the next campsite makes excellent kindling.

It is entirely possible to spend your whole vacation on a winding mountain road behind a large motor home.

Bear bells provide an element of safety for hikers in grizzly country. The tricky part is getting them on the bears.

Good Grief

Smile

The loaded mini-van pulled into the only remaining campsite. Four children leaped from the vehicle and began feverishly unloading gear and setting up the tent. The boys rushed to gather firewood while the girls and their mother set up the camp stove and cooking utensils.

A nearby camper marveled to the youngsters' father, "That, sir, is some display of teamwork." The father replied, "I have a system—no one goes to the bathroom until the camp is set up."

Notice Regarding Bears

In case anyone is considering camping this summer, please note the following public service announcement. In Alaska, tourists are warned to wear tiny bells on their clothing when hiking in bear country. The bells warn away most bears.

Tourists are also cautioned to watch the ground on the trail, paying particular attention to bear droppings to be alert for the presence of grizzly bears. One can tell a grizzly dropping because it has tiny bells in it.

Not only did Burt love river rafting, including sleeping outdoors, he assigned me the happy task of booking additional trips on far more exciting rivers. Our friends quickly asked to be included, so all future trips were custom designed. Part of the fun of a rafting trip in the summer is challenging the other rafts to water fights. Burt was an awesome menace with a bucket of water, but his macho enthusiasm caused him to end up with "River-Rafter's Elbow."

As for me, I have accepted an invite to go glamping with a friend on the Alsea River and I just ordered some bear bells. Stay tuned for a full report.

Bobbie camping with Lizzie (left), Daisy, and Gina Nielsen

Small Goats And Smaller Windows

Last Saturday, I attended two memorial services, now commonly referred to as Celebrations of Life. The first one was held at Atonement Lutheran Church to honor Barbara Mate, beloved mother of Bruce Mate. The second one was held at the Hatfield Marine Science Center to honor Dr. Lavern Weber. Both services were well attended and the chosen speakers shared stories and memories that caused me to get teary-eyed or just plain laugh out loud. I appreciated that in both services there was more focus on humor than on sadness.

While driving home on Highway 101, I can never resist a glance toward the house on the beach where Burt and I spent 14 gloriously happy years. It no longer looks like the fixer upper we lived in and loved, but I look anyhow. In case you're curious, our old place is a quarter mile south of Lost Creek, with a poodle on the mailbox. If you're not speeding you might spot the small barn. On Saturday, with no traffic behind me, I slowed way down to savor the memories of the years we lived there (no, not in the barn) and had such fun raising miniature goats, a whole new experience for my Brooklyn-born husband. If you look closer, you can see a rather small window in the barn and, of course, now you get a story never before told.

One lovely summer day, I nagged my husband into helping me with hay and feed in the 8-by-10-foot barn. As usual, several goats followed us in there, hoping for treats. We locked the lower door to keep out the dogs and the remainder of the goats. Just as we were wrestling with a bale of alfalfa, the top part of the barn door blew shut, locking us in. We looked at one another in disbelief. We were trapped, and not a cell phone in sight, as they were yet to be invented. Our only neighbors lived too far away to hear us if we yelled.

Being a problem-solver, Burt eyeballed that little window, then eyeballed me. Oh no, I thought, surely he knows I can't fit through that little window. He ignored my protests, removed the screen, and gave me a look that said he had no intention of spending the rest of his life locked in a stupid barn with goats. (Once a New Yorker, always a New Yorker.)

I tried to make myself look too large for that window, but it didn't work. Burt had already decided it was our only chance of survival. He shoved me bodily out the window, holding onto my feet while ignoring my moaning about being dumped head first into an overgrowth of blackberry vines. The drop from window to vines was at least six feet, but maybe I'm exaggerating. Believe me, it was no fun, and only made worse because I could hear Burt laughing his head off. Later he said he wished he had a camera to capture a shot of me, flat on my back, all tangled up in blackberry vines. Before you write to me, please know that a strong fence kept the goats from getting to that patch of blackberries.

Our daughters will be surprised to read about this unknown-till-now barnyard experience. Not long ago, while visiting my daughter Rocki and her husband Glen in their hilltop Camarillo, California, home, they tossed parties for me. Somehow, during the peak of pool party frivolity, someone suggested I should consider moving because Glen would happily build a "granny flat" for me. "And just think, Mom," exclaimed

Rocki, "you could have goats again, and a miniature donkey, and dogs and even a horse because we're surrounded by bridle trails."

Glen grinned at me like this was all even remotely possible, which of course it isn't, but the granny flat for Bobbie subject got kicked around by old friends who seemed to think the idea was better than sticking me in a nursing home. I finally had to remind everyone that the Oregon Coast is where I belong, that the people here are my village, and I will make trips back to LaLa Land when they can stand another visit.

Since I've made a pact with myself to focus on the fun times now in my new life without the guy who occasionally drove me nuts but mostly filled my life with joy and laughter, here are some "goat funnies" to leave you smiling:

Why did the goat run over the cliff? He didn't see the ewe turn.

Why is it hard to carry on a conversation with a goat? Because they are always butting in.

How do you keep a goat from charging? You take his credit card away.

And finally:

The young couple invited their pastor to Sunday supper. While they were in the kitchen preparing the meal, the pastor asked their young son what they were having.

"Goat," the little boy replied.

"Oh," said the startled man of the cloth. "Are you sure about that?"

"Yep," said the youngster. I heard my parents say that today was as good a day as any to have the old goat for dinner."

Burt Lippman with miniature goat (circa 1990)

Underground Beeping And Chomping

This column is for those of you "W" people who write to me (I still can't use the W word for my new status), and also for those who think I'm someone who is rarely intimidated in social situations. Wrong!

I was recently invited to a garden party held at the lovely home of Tonja and Bob Bergeron. It was one of those magical, windless summer evenings we so rarely have on the Oregon Coast. While strolling the grounds with other guests, I thought of all our years in southern California where outdoor entertaining goes on and on, because it can. I thought of our move to South Beach from L.A., and mentioned to a neighbor that we planned to put our old, lightweight patio furniture out on the deck.

"If you do," said the neighbor, "it will end up in Indiana!"

Well, duh!

There are many differences between life in a warm climate and life here on the coast. For example, we were clueless about slugs and I was horrified to see 6-inch, butt-ugly banana slugs. Yuck! My husband went after them with saucers of beer, but soon decided it was a waste of perfectly good beer. Since I can't bear to kill a critter, I used a pooper-scooper and threw the slugs across Highway 101 into the forest. Burt said this was a dumb idea when he noticed the slugs crawling back only to be squished by logging trucks on the highway. Double yuck!

Now, on my present Seal Rock property, I use the same old

pooper-scooper to pitch the slugs into the wetlands. My throwing arm is good enough to fling them so far they will die of old age before making it back to the yard. However, this year a new problem presented itself—a dozen molehills in the front lawn.

For a week, I went out there with shovel and wheelbarrow to collect all that nice aerated soil, which is perfect for planting if I ever feel in the mood again. (Many activities are no fun without Burt, and gardening is one of them). But the moles made me mad enough to ask friends for advice.

The first person I called said they hired someone to kill the critters at 35 bucks per mole. I called my California daughter, who lives on six acres of hillside property where moles and gophers can do (and do do) considerable damage, so they use a special mole service. (I did not ask the cost). I went to a local store and paid $30 for a two-pack of those long, yellow pointy things you load with D batteries and shove into the ground. They beep like a smoke alarm, which, supposedly, drives the moles crazy enough to pack up and leave. Guess what? No more molehills except for just a few small ones popping up near my greenhouse, so I figure Mr. and Mrs. Mole had invited cousins to visit.

The mole subject came up not long ago when I was with a group of walking friends and I overheard one woman mention the miracle of Juicy Fruit gum. Really? She claimed it works wonders, but you must only use Juicy Fruit, the real deal, because no other flavor works.

I immediately bought Juicy Fruit gum, which I have not chewed since high school. You cut a stick of gum lengthwise and poke a piece down each hole. Apparently, moles love the sugary taste. I don't want to know the end result, nor do I want to hear little choking/gagging sounds beneath the ground, but so far, the mole family and their annoying cousins have all gone bye-bye.

Good Grief

Meanwhile, back to the garden party. Somehow, I found myself separated from the women and in the midst of three guys looking at the greenhouse, which I was determined to see. There I stood with two master gardeners—Bob Bergeron and Art Bradley—plus local contractor, Mike Clark. During a lull in admiring some exotic species of plant, I asked the guys what they did about moles.

Have you ever brought up a subject and wished you'd kept your mouth shut? I found out more than I ever wanted to know about moles, gophers, slugs, and assorted other garden pests. I heard about the use of flares, traps, bait, bullets, shovels, and (oh no) sharp scissors for cutting slugs in half.

Did I dare mention to these learned men my smoke alarm beeper things or, worse yet, the wonders of Juicy Fruit gum? I did not! I excused myself to go rejoin the women who were discussing the joys of golfing and gourmet cooking.

I almost didn't go to this party knowing it would be all couples, but when you are "single," you sometimes have to get out of your comfort zone and make yourself do things—or stay home and wish you did.

It was a great party, full of scintillating conversation, and I smiled internally during the delicious dinner knowing a column was already writing itself in the back of my head. At that point, the subject was either going to be about garden pests or being single in a couples' world. Maybe both.

Every morning I go out to inspect my lawn with gum in a pocket, just in case. But seven mole-less weeks makes me very happy. Juicy Fruit gum anyone?

You Betcha

When was the last time you saw a lady smoking a pipe? Have you ever gone somewhere—anywhere—and found yourself immersed in reminders of your roots? If you are Scandinavian, or even if you aren't but are a computer person, you have surely received email jokes about Ole and Lena. There are hundreds of these type jokes floating from computer to computer, many X-rated, and I get them all because people seem to think I need reminders of my roots.

Here is a clean one: The judge had just awarded a divorce to Lena who had charged non-support. The judge said to Ole, "I decided to give your wife $800 a month for support." Ole thought about it and said, "Vell, dat's fine Judge, and vunce in awhile I'll try to chip in a few bucks myself."

Today's subject was born on a bus (actually a large and comfy van) because last Friday I went with Club 62, affiliated with the Newport Senior Center, on one of their outings. This time we headed out to the annual Scandinavian Festival in Junction City. The van was full of happy wanderers like me who love doing interesting things at very reasonable rates while leaving the driving to someone else. Perhaps you read my account about a trip to explore the famous Willamette River Sternwheeler with Club 62 not long ago.

If you enjoy getting out with a group, I highly recommend these creative excursions. You may not know anyone when you board the van, but you soon will. Although I was not the only

Scandinavian, no one shared a single Ole and Lena joke. But I was tempted to tell this one: Ole and Lena bought a new car. They were so excited that when they got home they locked the keys in the car. Ole says to Lena, "I thought you had the keys." Lena says, "You were driving, and the driver always takes the keys." Ole claims it doesn't much matter because the point is—what are they going to do about it. Lena says, "Vell, you better come up with someting because it looks like rain and you left the top down!"

So okay, that one's a groaner. Keep reading.

At Junction City, we piled out and headed for one of the booths serving freshly made aebleskivers, a kind of Swedish pancake in the shape of a large golf ball, served with lingonberry yam (oops, make that jam). Although it was a hot day, there were shady places to sit and enjoy big and little people dancing in costume to toe-tapping music, and an excellent storyteller where we listened to old familiar tales by Hans Christian Anderson.

My new friend Julie and I wandered in and out of the various booths selling ethnic goodies. I had not thought of my mother's sewing box in years, but there on a table was an exact replica of a colorful, hand-painted sewing box my grandmother brought with her from Sweden. Grandma bore eight kids in America, and somehow my mom inherited that sewing box. Unfortunately, my Swedish grandmother died before I ever got to know her. Now I'm wondering—whatever happened to that sewing box?

Although we pigged out on aebleskivers, we were soon seduced by the aroma of Swedish meat pies, so of course we had to try one—with piña colada lemonade. If you read the column about the Sternwheeler trip, you know these outings can turn into a feeding frenzy, especially the universal need of tourists to find ice cream. This trip was no exception because most of us were whining that we needed our ice cream fix.

True to form, we stopped at the Philomath Dairy Queen and once again, I confess to having ice cream for dinner. During the drive back to Newport, we were a quiet group due to full tummies, a hot day, and a lot of walking. If I'd had an ounce of energy left, I might have shared this dumb joke: Ole and Lena got married. On their honeymoon, they were nearing Minneapolis when Ole put his hand on Lena's knee. Giggling, Lena said, "Ole, you can go a bit further now that ve are married." So he drove to Duluth.

I bet by now you're wondering about the lady pipe smoker, and I know better than to disappoint you. Years ago, I got my husband to travel through Europe by train and, of course, we had to visit Scandinavia. In Stockholm, we went to a Swedish Festival, much like the one in Junction City. While we were people watching, we spotted a woman in the crowd happily puffing on a pipe. Burt knew I wanted to take a picture of her, but I had no idea how to do it without her knowing, so my brilliant guy said, "I'm going to go stand next to her. Act like you are taking a photo of me, then move the camera and snap one of her instead."

I still have that picture. I wish you could see it, but for all I know she wasn't as old as she looked and since this column travels, it would be just my luck that some relative of mine in Sweden would show it to her and the *News-Times* (and I) would be dealing with a lawsuit.

Uff da, everyone. That's Norwegian, with many meanings— my choice is, "You betcha!"

Blame It On The Brass

We all have moments—some of them wild, weird and often downright embarrassing. When you are half a couple, there are moments, and when you are alone, there are other moments. I am trying to go with the flow, shift gears, and be open to new experiences. It has been a long time since I've had houseguests, but such was the case this past week—women friends who go off on trips, including the coast where they usually rent someone's house for girl-time. This year I said, "You are welcome to stay with me," and they happily accepted.

Subject change: Before going further, you need to know that my husband Burt brought his "music system" into our marriage—a large chunk of now outdated equipment, but it plays CDs and radio, although the remote control stopped working about the time Burt died. I wasn't into listening to music until recently when I sorted through a ton of CDs (music from the 1940s) and reloaded the CD five-packs with my own favorite music, which is pretty eclectic—from country to folk to classical and pop. It's important to add here that I am crazy about the Tijuana Brass with Herb Alpert. My love of this music goes back to my single years in a tacky Santa Monica beach house. Shoving a vacuum was always more fun to the zippy TJ Brass, and I still do it to this day—although not in a bikini.

The point of this story is that women get into subjects that men don't touch, as in "What's your most embarrassing moment?" To protect my friends' privacy I'm using only their first names—Peggy, Arlene and Jan, which really isn't relevant because I'm not blabbing anything they shared anyhow. We had a great time playing tourist, eating, talking, and being lazy around the house. They seemed happy with the accommodations after discovering Murphy beds can be comfortable.

Since you steady readers are used to my openness, here are my two most embarrassing moments. When Burt and I got married, our first home was a very private one, with a swimming pool, which means a pool guy showed up twice a week. We used Dan the Pool Man, who came consistently on Mondays and Thursdays. One day Dan told me he was going on vacation, but a replacement guy would keep the same schedule. So, one very hot TUESDAY, while Burt was at work and my daughter in school, I put on the Tijuana Brass full blast and, as was my habit in those days, started vacuuming in the nude. Truthfully, if you can stand the visual, I enjoyed frenetic dancing to the music while pushing the vacuum cleaner. Suddenly, I was aware of an extremely tall, skinny guy in a ball cap watching me through the large picture windows. On a Tuesday?! I stopped dead in my dancing tracks. I think my heart stopped, too. So what did the guy do? He smiled, tipped his hat, and went back to cleaning the pool while I ran to put clothes on, hoping desperately to never see him again.

Incident No. 2. Burt took me with him on a business trip to Los Angeles shortly after we moved to South Beach. We stayed at the Universal Hotel on the 17th floor. Burt went to work and I hit the shower, with plans to spend the day with old friends. I turned the TV up and while toweling off from the shower I suddenly heard Tijuana Brass music from the TV. Of course, I could not resist flying out of the bathroom, using the towel as a prop and dancing like an idiot to the music—until I noticed some movement at the window high above Universal City. Window washers! Two of them—standing on a platform watching the crazy dancing lady. Did I ever tell my husband? Are you kidding? He never knew about the skinny pool man in the ball cap either.

And here the story takes a really weird turn. Yes, my favorite music is now on the ancient music system, which only works if you turn it on manually and push two other buttons. The useless remote is somewhere in a drawer. Last Sunday morning I had just showered for church and I assumed my houseguests were sleeping in. Lap Sitter was curled up on the bed when suddenly the extremely loud sound of the Tijuana Brass came blaring through the house. The poor cat took a nosedive off the bed as I grabbed a robe and raced to the living room. There sat my friend Peggy in her jammies trying to work the TV remote to watch the news on *Sunday Morning* and just as shocked as I was about the loud music. Somehow, the Tijuana Brass turned on all by itself.

Or did it?

Because Of You—Suspension Bridge

"I have what I need to see my way through this—if you, my friends, are with me."
— *Martha Whitmore Hickman*, **Healing After Loss**

I bet you thought I was all better since the last few columns have been full of fun and humor. Nope, the Grief Journey over the loss of someone who means the world to you doesn't work that way. You don't "get over it" even though well-meaning people may think you should. The Grief Journey is full of peaks and valleys. Just when you think you are doing pretty darned good, something will trigger a memory—an unexpected hug from a person in the middle of a grocery store, or maybe something as simple as a beautiful sunset.

    I continue to hear from widows and widowers who share their feelings, sadness, and often their quirks. I hear from parents who have lost a child, not necessarily a little one, although I hear from those, too. Losing an adult child carries its own kind of unbearable pain. I hear from people grieving over the death of a beloved parent. Two friends have recently lost their mothers. Oddly enough, both these women have to hide their tears from husbands who don't understand because to these guys, living into one's 90s is a long enough life and doesn't warrant such ongoing sadness from grieving daughters. I treasure mail from readers, even though it often brings me to tears.

Good Grief

When someone shares an oddball habit, it helps me know I'm not alone or all that abnormal. One woman is still sleeping in her husband's T-shirt because his scent is on the shirt. The mom of a teenager who died in a car accident could not bear to see his clothes on a local kid, so she packed up his stuff and sent it to Goodwill in the next state. Who are we to pass judgment on what others do, feel or think?

Here are just a few of the things I can't do—or have done—since my husband Burt died in July of last year. I cannot watch *Jeopardy* or *Wheel of Fortune* because he loved those shows. I can't sit out on the deck for more than five minutes because he isn't next to me watching the birds and the ocean. I still can't park my car on his side of the garage, and here's a biggie—today I scrubbed out our kitchen refrigerator for the first time since he died. Burt loved Grey Poupon mustard, and there is an almost-full jar of it. I wiped off the jar and put it back. How long does that stuff last, anyhow?

I'm in reasonably good health, but my doctor yelled at me to gain some weight. That's one of the strange things about grief—people either can't stop eating or can't start. So far, I have little interest in food. In a few weeks, I'm going to Omaha to visit loved ones I haven't seen in years. My close friend, Teresa Cavenaugh, is organizing a get-together with our old classmates and I'm excited about this trip and the mini-reunion. Seems strange to think I now weigh exactly what I did on graduation night, but so many years have gone by for all of us I will be happily matching my wrinkles with everyone else.

What prompted returning to the grief subject today is because of you readers who have lost a loved one. Your mail lets me know this column helps you and I cannot in good conscience, let you down. I still think of the two ladies who quit reading because I have friends and they don't. How sad is that?

On July 18, my husband's one-year death date, I wanted to spend the day in a special way. I sent out an email to women friends, not giving much notice, but figured whoever joined me would help make the gathering the way it was supposed to be. I love the Drift Creek State Park three-mile trail to the waterfall. Once you find that place, which is not easy, it's like stepping into another world. I called it a "Heart Walk for Burt," and several good friends showed up. I didn't have to tell them I needed to walk alone to the waterfall—intuitively they just knew.

I walked on ahead, and they caught up with me at the waterfall where we sat on logs and talked about a great guy named Burt Lippman. I wasn't the only one with tears. Spending that day, another of the dreaded "firsts," with good friends certainly helped in my healing. I am no expert on this thing called grief, but if you're just beginning the journey, I assure you that the passage of time is critically important. You will never return to the raw, unbearable pain when your loss first happened.

Today you are here, you are alive, and your loved one would want you to soldier on and live your best life.

"Heart Walk for Burt." Standing on the suspension bridge above Drift Creek Falls (L to R) are: Lin Lindly, Rhonda Stansell, Pat Lewis, Louise Waarvick, Linda Kilbride, Gina Nielsen, Nan Wangerin, and Bobbie

Catching Up

This is an attempt to catch up with some of the responses from readers who follow my "Bobbie's Beat" column.

First of all, my gopher problem. There were two messages left on my answering machine, both from guys, neither of whom left his name. One man insisted I put mothballs down the gopher holes, and the other guy advised me to hire a professional. It's rather comforting that people care so much about my lawn (far more than I do). But I'm happy to report there has been no sign of gophers for almost three months. Those beeping yellow battery-powered spikes did the trick. The gopher relatives that arrived from out of town to make mountains out of molehills near my greenhouse must have gagged on the Juicy Fruit gum I shoved down each hole. End of problem, but I do appreciate your concern and will certainly keep mothballs in mind. (I am trying to forget some guy's message about using human urine.)

For you dear people who ask, "How are you doing now that you are alone without your husband?" my answer is usually that I'm doing OK, hopefully in the so-called normal range of the Grief Journey although there really is no "normal" and we all walk the walk in our own way. I have good days and not-so-good days. Twice, in different local stores, I spotted the back of a tall, white-haired guy who is a ringer for Burt. Both times, I started running toward this person, then stopping short realizing it is a pure reflex action on my part. An experience like that can really mess up your day. I was left with a sad longing for my husband

and all the things we used to do together. I do hear from grieving folks who tell me about very real visits from their lost loved one. One woman swears her young son (killed in a car crash) suddenly appeared next to her in church, but only for a moment. The "visit" left his mother with an overwhelming feeling of comfort and gratitude.

I continue to receive mail at the *News-Times* from people who do not use a computer. A recent letter asked me to repeat a long-ago column called "The Trouble With Toastmasters." If you spend seven years involved with this worldwide organization (as I did) you end up with a better, well-trained brain, and you get rid of your fear of public speaking. You also can't help but be irritated by public speakers (usually politicians) who use awful English, such as "me and him went to the board meeting," etc. Your ear picks up all those "ahs" and "umms" (known as fillers), and Toastmasters helps you get rid of this common habit. I probably won't be repeating that old column, and this one paragraph is not going to make much difference for those who butcher the language, but I felt a few words were appropriate for the reader who sent that snail mail to the newspaper.

Now for the lady who lives half way across the country and reads the *News-Times* online. She actually called me on the phone the other day and we had a lovely chat. Somehow we got around to age and she seemed convinced that I had to be years younger than she. I told her my age because it's no secret, but she was not convinced, so I gave up. While still thinking of this thing called "age," a day brightener arrived on this very subject. Here it is.

> A lady goes to the bar on a cruise ship and orders a Scotch with two drops of water. As the bartender gives her the drink she says, "I'm on this cruise to celebrate my 80th birthday and

it's today." The bartender says, "Well since it's your birthday, this one is on me."

As the woman finishes her drink, the lady to her right says, "I would like to buy you a drink, too." The old woman says, "Thank you. Bartender, I want a Scotch with two drops of water." "Coming up," says the bartender."

As she finishes that drink, the man to her left says, "I would like to buy you one, too." The old woman says, "Thank you. Bartender, I want another Scotch with two drops of water." As he gives her the drink, he says, "Ma'am, I'm dying of curiosity. Why the Scotch with only two drops of water?" The old woman replies, "Sonny, when you're my age, you've learned how to hold your liquor. Holding your water, however, is a whole other issue."

Old is when: your friends compliment you on your new alligator shoes but you're barefoot; a sexy babe or hunk catches your fancy, and your pacemaker opens the garage door; going braless pulls all the wrinkles out of your face; you are cautioned to slow down by the doctor instead of by the police; getting a little "action" means you don't need to take any fiber today; getting "lucky" means you find your car in the parking lot; an "all-nighter" means not getting up to use the bathroom.

Old is when: you are not sure these are jokes.

My Remarkable Margaret

About once a month, a friend brings over Chinese food, and we watch a movie. What I'm about to say may come as a surprise to my friend because she doesn't know this story, but she will now when she reads it in the *New-Times*. Every time I enjoy Chinese food, my thoughts drift back in time to an amazing woman named Margaret.

I met Margaret when I was a volunteer on a 10-bed hospice ward in a large Los Angeles hospital. She was in her early 60s and lived alone until her illness progressed to the point where she needed hospice care. Because her younger sister, Emma, arrived from Texas, I didn't get to meet Margaret until a week after she had been admitted. Emma was an overwhelming presence on the ward. She showed up every day and rarely left the room. She fussed over Margaret, talked incessantly, read out loud (very loud) from the Bible, and shooed away the volunteers. She drove the doctors and nurses crazy.

Nobody realized Emma was also driving Margaret nuts until the day Emma was sick and stayed away. When I walked into the room, there was Margaret, a tiny figure curled up under the blankets. Although the nurses had briefed me that Margaret was not interested either in eating or talking, I was determined to give it a try.

Leaning over the bed, I touched her lightly and said, "Hello Margaret, I'm Bobbie, one of the volunteers." She shifted slightly, turning her small face towards mine. "Do you need anything?" I asked. "Do you feel like talking?"

She said, "No. I'm just praying to graduate." It was not the first time I had heard the term "graduate" rather than die. Hospice training emphasizes that one must be a good listener, non-judgmental, regardless of personal beliefs and above all, never to tell someone not to feel what he or she is feeling—which is a pretty good rule to follow in any relationship.

When I smiled at her, she asked, "Did I shock you?"

"Not particularly," I answered, then she went on to explain the word graduate felt more reassuring to her than saying she just wanted to die. "But I can't say graduate OR die to my sister," Margaret added. "She keeps telling me how good I look and that I'm going to get well. Do you think I'm going to get well?"

This is where hospice training comes in handy.

I pulled a chair up close to the bed and said, "I don't know. What do you think?"

"Heavens no," she said, "I've accepted this, but my sister refuses to."

Then Margaret surprised me by asking if I would help her sit up against the pillows. She suddenly wanted to talk about her husband, Harry, who had died of cancer 10 years before. "He promised to be waiting when I cross over," she said, while she closely watched for my reaction, then added, "My sister thinks this is all nonsense, you know." Then she got a defiant look on her face, "Listen," she said, "Harry never let me down in all the years we had together. Why would he let me down now?"

She clearly wanted to talk. She looked around to make sure we were alone in the room. "You know what?" she asked, in a conspiratorial whisper. "I really feel Harry's presence sometimes, as if he is just waiting for me to join him. Last night I think I saw him up in that corner," she said, pointing toward the ceiling.

When I didn't react, she surprised me even more by asking for some sherbet from the nurse's station. As I fed her little bites, I kept thinking how rewarding this felt and how I did not want to leave that room. A special bond had taken place between this woman and me. I left the hospice ward that day on winged feet and started visiting Margaret in the evenings, to avoid her sister Emma.

One night Margaret told me that she had two last wishes. One was to taste Chinese food again, and the other was to escape the hospice ward and get back to Texas so she could see her three favorite nieces before she died. I was far from confident about the second wish, but I will never forget the night we shared a Chinese feast in her room, just the two of us. There were very few restrictions on that hospice ward, and nobody questioned my bag of Chinese food. With soy sauce on both our faces, we giggled like schoolgirls. I remember one of the nurses sticking her head in the room and staring at Margaret and me with a raised eyebrow and an amused smile.

I never knew how she pulled it off, but three weeks after our first meeting, Margaret checked out of the hospital, traveled by ambulance to the airport and flew back to Texas with Emma.

I don't know what else to call it, but we continued our "love affair" by telephone for five more days. I was not surprised when Emma called to say her sister had died peacefully with a smile on her face and her nieces at the bedside.

To this day, whenever I have Chinese food, I think of my remarkable Margaret and feel blessed that she crossed my path—if only for a short while. What a woman!

Nose Rings And Other Things

Caution: This column may contain shocking details that are not suitable for the faint-hearted. I just returned from a fast-paced week with my Midwest family, specifically my kid brother Paul and his wife Dot. Add to this time spent with nephews, nieces, Iowa relatives, and a luncheon with old high school friends. I use the word "old" because if you factor in the year 1951, maybe we are, but you wouldn't know it from the laughter and noise we made in that restaurant.

In case you haven't been following this column from the get-go (1985), you need to know that my parents instilled their hilarious senses of humor and "jokestering" in my brothers and me. I didn't dare pay them a visit without bringing Dad an outrageous gift, such as Groucho Marx glasses (with the big nose), or the latest in hand buzzers and whoopee cushions. He especially loved wild and crazy wigs. He would dress up and walk next door. If the neighbors weren't home, he drove their dog nuts. For my mom, especially after she lost her sight, I brought her sunglasses in the shape of hearts or pumpkins or silly animals. She knew of my radio campaign and the 1,000 bumper stickers Burt bought to hand out. I have a photo somewhere of the back of her wheelchair with the sign saying, "Practice random acts of kindness and senseless acts of beauty."

I will never forget arriving at the Omaha airport shortly after finishing my bucket list dream of bicycling the West Coast. My

Good Grief

friend Roz and I wore orange safety vests sporting the words "Canada to Mexico or Bust." Picture my parents driving toward their Omaha house with me excitedly checking out my hometown changes. Suddenly, up ahead, was a cyclist peddling along with a sign on his back that read: "Encino to Omaha or Bust." (Burt and I lived in Encino, California, at the time). I yelled at Dad, "Pull over, pull over, I have to talk to that guy!" I jumped out of the car and raced to the cyclist—only to discover it was my brother Paul, decked out like a long-distance bicyclist. They had all set me up.

Now that you know my DNA, fast forward to last week. Thanks to a suggestion from my friend Louise Waarvick, we visited a shop on the Newport Bayfront. I came out with two totally weird and wicked goodies, so now you get to visualize me getting off the plane in Omaha and being greeted by Paul and Dot. I was dressed like a normal traveler—except for the silver ring in my nose. The shocked look on their faces was priceless. Not for a second did they think it was fake.

My friend Gina Nielsen traveled with me for two reasons: I can't travel alone due to macular degeneration, and Gina was able to visit her daughter in Iowa. I do have photos of my nose with the ring in it, but the newspaper has standards. However, I will beg my editor.

I wasn't done with shocking my brother, and I needed Dot's help for trick number two. As some of you know, my husband loved my brother and left orders that Paul was to inherit Burt's Buick LaCross—a car loaded with bells and whistles. In a column five months ago, I wrote about Paul and Dot flying out for a visit and driving the Buick back to Nebraska. Needless to say, they are crazy about that car, which they refer to as "The Burt Mobile." It had only 12,000 miles on it, and I think by now it's up to twice that. One day, while Paul was teaching, Dot and I enjoyed a girl's day out, using the Buick. When we drove back into their garage mid-afternoon, Dot quickly pasted on the back fender "The Car Scratch," sold by the little shop of horrors on our Bayfront. The scratch looks as authentic as my nifty nose ring. Dot and I put on sad faces just as Paul opened the door to the garage to greet us.

"Oh sweetheart," said Dot, "we parked the Burt Mobile in what I thought was a safe place, but oh, just look what happened." Paul looked, and I was sure he was going to cry. I just kept snapping pictures as he went closer to the ugly scratch on the pristine paint job. I heard him mumble something about hoping their GM dealer could fix it. It wasn't until he felt the "scratch" with his fingers that it dawned on him. Another fake from big sister Bobbie. "Gotcha," says I. And you know what, folks? I think if Paul had to choose which "joke" was the least horrible of the two, it would have to be the nose ring. Messing with the Burt Mobile was way too heartbreaking for my brother.

Quote of the day: "You don't stop laughing when you grow old—you grow old because you stop laughing."

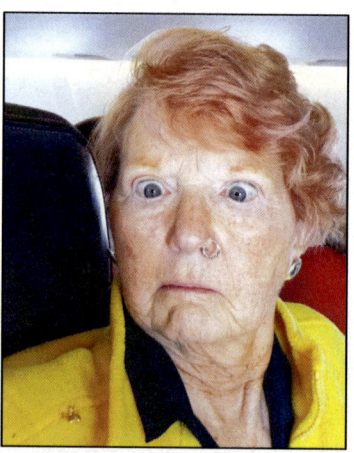

Bobby sporting her nose ring, prepares to greet family members at the airport

A Week In Chains

This column cannot begin until I clear something up with several of you readers. This past week, for eight days in a row, I was out and about attending meetings, lunches, dinners, and holiday parties. I kept hearing, directly, indirectly (or in emails) the following words in one form or another: "It's so nice that you have gotten over the death of your husband and moved on."

Really? The truth, for all of us who have lost a loved one, is that you do NOT "get over it." You do go through changes because it would be dumb to stay stuck indefinitely in a fetal position with tears rolling down your face. I can't speak for everyone, but I know my Burt is still watching over me and cheering me on to live life to the max, as we always did together.

Having gotten that out of the way, let us move on to some fun stuff, starting with the annual Scary-Okie gala thrown by Newport's energetic and creative Chamber of Commerce staff. Since I don't drive at night, I took my young friend Gina Nielsen as my "date."

I'm a firm believer in showing up in costume if you are going to a costume party. We decided to go as "Biker Babes" and we pulled out all the stops, including paste-on tattoos and the fake two dollar nose ring I recently wore to shock my relatives in Omaha. Then we raided a box in our garage marked "Dog Stuff"—a box full of dog collars, leashes, and training chains left over from years of large dogs who shared my life. I may be dog-less right now, but you never know. We must have looked pretty cool because we won the "Best Girls Costume" prize at the sold-out Scary-Okie party.

While you still have the Biker Babe image in mind, let us proceed to the night of Halloween. For many years, it was a Halloween tradition for Burt and me to go to the home of Judge and Patti Littlehales. They live on a street in Newport that is blocked off by the police because at least 900 kids know that is the hottest neighborhood in town for trick or treating.

This year I was going with Gina. Now comes the main chunk of this story—or perhaps the funniest part.

I had somehow forgotten to sign my voting ballot envelope and needed to get to the Courthouse and do it. I had to drive in early to meet up with Gina (who works there) so we could get to the Littlehales before the street was closed. This meant she changed into her costume in the ladies room while I strolled into the Courthouse in full biker babe regalia—chains and all—totally forgetting that you must go through security in a courthouse just as you do in airports. I might add that even my purse had dog chains wrapped around it.

I will never forget the look on the face of the oh-so-young officer on duty. I put my purse in the cat litter container, then walked through the golden arches setting off all kinds of bells and alarms. I mumbled something about being dressed for a Halloween party, and felt totally stupid wearing a spiked leather dog collar and a silver ring in my nose. The officer took his job seriously (as well he should) and asked me to place my feet on the floor within the feet outline as he passed the wand over my leather-clad body, setting off more whistles and alarms.

By this time, I was questioning my sanity and judgment while I'm sure the young officer on duty was asking himself, "Why me, Lord?" But hey, voting is an important privilege and I

Good Grief

was determined to have my vote count. I hurried up to the 2nd floor, signed my ballot, and zipped out of the Courthouse picking up Gina on the way, knowing this little vignette would have to be shared with you.

Yes, it was certainly fun celebrating Halloween this year and I know my husband would have enjoyed all of it, too. The reality is that he is no longer here but I am sure he was sitting up on a cloud somewhere laughing at his crazy wife draped in chains setting off alarms in the Lincoln County Courthouse.

Life is what we make it, folks. The following poem (author unknown) says a lot:

> There was a very cautious man, who never laughed or played.
> He never risked, he never tried, he never sang or prayed.
> And then one day he passed away, the insurance was denied.
> Because he never really lived,
> They claimed he never really died.

Bobbie and Gina Nielsen as biker babes on Halloween

JERICHO

Have you ever been to Israel? Have you ever wanted to go? When it comes to far off places, many of you today are probably, like me, armchair travelers. Thanks to television, you can relax in the comfort of home and enjoy the wonders of the world.

Today's subject got hatched when my daughter Rocki recently told me they were off on a whirlwind trip to Israel. Here are the two reasons they decided to go: (1) they have never been to the Holy Land, and (2) one of their favorite former AFS (American Field Service) students—Cilly—is now grown up and married to an Israeli with whom she has a year-old son. Rocki and Glen have hosted several AFS kids and stayed connected to all of them, especially Cilly.

When Rocki called to tell me they were off to Israel, my first thought was a memory of Jericho. Keep reading for the bizarre story. But first, here is the report Rocki sent to family and friends at the close of their recent trip:

> This has been quite an experience. We've never been in a country like this one. From riding bicycles for hours through Tel Aviv, staying five nights in Haifa with Cilly (Carmel Center) and walking the Wadi villages, celebrating Sukkot with Gal's family at their home, touring the Bahai gardens, the aquamarine colored grottos of Rosh Hanikra, exploring the Arabian markets of Akko, a picnic at Mt. Tabor monastery, putting my toes in the Sea of Galilee, staying two nights at a Bedouin camel camp in the arid desert, waking up early to

hike up Masada at sunrise and explore those historical ruins (this was epic), floating in the Dead Sea at Ein Gedi, hiking up to David Falls at the nature reserve, riding a camel at sunset, walking the old city with the perfect guide Yuval, praying at the Western Wall, Dome of the Rock, and Holy Sepulcher, wandering the Mehane Yehuda market, and exploring the narrow streets of Old Jerusalem at night in the Christian quarter with Cilly, Gal, and little Erri. And I haven't even mentioned all the delicious food we ate, which was almost continuous. It's been a wonderful cultural, visual, culinary, and deep adventure in this land of love, passion, and conflict. Tomorrow we drive from Jerusalem to Tel Aviv at dawn to catch our plane back home. Love to you all.

I am so grateful they are safely back home, and I am also glad that Burt and I once spent nine incredible days in the Holy Land. Of all the places in this world, Israel is at the absolute top of my travel memories. But for today, let us focus on Jericho. We hired a driver and within five minutes, he and Burt were best friends. I sat in the back seat, my eyes bugging out as we traveled across this amazing land. When we drove into the little town of Jericho, I spotted a ram tied to a tree in the parking area. "Oh look, Burt," I said, not that you could miss seeing a rather large animal with horns tied to a tree in a parking lot. Burt said to the driver guy, "My wife loves animals." (Thanks a lot, Burt). We piled out of the car and the guide said to me, "Bo-bee, why don't you go pick up that ram." Now, a normal person might hesitate, but you readers know I'm a bit off-course at times and subject to doing things spontaneously. I walked over to the animal whose fleece made him look a lot bigger than he was. He gave me a bored looked. I noticed the guide grinning like an idiot as I put my arms under the ram and lifted him off the ground as Burt took pictures. That's when it dawned on me how wet my arms were. I did not realize that male sheep (and related critters) pee all over themselves to attract females. I could have smacked our guide, Burt, AND the damn ram. I found a restroom of sorts and managed to scrub off most of the smell. I can still hear Burt and the guide laughing their heads off. As for Jericho, it was an interesting place to see but, of course, what I remember most is that ram. In case you didn't see the humor in my Jericho experience, here's a day brightener:

A young Sunday School teacher was telling the class the lesson about Jericho and the walls and how it all came about. She asked little Phillip, "Who tore down the walls of Jericho?" Phillip looked at her with big eyes and said, "I didn't do it!" She was taken aback and said, "Phillip!" and he said, "I told you. I didn't do it." So when Phillip's parents came to get him that day, she told them and the father said, "All I can tell you is that we just moved to the neighborhood, and we don't know what happened." With that, she went to see the head of the Sunday School and explained the experience, not only with Phillip but with his parents, and the head of the Sunday School said, "All I can tell you Miss Smith is that I personally know them, and if they said they didn't do it, they didn't do it." Miss Smith couldn't stand it so she wrote to the district superintendent. He wrote back to her and said, "I'll give you a suggestion. Have a fundraiser and repair the doggone wall!"

I think these people need to talk to Joshua.

Winter

My poor computer often chokes on mail from you readers. Forgive me if you don't get an answer, but (due to vision fatigue) it has become impossible to keep up, although I try my best. Once in a while a gem arrives that needs to be shared. I figure if it is full of food for thought for me, it may have some value for you. The author of these words of wisdom is unknown.

Time has a way of moving quickly and catching you unaware of the passing years. It seems just yesterday that I was young, newly married, and embarking on a new life with my mate. Yet, in a way, it seems like eons ago and I wonder where all the years went. I know that I lived them. I have glimpses of how it was back then, of all my hopes and dreams. But here it is, the winter of my life and it catches me by surprise. How did I get here so fast? Where did the years go, and where is my youth?

I remember seeing elderly folks and thinking that those older people were years away from me and that my winter was so far off that I could not imagine fully what it would be like. But here it is, my friends are retired and getting gray, they move slower. Some are in better and some in worse shape than I, but I see the great change. Like me, their age is beginning to show. We are now those older folks we used to see and never thought we'd be.

Each day now, I find that just getting a shower is a real target. And taking a nap is not a treat anymore, it's mandatory because if I don't lie down of my own free will, I just fall asleep where I sit. And so now I enter this new season of my life, unprepared for all the aches and pains and the loss of strength and ability to go and do things I wish I had done, but never did. But at least I know that though the winter has come and I'm not sure how long it will last, when it's over on this earth, it's over. A new adventure will begin.

Yes, I have regrets. There are things I wish I hadn't done, things I should have done, but indeed, there are many things I'm happy to have done. It's all in a lifetime. If you're not in your winter yet, let me remind you that it will be here faster than you think. So whatever you would like to accomplish in your life, do it soon. Don't put things off too long. Life goes by quickly.

Do what you can today, as you can never be sure whether this is your winter or not. There is no promise that you will see all the seasons of your life, therefore live for today and say all the things that you want your loved ones to remember. Hope that they appreciate and love you for the things you have done for them in years past.

Life is a gift to you. The way you live your life is your gift to those who come after. Make it a fantastic one. Live it well. Enjoy today. Do something fun. It is health that is real wealth, not pieces of gold and silver.

Today is the oldest you have ever been, yet it is the youngest you will ever be again. So enjoy this day while it lasts.

Your children are becoming you, but your grandchildren are perfect. Going out is good, coming home is better. You forget names, but it's OK because other people forgot they even knew you. You realize you're never going to be really good at anything again... especially golf. The things you used to do, you no longer care to do, but you really do care that you don't care to do them anymore. You sleep better on a lounge chair with the TV blaring than in bed. This is called "pre-sleep." You miss the days when everything worked with just an "ON" and "OFF" switch. You tend to use more four-letter words like What? and When?

What used to be freckles are now liver spots. Everybody whispers. But old is good in some things: old songs, old movies, and best of all, old friends. It's not what you gather, but what you scatter that tells what kind of life you have lived.

Three generations skydiving
Bobbie, Autumn, and Rocki

Meltdown with a Message

Maybe it's the holidays. Maybe it's because I started plowing through boxes of photographs. Maybe it's because I went to the annual Oyster Cloyster at the Oregon Coast Aquarium. Maybe I need to quit analyzing what triggered a recent four-day meltdown. It happened—out of the blue. I tried to write something upbeat and funny today, but then the thought of all you readers out there who have written to me about your losses of loved ones forced me to fess up. I had been doing so well, for weeks, maybe months, getting out and about, carrying on alone without my husband at my side, then BAM—a super major case of the blues, almost as painful as being thrown back into those first horrible weeks following Burt's death.

Perhaps I needed another lesson in the Grief Journey. Those four days were humbling, and I was forced to find my way out of a black hole pity-party for one. I closed myself off from the outside world, tried to stop crying, and made a list of constructive and positive things to do. Before putting pen to paper, I looked up and out over the ocean and uttered the words "Help me, Lord." I almost hate admitting being surprised to get immediate answers when a big part of me just wanted to feel sorry for myself. I reached for the telephone and made a call. Half way across the country, my beloved cousin Kay answered the phone. We were close as kids and have stayed in touch through the years. Kay is not only dealing with Parkinson's Disease, but her husband Rod just went on hospice care. The call seemed to mean a great deal to Kay, and I think it helped that I reached out to someone so much worse off than I am. Then I wrote a long list of things for which I am grateful. I used to do this practice at bedtime, writing down five gratitude items for the day—then somehow got out of the habit. Now I'm doing it again.

I went back through mail from you readers and found several that mentioned meltdowns, although no one used that word. A local lady wrote that if she wasn't a woman of faith, she would not have been able to survive the recent loss of her mate. A young widower wrote about how the grieving pain eases up, but never entirely goes away.

I do tend to over-analyze things and have decided to blame my meltdown on the Oyster Cloyster. I went with a friend and it was the first time I walked around the Oregon Coast Aquarium without Burt. We were there so many years ago when ground was broken. We were there for all the fundraisers. We were there that night the famous whale, Keiko (of *Free Willy* fame) was delivered by airplane. The Oyster Cloyster is a gala evening affair and others probably thought I was having a wonderful time. What a sham! I kept pretending Burt would appear at any moment—that he was simply off in the crowd schmoozing with people as he always did so well.

On the fourth day of my meltdown, I found myself at Burt's desk, which is exactly as he left it. I sat down in his office chair, having no idea why I was doing this. That's when I saw a little piece of paper poking out from under his computer keyboard. I had never seen it before, but I feel the words on the paper obviously meant a lot to my husband and are somehow connected to my meltdown cry for help.

(Author unknown)

Have I prayed for someone today?
Have I thanked God today?
Have I lived up to my capacities today?
Have I been friendly today?
Have I smiled today?
Have I praised anyone today?
Have I affirmed life and strength today?
Have I conquered fear today?
Have I kept serene and calm today?
Have I looked to God for my supply today?

Since this is Thanksgiving week, the only words that feel appropriate to wind up this column are, "Thank you."

Bobbie and Burt Lippman at the Oregon Coast Aquarium, 2012

Loretta

When you lose someone who has been part of your life for a long time, you can either wallow around in sadness (I am guilty of this) or you can open your heart to lessons in how best to handle the Grief Journey. The death of my husband Burt, 17 months ago, has been—to say the least—educational, and you steady readers have followed along as I've written honestly about my grieving process. One of my biggest lessons for healing is to focus on the good times shared with the one who went on ahead.

Today, many of us are mourning the loss of Loretta Macpherson who died unexpectedly on December 3. She was one of the first amazing women I met shortly after moving to the Oregon Coast in 1983. As I mentioned in an earlier column, Burt and I had barely unpacked when we were invited to Alice Silverman's annual "ball."

As we were being introduced to local people, trying to keep names straight, a pretty, young woman came up to me, introduced herself, and asked if I played tennis. When I said yes, she invited me to join a group that played regularly at Salishan Golf Resort. The woman was Loretta MacPherson. It was instant friendship and the following week my coastal tennis life took off. Gracie Strom, owner of the Sea Hag in Depoe Bay, was part of the group. Let it be known here and now that Gracie was an awesome tennis player. I never could beat her or Loretta. After two hours of tough tennis, we all headed to the Sea Hag for lunch and laughter. Those tennis times are very happy memories.

Burt and I socialized with Loretta and her husband Gordon on Thanksgiving at their home, and every year went to the St. Paul Rodeo. We were in on their plan to adopt kids, and we were there when Pete arrived, and later when little Mark joined the Macpherson family.

The fixer-upper we bought in South Beach was sorely in need of fixing up. At the time, Loretta owned Wildflower Design in Newport, and we hired her to work her magic on our house. Those days were such fun as Loretta guided us with her professional ideas in snazzing up our home. By this time, I was involved in helping get a hospice organization up and running. My dream was to have a special homey hospice room available for people who could not be cared for at home. Hospice was all volunteer-driven back then, and Loretta was quick to help make my dream happen. We were given a room at the local rehab facility and it was sheer joy decorating that room. Local merchants donated things we needed, like a sofa bed (for family members), other pieces of cozy furniture, a small refrigerator, and a music system. Decorating, be it a home or a hospice room, calls for discussions and decisions, and this we did every week over lunch at Canyon Way. Can you tell I'm trying to focus on all the good times?

I'm not sure of the year, but Loretta and I were asked by the Loyalty Days committee to be emcees for the Pageant of the Princesses and crowning of the Queen of Loyalty Days. This gala evening took place to a full house at the Newport Performing Arts Center. When the committee decided to dress us in rented white tuxedos (with tails), we thought it was a total hoot and tried to take the occasion seriously. But Loretta had her silly side, as I do, and we camped up our performance that night, probably to the dismay of the Loyalty Days committee. Actually, we were told we did a good job, especially at calming the nerves of the young girls who had to perform on stage that night.

I am trying hard as I write this to avoid any gloom and doom, but it's only fair to mention the long illness and passing of Gordon MacPherson. Loretta eventually sold their Newport home and moved to Sisters where she started picking up the pieces of her life. We saw her there, and she visited us here in Seal Rock. She drove to Newport for Burt's Celebration of Life last year.

I wish there was a way to end this with something upbeat, but I'm surrounded by heavy hearts over the unexpected death of Loretta Macpherson and she will be missed by many. Hold on. I just thought of the time Loretta was on a ladder hanging a wallpaper border. When I reminded her to keep it straight, she looked down and said, "Look, you are the writer, I am the decorator. Just hold the damn ladder!"

**Bobbie and Loretta Macpherson in white tuxedoes.
Emcees at the Newport Loyalty Days Queen's Pageant**

Knocking The 'Stuffing' Out Of Christmas

Some of you readers have amazing memories regarding various subjects that have appeared in this column over the years. During the past few weeks, I've attended several community events and half a dozen people wanted to talk to me about "Unplugging the Christmas Machine." Four of them wanted me to know they did it because I did it. Yep, I'm guilty, but I don't feel a bit guilty. Here is the back-story.

Thirty-four years ago, my husband and I were incredibly caught up in the hassle of the holidays—the shopping, the baking, the decorating, composing a newsletter to enclose in 250 cards. In the race to keep up with that every year, I ended up getting sick. Let me paint a picture for you of what pushed me over the edge.

One Christmas Eve, an executive in Burt's company insisted we stop by to watch their nine-year-old son open his presents. It wasn't what we wanted to do, but the pressure was on. There we stood in their living room, eggnog in one hand, rum ball in the other while little junior ripped open his gifts. I counted 23. Not once did he say, "Oh boy! Just what I always wanted!" Not once did he say, "Thank you." He ripped stuff open, threw it aside, and grabbed the next present. I felt myself getting nauseated—not from the eggnog and rum ball, but from this scene of overkill, greed, and commercialism.

Three weeks later I told Burt I wanted to try not doing

Christmas at all, just to see how it felt, because I was sick and tired of the stress, and sick and tired of getting sick and tired. My husband had such a generous, giving heart and was not happy with my decision but he agreed to try it just once. The next August, I told everyone to take us off their list because we weren't making one. A few people called me "Scrooge." But that first non-commercial Christmas was heavenly. Instead of buying stuff for people who already had a lot of stuff, we gave to charities and those less fortunate. It felt great, and I did not get sick. There's an old saying, "If something hurts badly enough, you do something about it."

As time went by, we returned to celebrating the holidays, but in moderation. We did a little decorating, gave small gifts to the little ones and to the elderly, and eliminated the newsletter and 250 cards.

Then in 1983, we moved to the Oregon Coast. Burt's huge collection of Christmas lights came with us and our South Beach house was ablaze with strings of lights that somehow managed to make it through December storms for about three years.

What neither of us expected was during that first Christmas on the coast, Burt was asked to be Santa Claus for a charity event held on a rust-bucket floating restaurant in Yaquina Bay. Children were to come aboard, sit on Santa's lap and tell Santa what they wanted. That boat (referred to by locals as the SS Bilge Water) was a total tub, freezing cold, and I remember only too well helping Burt shiver his timbers getting into the Santa suit in some dingy little room. We heard years later (big surprise) the boat eventually sank.

I doubt that Burt ever turned down a request to help any charity or community cause. From then on, my husband was asked to be Santa on such a regular basis that he started letting his beard grow in October so he wouldn't have to wear what he called that "phony white cotton candy." Children thought he was the real deal, and many adults could not resist climbing on his lap too. His favorite "gig" was Santa Dog Night for Sue Giles Green and her 4-H kids.

When this column started appearing in the *News-Times*, I wrote, usually in August, about our stand on not giving stuff for Christmas, in case readers wanted to start making changes, (There is an excellent book called *Unplug the Christmas Machine: A Complete Guide to Putting Love and Joy Back into the Season.*) I also wrote about people who send Christmas cards with just their names embossed in gold and no message. To me this is as meaningful as getting a piece of mail marked "occupant."

I wrote a few columns spoofing the people who write long, boring, bragging newsletters. Yawn. This would sometimes get me in trouble with the newsletter writers, but not nearly as much trouble as my take on fruitcake. I have quoted the humorist Erma Bombeck who wrote, "A fruitcake weighs as much as the oven it was cooked in!" I think she also said, "Fruitcakes make dandy door stops." I had to quit complaining about fruitcake on my old radio program because women listeners were convinced their fruitcake was the best and would deliver chunks of it to the station in an attempt to convert me. You would think I had attacked their first-born child!

My current stand on Christmas hasn't changed much, although the holidays without Burt are certainly a major change. But I'm trying to carry on his legacy of giving to needy causes and those less blessed. He set an amazing example in helping others. Merry Christmas, everyone.

Gordon Macpherson on the lap of Santa (Burt Lippman), accompanied by Mark Collson (front) and John Clark

The Consummate Romantic

"What is there to do when people die—people dear and rare—
but bring them back by remembering?"   —May Sarton

Today began as a very painful day. I woke up crying and then I stood in the shower with my face to the force of the hot water in a feeble attempt to wash away the tears—and the pain. I walked through the house like a zombie, turning on lights, making coffee, standing by the windows watching the rain beat on the glass, staring out at the ocean hoping it would bring me some kind of joy as it has for years. Nothing helped, not even Lap Sitter rubbing against my legs asking to be picked up and petted. As so many of you have shown me, there isn't a "one size fits all" way to deal when you have lost a loved one.

I opened my favorite book on grief (*Healing After Loss*) and saw the quote that begins today's column. Today would have been our 45th wedding anniversary. That quote turned me around (as did a long walk in the rain), and I knew what I wanted or needed to write about today—the good times, focusing on the ones having to do with our anniversary.

I didn't realize Burt was such a romantic until I married him on December 27, 1969—in a private airplane at 10,000 feet over Portuguese Bend, California. The following month, on the 27 of January 1970, a dozen red roses arrived with a note saying, "Happy month-aversary." My first reaction was "wow!" But then he kept it up every month for two years, until I begged him to stop. My frugal side knew how much all those flowers were costing and he reluctantly slowed down, but never ever did he come to a full stop. Every month, on the 27th, he made it special, and so I had to get with the program. Yes, I know there are guys reading this who suffer from a lack of romanticism. My husband's blatant show of how he felt about me was no secret to anybody. Burt's out-and-out demonstrations of his love made some husbands squirm while their women were ticked at them for not being more like Burt.

My attempts at reciprocating were pathetic by comparison, but I often made my guy a special dinner or got him a love gift of some kind. He was terrible at receiving. He only wanted to give—and I wasn't the only one on the receiving end of his generosity, as everyone who knew him is aware.

One night, on the 27th, Burt quietly came in from work, snuck up behind me as I stirred a pot on the stove, gave me a hug, and said, "Quick, what number is today?" He was the consummate numbers man and had tricked me a few times, but not that night. I had learned to write the month-aversary number on my arm. I turned around, kissed him, and said, "Eighty!" At which point he handed me 80 bucks in cash. Believe me, from then on I maniacally kept track, although the gift of cash happened only once more during our marriage, right in the lobby of the Newport Performing Arts Center as we were chatting with Bernice Barnett and her husband Bruce. For some reason, Burt told them it was our month-aversary and, for some reason, I blurted out the story of the 80 bucks. I jokingly said, "Yeah, like that was ever going to happen again." Burt then told me to go out to the car and look under the floor mat. I ran to the car and came back clutching $398 in cash! I will never forget the look on Bernice's face.

If she is reading this, she will well remember that night.

There were so many monthly events, but let me share one more. We had a houseguest who, to be honest, did not share our offbeat sense of fun. It just happened to be the 27th of that month and she wanted to take us to a restaurant where she could order Scotch. During dinner, Burt pushed a small gift box across the table. While our guest watched me open it, Burt explained about our month-aversary. Inside the box was a pair of gold earrings in the shape of tooth crowns! Burt had taken his own crowns to a jeweler who made them into earrings. I love those earrings. No one but dentists and dental hygienists recognize them for what they are, but our houseguest was horrified. Such a gift was way too bizarre for her.

Writing this column has always been a great outlet for me, and since Burt's death, it has been downright therapeutic. I'm not sure if today's take on celebrating month-aversaries will be of help to all the bereaved folks who write to me. All I know is this day is coming to a close and I'm no longer depressed and crying. Remembering the great moments is truly the best medicine.

Burt and Bobbie Lippman on their wedding day

Have You Ever Been In Secure?

"It's the nature of grace always to fill spaces that have been empty."   —*Goethe*

I don't know what to call this past year except an emotional roller coaster. Today, as I look back, it seems there were more good times than sad ones. Maybe it's my nature to look on the sunny side—or maybe there is truth to that axiom "time heals." To be honest, though, I still can't label my status with the "W" word, but who says I have to?

Here is a brief recap of this past year, although much of it ended up as column fodder. I never thought I would laugh again until my daughter Rocki showed up for my birthday on January 1, 2014. I did not ask her to come, but apparently, she was sick of a mother who was wallowing in grief. Rocki made me open four gifts: the first I've mentioned before—matching leopard print pajamas for us, plus the same for Charley the aging poodle and Lap Sitter the cat. She used her phone, with timer on a tripod.

Photographing humans is one thing, but trying to get a good shot of us, plus two pets in PJs, sent us into hysterics. Charley was so old he kept falling asleep, but the cat went ballistic. For a change, I had tears from laughing. Yes, the photo (ninth try) made it into the paper much to the delight of readers.

I also never considered traveling, not with an old dog at home. Then one day Charley could not get up, and he looked at me as if to say, "I'm old and I'm tired. Please do the kindly thing and let me go." Dr. Eric Brown and Kim came out to the house, some close friends arrived for moral support, and Charley went peacefully to that great poodle place in the sky. This left me with only a cat to worry about, but cats are self-sufficient and I'm blessed with feline-loving friends who are willing to take over. Before long, Kath Schonau talked me into joining her and daughter Hannah for three days in Redwood country. Kath knocked down all my resistance. The drive on Highway 101 was beautiful, and the trip was great therapy. Before I could put my suitcase away, Kath and Don Taylor insisted it would be good for me to visit family and friends in Los Angeles. Since I'm challenged with macular degeneration, I was a nervous wreck, but that trip could not have been a better confidence builder. My suitcase never made it back to the attic because I soon took off for a girly getaway in Portland with Patti Littlehales and Louise Waarvick. Traveling with friends was becoming addictive. Marylou and Bruce Mate took me along to Seattle and Whidbey Island for a few days of fun with their family, followed by a "glamping" trip on the Alsea River with Gina Nielsen. Glamping means she did all the camp chores, while my job was to supervise her three dogs at which I failed miserably. Of course, all this got documented in columns. My life—the merry and the miserable—somehow seems to keep being shared with you readers.

Since I gained confidence on the L.A. trip, I was soon off to Omaha, accompanied by Gina, who visited a daughter in Iowa. It wasn't just family luring me to my old hometown. My kid brother Paul has a Harley, and riding a Harley has been on my bucket list for years. Fortunately, my sister-in-law, Dorothy, is my size, and her "leathers" fit me fine. Did I love getting to be a biker babe? Do you have to ask? With trust in my brother, we varoomed out into the country on the Interstate and visited the Elkhorn River where our family played for years. I would hop on that Harley again in a heartbeat.

Before year's end, there were more girly getaways, and a four-night sleepover here with gal pals who appreciated a place to crash. In December, I took off on a two-day trip to view the Shore Acres holiday lights in Coos Bay with Laramee Ward and Gina. Now, after a look back at this past year of living out of suitcases and duffle bags, I might need a nap. But a whole new year is beckoning and there are things still to do on my bucket list. Speaking of going places, here is a silly day brightener:

My travel plans for 2015.

I have been in many places, but I've never been in Kahoots. Apparently, you can't go alone. You have to be in Kahoots with someone.

I've also never been in Cognito. I hear no one recognizes you there. I have, however, been in Sane. They don't have an airport; you have to be driven there. I have made several trips there, thanks to my children, friends, family, and work.

I would like to go to Conclusions, but you have to jump, and I'm not too much on physical activity anymore. I have also been in Doubt. That is a sad place to go and I try not to visit there too often.

I've been in Flexible, but only when it was very important to stand firm. Sometimes I'm in Capable, and I go there more often as I'm getting older. One of my favorite places to be is in Suspense! It really gets the adrenalin flowing and pumps up the old heart! At my age, I need all the stimuli I can get!

I may have been in Continent, but I don't remember what country I was in. It's an age thing. They tell me it is very wet and damp there—like Oregon.

Computer Dating

Today's subject is computer dating, and maybe you will be surprised to know I have tried it. Or maybe not. I recently listened to a radio program about the increased action on dating sites (from December through February) of people searching for that significant other. I'm not kidding. The Internet is loaded with dating sites for every imaginable category of people—all colors, ages, religions, interests, you name it. I find the subject utterly fascinating.

Not long ago my friend Angie Rozell walked into my house, and she was absolutely glowing. She held out her left hand to show me her beautiful engagement ring. Angie has been a divorced mom (two teenagers) for a long time, and she decided it was long enough to be alone. Of course, I wanted to hear her story. She went on Christian Mingle and met the man of her dreams. I could not be happier for Angie. Through her I learned there are people who call themselves Christian but are really "C and E's,"—those who go to church only on Christmas and Easter, which is not what she was looking for.

Another young friend tried a dating site and has already gotten 104 "hits." She showed me photos on her iPad and some of the men look like they stepped out of Duck Dynasty. I guess if a crusty-looking guy with a beard to his belly button rings your chimes, why not? Who am I to judge? She showed me the place where you click yes, no, or maybe. I think she is clicking no a lot.

It must be that time of the year because I am suddenly

receiving mail on the subject of computer dating and I am having such fun getting an up-to-date education. I received an email from an Arizona reader who reports that women looking for love send out pheromones, and guys pick up on the signals. An older widow, having been told this by a well-meaning friend, said, "I didn't realize I had any pheromones left!"

And now, true confession time. In the 1960s, B.B. (before Burt) my little girl, age 7, and I were living happily in a drafty Santa Monica beach house. Picture us curled up together early on a Sunday morning, me reading the *Los Angeles Times* and Rocki reading the comics. She glanced at my paper and leaned over to read a full-page ad with this headline: "Meet the Person of Your Dreams." I hadn't even noticed it, but Rocki did. If interested, you were to fill out a profile about yourself, what you were looking for in a person, then mail it to an address with your check for $15. "Let's do it, Mom," said my daughter. "You aren't getting any younger and you need to meet somebody." Huh?

She wore me down, and together we answered all the questions with honesty and mailed it with a check. No photo required, and no home computers back then, either. After this company banked my money, I was to receive postcards with names of guys who would be calling me. Then I forgot all about it until Rocki called me excitedly at my office in Beverly Hills. She had picked up the mail after school. "We got one, Mom! We got one!" You'd think we were on a fishing trip and had snagged an albacore. I guess in a way we were on a fishing trip.

The phone calls started coming in. Most of them sounded like total dorks, so those guys were told I had suddenly become engaged, until a voice on the phone sounded rather interesting. I agreed to meet him at a well-lit coffee place and told him my little girl would be with me. He said he loved kids. Rocki was beyond excited, especially when a loud motorcycle roared into the parking lot. We could see the guy through the window. *Oh no,* I thought. "Yippee," said my daughter. The guy came clanking into the coffee shop, all decked out in leather and chains and a big smile. He was easily 10 years younger than me, admitted to lying on the questionnaire but added that he preferred "older women." He was definitely interested, but I could not get out of there fast enough. Rocki kept asking why I had a problem with him.

I decided no more computer guys until the day she called me at the office, laughing hysterically. She said the name on the postcard was so funny—and all I'm going to admit here is that we still refer to him as Percy from Pasadena. I wish I could print his last name but you would not believe it. Out of sheer curiosity, we let him come over. Picture Percy at 6-feet-8-inches tall, weighing maybe 135 pounds. He resembled a very tall stork. While Rocki and I sat down on a low Swedish sofa, Percy sat across from us (on a matching low sofa), peering at us over his knobby knees. He was terrible at making conversation, so I finally asked him if he had done anything interesting lately.

"Wulp," he said, "I guess it was my trip to Waaa-ki-ki."

At which point Rocki jammed an elbow into my ribcage while not exactly stifling her giggles. She knew full well he had mispronounced Waikiki. I soon ushered him out of our house and said goodbye to computer dating forever.

My current plan is to live vicariously through friends who are looking for that person of their dreams. I looked up pheromones and decided if I have any left, I'm keeping them to myself.

Don't Hold Back

An amazing moment happened the other night, and I haven't been able to stop thinking of it. Since that moment meant so much to me, I take it as a sign, maybe even a lesson that needs to be shared with you.

Every month the Newport Chamber of Commerce does what is called "Business after Hours." It's a short, social evening that people can attend right after work. Each month this event is held and sponsored by various businesses and organizations. Last week was hosted by the Newport Symphony Orchestra and held at the Newport Performing Arts Center. I try to attend and support Chamber events when I can, as a way of carrying on my husband's legacy and his love for this community.

The lobby of the PAC was already crowded when I walked in, and to my amazement, several people suddenly reached out en masse with friendly hugs and greetings. Their names aren't relevant for this story—in fact, I'm a little fuzzy about who all was in the group. What matters and means so much to me is what was said. Each one wanted to tell of how my husband impacted their lives. A couple of stories went back 25 years. This magical moment was probably no longer than 12 minutes, barely long enough for me to get all misty eyed, but I left there feeling such joy and gratitude about Burt's memory living on, realizing again that he has clearly not been forgotten. Knowing this would mean so much to his daughters, I sent them an email, trying hard to put those 12 minutes into words. Here are their replies:

"Thanks so much for sharing. What a wonderful and heartwarming tribute to Dad and you. You both have given so much to the community and have been such a big part of it. I am so grateful to know that Dad is remembered and honored." Love, Meryl Lippman Perutz, Montecito, Calif.

"Remembering is the greatest way to keep him with us. I wish I could have been there. So glad you had that moment. Dad lives on." Love Robin Lippman Scharf, Niskayuna, New York.

Whenever I go out in this community, whether attending an event or just getting groceries, I am often stopped by someone wanting to share a happy story about Burt. The unusual thing about the other night was the number of people in the lobby of the PAC, all wanting to talk about Burt. Here is the really big lesson in this column today. If you haven't lost a loved one yet, you will. For those of you on the Grief Journey, you know how much it means when memories are shared and your loved one is talked about. Unfortunately, it is human nature that most of us hold back on mentioning the name of the one who has gone on ahead for fear of making someone sad or, worse yet, cry. On the contrary, one of the many lessons I have learned since Burt died is an almost insatiable need to hear stories about him and his name used with such respect and admiration. Those people at the PAC may read this and not even remember all that was said. The important thing is how much their words meant to Burt's daughters and me.

Bobbie with Burt's daughters Meryl Perutz on left and Robin Scharf on right

"The Thing"

On my right wrist is a funny looking bracelet with a recessed button that is to be pushed in case of trouble. This waterproofed bracelet is called the Lifeline Medical Alert and I have been wearing it for over a year. I did not want the darn thing, but my friend Kath Schonau of Aging Wisely With Heartfelt Hands can be very persistent. I tried telling her I am not a fall risk, but she kept pointing out that I could tumble off my treadmill, my exercise bike, trip over the cat, slip in the shower, or get cornered by a porcupine. Then she added the possibility of thieves breaking in during the night and other horrors of living alone, so I caved in and got the Lifeline. Kath said my family would feel better if I wore "the thing." It works 800 feet from the house, so if I grow a man-eating plant in my greenhouse and it attacks in a fit of hunger, I can activate "the thing." It's cheap insurance, and I now recommend it to anyone living alone.

So why this subject today? Because Patti Littlehales has this really cool friend from childhood who writes a column for *The Nugget*, a newspaper in Sisters, Oregon. Patti sent me some nuggets from *The Nugget*, and I now also have a very cool and new friend. Judy Bull's column is called "Bull By Bull." Judy and I have discovered we have a ton of things in common. We both live at the end of a road, but I am jealous of Judy because she lives with horses, goats, a cat and dog, while all I have left to cuddle is Lap Sitter. I can hear my granddaughter Autumn saying, "Well hey, Beverly Jo, would you like some cheese with that whine?"

Here is a recent bit from Judy's column: "I was out at the barn early one morning when I saw trucks and cars racing up to my house. Having unknowingly pushed my "Help, I've fallen and I can't get up" button, I can vouch for said system including a fantastic turnout from the Cloverdale Fire Department, Deschutes County Sheriff, Sisters/Camp Sherman ambulance and two neighbors."

I emailed Judy for more information because this was obviously good column fodder. Judy wears "the thing" around her neck and, at the time of the above incident, the button was pointing outwards. Judy was clutching a bale of hay to her chest, and the button got pushed, consequently all the action arriving at her house. She now wears "the thing" with the button facing in. Smart girl.

Similar story number two. During our temporary return to Los Angeles (1997 to 2005), a dear friend of 35 years—also named Judy—was diagnosed with stage 4 lung cancer. We saw one another a lot. I took her to doctors and chemo appointments until she decided to quit fighting the cancer and just milk life to the max. Since Judy lived alone, I nagged her into getting "the thing," although she fought me for months. She finally got tired of my daily nagging and signed on for "the thing," one she could wear around her neck. I called every morning to see how she was doing, and here is the typical exchange:

Me: "Are you wearing 'the thing'?"
Her: "No."
Me: "Where is it?"
Her: "Upstairs, in my bathroom."
Me: "Ohforheavensake, give me a break!"

The next day she said I had worn her down and she was wearing the darn thing. *Great*, I thought—until a few days later when she called me, laughing her head off. She told me she had accidentally activated "the thing" and ended up with "seven handsome hunky paramedics in her kitchen." She loved every minute of it and she had me laughing, too. When I finally caught my breath, I asked how on earth she managed to accidentally push the button.

"Because," she said, defiantly, "I was trying to open a bottle of vodka, that's why!"

Sometimes it's better not to ask. Meanwhile, my old friend Judy has passed on, but I am exchanging columns with my new friend, Judy Bull, and it's only a matter of time before we meet in person. Here is how she wound up a recent column:

> "Of course, where you find yourself is the best place to be. Of late, I am making a concerted effort to think more about today. I've already lived yesterday and I don't know a thing about tomorrow."

My philosophy exactly.

Don Taylor and Kath Schonau with Burt

JUST IN TIME

The subject of love is universal and we all need a reminder now and then to let our loved ones know how we feel—while we still can. The following story was originally written for the Newport *News-Times*, then sold to the first *Chicken Soup for the Woman's Soul* book, and eventually went on to appear in newspapers across the country.

A Valentine For Connie

Most people need to hear those "three little words." Once in awhile it happens just in time.

I met Connie when she was admitted to the hospice ward in a large Los Angeles hospital where I worked as a volunteer. Her husband, Bill, stood nervously nearby as Connie was transferred from a gurney to the hospital bed. Although Connie was in the final stages of her fight against cancer, she was alert and almost cheerful—one of those patients who are a joy for caregivers.

We got her settled while Bill was off filling out the usual forms. I finished marking her name on all the hospital supplies she would be using, then asked if she needed anything.

"Oh yes," she said, "would you please show me how to work the television? I enjoy the soaps so much and don't want to get behind in what's happening."

Connie was a romantic. She loved soap operas, romance novels, and movies with a good love story. As we became acquainted, she confided how frustrating it was being married 32 years to a man who often called her "a silly woman."

"I know he loves me," she said, "but he has never been able to say he loves me or send me cards." She sighed and looked out the window at the trees in the courtyard. "I would give anything if Bill would say 'I love you,' but it's just not in his nature."

Bill visited Connie every day. He sat next to the bed while she watched soap operas, or else, when she began sleeping more, he paced up and down in the hallway. Soon, when she no longer watched television and had fewer waking moments, I began spending more of my volunteer time with Bill.

He talked about having worked as a carpenter, and he loved fishing. They had no children, but had been enjoying retirement by traveling—until Connie got sick. Bill could not talk about the fact his wife was dying.

One day over coffee in the cafeteria, I got him on the subject of women and the need for romance in our lives—how we love to get sentimental cards, maybe even a love letter.

"Do you tell Connie you love her?" I asked, (knowing his answer), and he looked at me like I was crazy.

"I don't have to," he said. "She knows I do!"

"I'm sure she knows," I said, reaching over and touching his hands—rough carpenter hands that were gripping the coffee cup as if it was the only thing he had to hang onto. "But she needs to hear it, Bill. She needs to hear what she has meant to you all these years. Please think about it."

We walked back to Connie's room, and Bill disappeared inside. I left to visit another patient and later saw Bill sitting by the bed, holding Connie's hand as she slept. The date was February 13.

The next day I walked down the hospice ward at noon. There stood Bill, leaning against the wall in the hallway, staring at the floor. I already knew from the head nurse that Connie had died at 11 a.m.

When Bill saw me, he allowed himself to come into my arms for a long hug. His face was wet with tears and he was trembling. Finally, he leaned back against the wall and took a deep breath. "I have to say something," he said. "I have to say how good I feel about telling her." He stopped to blow his nose. "I thought a lot about what you said, and last night I told her how much I loved her, and loved being married to her. You shoulda seen her smile!"

I went into the room to say my own final goodbye to Connie. There, on the bedside table, was a large valentine card from Bill. The sentimental kind that says, "To my wonderful wife—I love you."

Try Anything Once

Last year on Valentine's Day, I remember nothing. Last year felt like living inside a dark cave. Since being a masochist is not very attractive, I have made a concerted effort to emerge from that miserable dark cave called Grief. This year I woke up on Valentine's Day with the blues, then reminded myself how my husband Burt would yell at me for being a Gloomy Gus. He would want me to think of all the good times we had together.

I dressed, got my coffee, and sat down with my iPad to lurk around on Facebook. What to my wandering eyes should appear but a photo of Burt's daughter Robin, cross-country skiing near their home in Albany, New York. That photo uprooted a fun memory and Robin might be surprised that her dad once tried cross-country skiing.

When Burt and I got married, he assigned me the job of social director. He was not born with my sense of adventure, and he promised to try anything once. I told you about our river rafting adventure earlier when he thought I had said, "shooting rabbits" when I had actually said, "shooting rapids." He ended up loving that first river trip to the extent that we went on to conquer a few more challenging rivers.

That winter, we headed to California snow country with several friends. We stayed in a large cabin and most of us wanted to try cross-country skiing. After renting the equipment, we headed out on a designated trail, having no idea what we were doing. Burt, being an alpha male, took the lead, and we trudged after him in single file. We did okay as long as the trail was flat, but when we tried going uphill or down, it was such a disaster we all ended up flailing in the snow. The guys swore a lot, and two of us females needed to find a restroom. We called it quits, turned in the equipment, and spent the rest of the weekend by a roaring fire playing word games. So much for fun in the snow, which conveniently leads me to the following day brightener.

A ski story. (Author unknown)

Conditions were perfect—12 degrees below zero, no feeling in the toes, basic numbness all over, the "Tell me when we're having fun" kind of day.

One of the women in the group complained to her husband that she was in dire need of a restroom. He told her not to worry, there was relief waiting at the top of the lift in the form of a powder room for female skiers in distress. He was wrong of course, and the pain did not go away. If you've ever had nature hit its panic button in you, then you know that a temperature of 12 below doesn't help. With time running out, the woman weighed her options. Her husband, picking up on the intensity of the pain, suggested that since she was wearing an all-white ski outfit, she should go off in the woods and no one would even notice. He assured her, "The white will provide more than adequate camouflage."

So she headed for the tree line, lowered her ski pants, and proceeded to do her thing. If you've ever parked on the side of a slope on skis, then you know there is a right way and wrong way to set your skis so you don't move. Yep, you got it. She had them positioned the wrong way. Steep slopes are not forgiving—even during the most embarrassing moments. Without warning, the woman found herself skiing backward, out of control, racing through the trees, somehow missing all of them and onto another slope. Her derriere and was still bare, her pants down around her knees, and she was picking up speed. She continued backwards, creating an unusual vista for the other skiers. The woman skied back under the lift and finally collided with a pylon.

The bad news was that she broke her arm and was unable to pull up her ski pants. At long last, her husband arrived putting an end to her nudie show, then summoned the ski patrol. They transported her to a hospital.

While in the emergency room, a man with an obviously broken leg was put in the bed next to hers. "So, how'd you break your leg?" she asked, making small talk.

"It was the wildest thing you ever saw," he said. "I was riding up this ski lift and suddenly I couldn't believe my eyes! There was this crazy woman skiing backward, out of control, down the mountain, with her bare bottom hanging out of her pants. I leaned over to get a better look and fell out of the lift. How did you break your arm?"

The Power of Words and Hugs

"As for inflicting our sorrow on other people, one does not want to go around blathering and crying all the time. But perhaps it is our gift to others to trust them enough to share our feelings with them. It may help them to deal with some of their own."
—Martha Whitmore Hickman, author of **Healing After Loss.**

The above wisdom might have helped me that day 18 months ago when I drove into town for the first time after my husband's death. It wasn't easy venturing out of my dark cave, but I was in desperate need of a few groceries and a long way from learning to ask friends for help. I parked my car, walked into the store, and was honestly shocked to see people filling their carts, chatting happily with one another and acting as if life was just dandy. Did they not realize my life as I had known it for 45 years had just come to a crushing halt? It takes a lot to make me angry, but I was furious at those people. I wanted to scream at them. How dare they not realize a pathetically miserable person was in their midst?

In the many columns documenting my Grief Journey, I haven't written about that day and my anger, not out of an attempt to hide what I now know is a normal, human reaction to great loss, but the anger was quickly replaced by a deep and ongoing sorrow that continued to be written about in this column for months. The process of writing is therapeutic for many people. It certainly has been for me. What I did not expect was the response from readers. Emails poured in from near and far. This column has always traveled, but never to this extent and it is still happening. Much of the correspondence is from folks I didn't know, but I know them now because of a shared human condition called grief.

For those of you wondering why I'm back on this subject, chalk it up to what I call a "hug fest." As I continue to move about this community and attend various events, it is not at all unusual for someone to tell me how much this column has helped them deal with the loss of a loved one. They say I put into words what they are thinking, and that now they no longer feel so alone. Whether or not I know these people a handshake somehow seems cold and stupid, but a hug is warm and nurturing. I ask for names and try to remember, but we all know how fleeting this can be when someone tells us their name. I made a special effort this week because three women, previously unknown to me, took time to say thanks for this column, and I got warm hugs from all three—Clair Finnegan (church), Page Zeman, (J.C. Market), and Andrea Sachs (at the symphony concert). These women will recall the moment we spent together and, I hope, forgive me if I misspelled their names.

The important message today is a reminder to reach out to those who have a heart full of hurt, whatever the reason may be. When I told one of these women about my anger that day in the market, she said she cannot bear to go down the cereal aisle because her husband loved Raisin Bran, and he is no longer here to enjoy it. A woman told me how much the "Coffee Cup" story meant to her because she felt the same way. A most interesting email arrived months after the column about Burt's coffee cup. The person who wrote said she could not move her husband's shaving mug. Shaving mug? The last man I knew who used a shaving mug was my dad, so I figured this woman's husband had to be 100 years old. Not so. Out of curiosity, I had to know more. Putting it into tactful words was a challenge, but now I know that shaving mugs are back in style and young(er) men are now happily whipping up a lather.

Since this is a thank you to the three women who inspired today's column with their words and hugs, I need to admit how I love getting a guy hug. There is nothing inappropriate about a hug from a guy who has known you for a long time and the hug is clearly delivered with affection and respect. During this past week, a dose of male energy in the form of hugs was delivered by Dave, Mike, Will, Mark, and Steve (church, Chamber of Commerce luncheon, and Newport Symphony).

As this column continues, there will most likely be more on the subject of grief and loss. But for the couple who made a big deal of telling me (in a Nye Beach restaurant) that they "rip their Friday paper apart to find the humor," I promise to keep you laughing if you promise to keep on reading.

Food, Feathers, Fun And Frolic

Belated happy greetings to those who just celebrated Easter and Passover. We all know these holidays are based in religious beliefs, but today the focus is on food, not faith. Food is a safe subject, a universal one, and nobody survives without food. I have realized for a long time that I am in the tiny minority of folks who are not passionate about food and cooking.

My 45-year marriage to Burt introduced me into the world of Passover and Seder celebrations. In fact, I was so utterly amazed with my first Seder experience at the home of a close friend that I wrote about it—a story called "Passover in the Playroom," from a Shiksa's point of view. (Shiksa: a female gentile.)

That story appeared in the Newport *News-Times*, *Chicken Soup for the Soul*, and a dozen national newspapers. The story described all the traditional Passover foods, such as moror, (bitter herbs to recall the bitterness of life in Egypt). My 9-year-old daughter Rocki eyeballed the unfamiliar foods with such suspicion I had to poke her under the table. Today, she has Jewish friends who make sure she is seated at their Seder table. This year a part of me wanted to fly east and join Burt's large and loving family as they celebrated Passover. Maybe next year.

Food was a big part of this past weekend, and I have to give kudos to Lorna Davis and her Chamber of Commerce crew (plus volunteers) who put together the annual banquet and balloon gala. The theme this year was Mardi Gras, and most people were decked out in wild costumes. My "date," Gina Nielsen, got really creative, which you can tell from the photo. I realized how many read last Friday's column because the hugs just kept on coming from men and women alike on Saturday night. Consequently, most of my beads and feathers fell off probably to the dismay of whoever had to vacuum the Best Western ballroom. Since Mardi Gras was the theme, dinner was completely Cajun. Have you ever tasted Jambalaya or Bananas Foster? Yummy!

I was delighted to be invited to Easter dinner at the home of friends. It was an Italian-theme dinner and everyone, except me, contributed food. Although I don't cook, I do know how to bring wine. The dinner was gourmet delicious, and every person at the table seemed to be a foodie. It's not the first time I've listened to passionate discussions of various cooking shows on TV. These table talks always make me realize I have never been interested in cooking. My poor mother tried to chain me to the stove to learn something, but the outdoors was always calling and, to her dismay, I would sneak away to play. It's not that I can't cook, I just don't enjoy it like normal people. During marriage to Burt, I made an effort to whip up good meals because he truly enjoyed food.

I can't leave this subject without sharing the following day brightener, which has been showing up in my mail for ages, and it always makes me laugh. Here it is:

The Pillsbury Doughboy: In Remembrance. (Author unknown)

Please join me in remembering a great icon of the entertainment community. The Pillsbury Doughboy died yesterday of a yeast infection and trauma complications from repeated pokes in the belly. He was 71.

Doughboy was buried in a lightly greased coffin. Dozens of celebrities turned out to pay their respects, including Mrs.

Butterworth, Hungry Jack, the California Raisins, Betty Crocker, the Hostess Twinkies, and Captain Crunch. The gravesite was piled high with flours. Aunt Jemima delivered the eulogy and lovingly described Doughboy as a man who never knew how much he was kneaded. Born and bread in Minnesota, Doughboy rose quickly in show business, but his later life was filled with turnovers. He was not considered a very smart cookie, wasting much of his dough on half-baked schemes. A little flaky at times, he died a crusty old man, yet was considered a positive roll model for millions.

Doughboy is survived by his elderly father, Pop Tart, his wife Play Dough, three children: John Dough, Jane Dough and Dosey Dough, plus, they had one in the oven. The funeral was held at 3:50 for about 20 minutes.

If you smiled while reading this, please rise to the occasion and pass it on to someone having a crummy day and kneading a lift. If you think someone can use a hug, do it.

Bobbie with Gina Nielsen, dressed for Mardi Gras at the Newport Chamber of Commerce banquet and balloon gala

Any Lap Will Do

Dear Mimi and Teddy: This is my first letter dictated to my human who is frowning because apparently it's not easy to take dictation with me on her lap. You are hearing from me because your human, Sharon Beardsley, recently told my human in the lobby of the Newport Performing Arts Center that you are interested in knowing about my life. (Does your human really read the newspaper to you every Friday?)

All I know is that our humans must be avid book readers and were at the PAC for a community function called "Newport Reads." If you are anything like me, you appreciate owning a human who reads because a book forces them to sit down and make lap room.

I'm a little vague about my history because I am elderly now and my memory is not as sharp as my claws. I can't remember my original humans, but they either dumped me at the local animal shelter or maybe I got confused and wandered off. At any rate, there I was, nicely cared for because that's what the animal shelter people do. They claimed my ethnic background is a Snowshoe Siamese, which meant. I could not go to a forever home with other cats. So there I stayed for three weeks until this nice lady walked in, took me out of the arms of a volunteer, and sat down in a little glass booth so we could have a cat chat.

She has always had cats, so she knew right away I was what she was looking for. But she would not commit until going out to the car and bringing in this tall, bearded male human so he could

Good Grief

be in on the decision (like he had any choice). The lady human stood at the counter while the male human sat down in the little glass booth. Someone put me in that room and, of course, I immediately had to do a test drive on his lap, which, frankly, was far more ample and soft than that of the female human. I could tell he had already learned to pet a cat in all the right places, so I purred loudly to show my pleasure.

They signed the adoption papers and took me to a nice man named Dr. Steve Brown. Although the doctor was very gentle, I hated that metal table and all the strange smells. He said I was about six years old, needed my teeth cleaned, and did not have a hysterectomy tattoo or scar. What a bummer, and oh how I wanted to tell these humans that I had already been through this surgery a long time ago by some yahoo veterinarian who should have stamped proof on my tummy.

The next day, my new humans came back to take me to my forever home, but I overheard their concern about a dog named Charley who lived with them. I quickly let curious Charley know who was boss by whacking his nose once, and that was that. We know, don't we, Mimi and Teddy, that cats rule.

The years have been really good here although it was a challenge comforting my female human after her male human went away. I could tell Charley was getting old and tired, and I kind of missed him when he also went away. It's not really extra work for me when my human gets sad because it means she needs to cuddle and hold me close, which works for me.

And that bit about Snowshoe Siamese cats not liking other cats, well, that's a lot of horse pucky! I enjoy being outside in the sunshine and the cats next door (Sam and Emma) usually wander over to visit. They tell me wild stories about how much fun they have bringing half-dead critters into their house as gifts for their humans, but that is a messy pastime and seems like too much effort at my age.

My human thinks I'm at least 15, and she worries because I am now sleeping until noon. I do enjoy messing with her. When I think she is worrying excessively about me getting old and leaving her, I wait until I know she has gotten into bed with a book. Then I finish my nice big dinner, hit the litter box (very satisfying), then run like crazy all over the house. I know she is listening to my galloping feet and feeling relieved that all is well. Finally, I hop in bed with her, curl up close to her cheek, and activate my purring machine. This makes her happy, and she knows I will be right there in that same place when she wakes up. I wish she would stop being concerned about me sleeping until noon. She will too, when she gets to be a geriatric case like me.

Thank you, Mimi and Teddy, for your interest.

Sincerely, Lap Sitter Lippman

Lap Sitter Lippman

I'M KEEPING MY FORK

I hit the pits the other day, as I am sure all of you have at one time or another when problems pile up in such a cluster you wonder if you can dig yourself out of the pit. Readers often say they appreciate my honesty and I'm not backing off now.

Here's a summary: I'm facing major surgery (complete shoulder replacement), major dental surgery (implants), and I'm fighting like crazy to hang onto my vision (macular degeneration). It is really hard trying to make decisions without my husband's wisdom and loving support.

I was barely holding it together when the final blow fell, which may seem trivial to you but it felt major to me. A couple of days ago I was driving home and, as always, took a quick look at the house on the beach where we lived so incredibly happily for our first 14 years here on the coast. I knew it was inevitable the new owners would remove the little barn visible from the highway, but suddenly it was gone. Burt and I spent so much time in that barn, raising miniature goats, mucking out the barn while our various dogs and goats played their goofy games that broke us up in laughter. Maybe you saw the column not long ago about the day the animals locked us inside the barn and Burt shoved me out a small window—head first—into a blackberry patch. He thought this was a lot funnier than I did, and I think the animals were laughing, too.

When I got home, I sat in the car and cried. I felt sad, alone and scared. I went in the house, flopped down in my lazy girl chair with the cat on my lap, and opened my iPad. A day brightener popped in from my Arizona friend Susan Fox. The DB has been floating around for years, but it never spoke directly to me until now. Here it is:

Keep Your Fork. (Author unknown)

A young woman had been diagnosed with a terminal illness and given three months to live. As she was getting her things in order, she contacted her pastor and asked him to come and discuss certain aspects of her final wishes. She told him the songs she wanted sung at the service and the scriptures she would like read. As the pastor was preparing to leave, the woman suddenly remembered something.

"This is very important," she said. "I want to be buried with a fork in my right hand. My grandmother once told me a story and from that time on, I have always tried to pass along its message to those I love and those who are in need of encouragement. Grandmother said, 'In all my years of attending socials and dinners, I remember that when the dishes of the main course were being cleared, someone would inevitably lean over and say keep your fork. It was my favorite part because I knew that something better was coming—like velvety chocolate cake or deep-dish apple pie—something wonderful!'

"So," the young woman continued, "I just want people to see me there in that casket with a fork in my hand and I want them to wonder, What's with the fork? Then I want you to tell them Grandmother's story and remind them to 'Keep your fork—the best is yet to come.' "

The pastor had tears of joy as he hugged the woman goodbye. He knew this would be one of the last times he would see her before her death. But he also knew that the young woman had a better grasp of heaven than he did—better than many people twice her age, with twice as much experience and knowledge. She knew that something better was coming.

At the funeral, as people walked by the casket they saw the fork placed in her right hand. Over and over, the pastor heard the question, "What's with the fork?" And over and over, he smiled. During his message, the pastor told the people of the conversation he had with the young woman shortly before she died. He told them about the fork and about what it symbolized to her. He told the people how he could not stop thinking about the fork and that they probably would not be able to stop thinking about it either. He was right.

So the next time you reach for your fork let it remind you, ever so gently, that the best is yet to come. Cherish the time you have and all the memories. And just remember to keep your fork. The best is yet to come!

I will manage all the medical stuff with the help of friends and somehow muddle through six weeks with one arm in a sling. I do keep thinking of that day brightener and one thing is for sure, I'm hanging onto my fork!

Meet Waldo

True confession time. Two weeks ago, I decided a little extra help was needed around here and I hesitantly agreed to allow Waldo to move in with me. He is still on probation but I'm leaning toward letting him stay. After all, he does make me laugh, but he also has some strange quirks—don't we all?

For instance, I'm never quite sure where he is, which explains why I dubbed him Waldo. I can hear the low-humming sound he makes, which is not annoying but sort of like what you might notice if you got too close to a beehive. If his humming suddenly stops, I go check on him. He is very short, but he has a cool way of telling you why he stopped working. For example, "My vision is blocked," means he has gotten himself into a predicament and wants to be moved. When he first started on my carpeting, he would suddenly stop after a half hour and let me know his filter was full. He seems to be exceptionally strong, and I'm suspicious he is sucking up dog hair left over from the two Corgis who lived here 10 years ago. (Just kidding. I'm not THAT lousy a housekeeper.)

You have probably figured out by now that Waldo is a robot. My friend Sue, whom I met on an amazing gray whale expedition to Baja, treated herself to a robot and her stories broke me up. I spent several days obsessing about such a seemingly silly investment, then decided what the heck, life is too short, and I can use more laughter around here. When my husband Burt sat in his favorite place on the sofa, he would lift his feet onto the coffee table so I could vacuum all his crumbs. Now I sit in my lazy girl chair and wait for Waldo to come humming toward me. I lift up my legs out of his way and laugh as he happily sucks up all the crumbs under my chair. Burt might think I've gone around the bend, but then again, maybe not. He kind of lived vicariously through all my wild and crazy ideas.

I am not disclosing Waldo's official name because I have gotten into trouble mentioning brands in this column and there are a few competitor robots on the market. But if you ask me off the record, I'll be happy to share. So far, Waldo has vacuumed this entire house, but I still worry about him committing suicide tumbling down the stairs. However, he seems to have a slick internal sensor that tells him when he gets too close to an edge. If you think it's odd that I have given him a male identity, you should go online and read reviews by other people. Most folks name their robots because it really does seem like having a very short funny little person running around your house. One guy calls his robot Toto. My Waldo is so smart he knows when his battery needs charging, and he heads for his home base, which is in my bedroom. I love watching him back up to his charging unit and wiggle his little behind to get exactly in position to power up. It does not take long before he is ready to go back to work. You would be impressed at how well he cleans my kitchen floor and laundry room. No longer do my feet crunch on scattered kitty litter.

I know you are dying to ask about Lap Sitter's reaction to Waldo. She finds a high, safe place to perch and watches this mysterious thing moving and humming around the house. Maybe she is laughing, but it's hard to tell with a cat. I know Burt would laugh, and if he were still here, we would both be sitting with our legs up while Waldo vacuums under our feet.

Is my robot perfect? No. He gets ticked off if strange stuff gets in his way, like cords and fringe and low-hanging drapes (which I don't have). He doesn't cook or clean my fridge, but I saw a bit on TV about scientists trying to program a robot to fold towels and socks. I can fold my own, thank you very much. I do have another friend who is on her third robot vacuum. Her first one worked himself to death, her second one went out an open door on a rainy day and expired (no warranty covers a drowned robot). Her third one is performing nicely, but he doesn't have Waldo's brain—her robot does not know to return to home base or (get this) remember where he left off during the last cleaning cycle. If you want to laugh your head off, go online and type in "Shark Cat You Tube," which is a video of a cat in a shark costume riding a robot all around some lady's kitchen floor. Hysterical!

Yep, I'm thinking my Waldo is here to stay.

WALDO REPORT

I looked up the word "avalanche," but it seems a bit of an overkill word for describing the amount of reader response from last week's Waldo the Robot subject. Let's just say there has been a surprising amount of feedback from folks interested in robots. Here is a bit of it:

Julie, Big Bear, California: "Wow! I had no idea robots were so smart."

Richard, somewhere east of the Rockies: "If I had one, I'd name him Clyde." Then Richard wrote a hundred more words about the Boston Red Sox and a ballplayer named Clyde.

Rhonda, Corvallis: "So funny you did this article. Just a few days ago, Bill and I were talking about getting a robot. What brand did you get? We want to get a smart one like yours."

Susan and John, Newport: "We have one and we have no idea how we ever got along without her."

Jackie, Seal Rock: "I have had a robot vacuum for over 10 years and he's spent the last nine years in storage. You inspired me and I am going to get him out and let him do his stuff."

Teresa, Omaha: "You are so talented. I would have conveyed my robot vacuum using just a few words, not a whole column, i.e. 'I have a robot vacuum, and it is great.' I would like to know the brand because I am thinking about getting another one."

Have you noticed that people refer to robots as "him," "her," or "it"? A few readers asked if Lap Sitter has hopped on Waldo to ride. Seriously? She has reached the elderly age where she doesn't hop, but she does perch, which, I guess, requires a hop in order to perch.

Barbara, Laughlin, Nevada: "What a great topic! Waldo sounds like a big help to you. I can picture the cat watching him work and I have seen the video of the shark cat that rides on the robot. Too funny!"

Patti, Newport: "I love the anthropomorphic attributes given to your new friend. The best view must be that of Lap Sitter perched on the counter wondering, *What in the world is this thing?*"

Edna Abbott Lemmon, Lincoln City: "Just to let you know Mother is doing well." (Edna Abbot Sr., for those who knew her all the years she lived in Toledo, will enjoy knowing that Edna is being lovingly cared for in a private home up the coast.) "Mother looks forward to me bringing the *News-Times* and, of course, she wants me to read your column to her. Today I had fun telling her I have two robots—one for vacuuming and one for scrubbing and mopping my hard-surface floors. I get a kick out of Zach, my 95-pound Golden Retriever—he ignores the robot as it bounces off of him and heads in a different direction. My biggest problem is when the robot runs out of energy. He hides under my king-size bed and I have to get under there and pull him out. Yes, mine is also a male."

My latest Waldo report is that he "found" one of my favorite earrings, lost here in the house months ago. I heard him clinking and clanking and went running to rescue whatever he had swallowed. Hooray, my earring. I almost hugged him, but we don't have that kind of a relationship.

As a contrast to his cleverness, I can't resist leaving you with a dumb day brightener. I receive Ole and Sven jokes every week from a Minnesota reader:

One day Ole and Sven were paging through the Sears catalog admiring all the beautiful models. Ole says to Sven, "Haf you seen da perdy girls in dis catalog?"

Sven replies, "Ya. Dey sure are bootiful, and yust look at da prices!"

Ole says, "Yumpin' yimmy. Dey ain't very expensive. At dese prices I'm buyin me vun."

Sven says, "Me, too."

Three weeks later Sven asks Ole, "Did ja ever get dat girl you ordered from dat Sears catalog?"

Ole answers, "No, but it von't be long now. Her clothes came yesterday!"

Shredding My Life

Do you remember what your life was like at age 10? How about 12, 14, or better yet, your entire daily drama as a 16-year-old? I do, because it is all written down in journals, diaries, and faded old blue-lined notebooks. Writers write, and compulsive writers simply can't help it. My mom saved it all. I know there are mothers who read their daughters diaries, but I can promise you that it would never have occurred to her to invade my privacy. I inherited her ethics and never opened my husband's mail or his wallet—until the day he died.

As for all those written words, it is time to let them go. The other day I was sitting at Burt's desk with his shredding machine grinding away. The phone rang and a friend asked, "How are you doing, and what are you up to?" I get a lot of calls like that—not unusual if you are lucky to have a circle of caring friends or what my daughter refers to as "your village."

"I'm shredding my life," I answered, maybe a bit flippantly but not meaning to be. I heard a gasp from the friend on the phone. I explained how it does not make sense to leave all this behind, but I could tell she did not understand.

Before stuffing pages in the shredder, I did take time to randomly read parts of my teen years, wondering how on earth my poor parents survived.

Life before my husband Burt was easy to shred, but our 45 years together, recorded in leather-bound journals he gave me every January 1 on my birthday caused an emotional meltdown and a pile of tear-soaked tissues. I could not resist stopping to read, remember, reminisce, and realize what a huge blessing it is to be married to your best friend, lover, and soul mate. I am far from done with the shredding of those 45 years—years of youthful energy and passion, helping one another deal with the loss of loved ones and pets.

Best of all are the adventures. Did we really ride bikes after touring those breweries in Amsterdam and Copenhagen? (We didn't even like beer, but hey, when in Rome...) Did I really beat him to the Wailing Wall in Jerusalem while he hung back schmoozing with our Arab guide? The gentleman was clearly baffled about this tall, friendly, bearded Jew whose non-Jewish wife was already inserting a prayer in the famous wall. Did we really throw all those wild and crazy costume parties? The journals are written with way too much intimate detail, certainly not meant to be seen by our kids and grandkids.

I shut down the shredder feeling depleted and sad. As many of you know, the Grief Journey does not stop—it only loses its original intensity. I went out on the deck to sit and think, with Burt's empty chair beside me, as usual. How overwhelming it feels to face major surgery without him by my side. And what about becoming even more visually challenged if the macular degeneration gets worse? My pity party was now in full swing and I reached the decision that it is no longer possible to continue writing this column.

Then I got dressed and attended the annual fundraiser dinner for Samaritan House, one of Newport's most worthy causes in meeting the needs of others. Of course, I felt like canceling. The shoulder pain was all the excuse I needed, but I had promised to be there and could not cop out. (Thanks Mom, for all your ethics... I think)

I truly believe there are reasons for everything. Never ever have so many people at one event approached me to introduce themselves, share their stories, and say what this column means to them. How could they possibly know I had decided that day to quit?

One woman waited patiently while I chatted with friends to tell me she had lost five of her six children and what she has learned from death and her faith. One gentleman stopped at our table, leaned down to introduce himself and told me—with tears—that his wife had Alzheimer's and that he got something of value out of the column every week. Before the evening ended, I realized I really do need to somehow continue—maybe reruns of old favorites for awhile during post-op, maybe eventually new stories dictated to a patient angel with normal vision who can type.

Shredding the history of my old life is one thing— disappointing you readers doesn't feel like an option as long as my heartbeats and my brain can put words into coherent sentences.

I know for sure what Burt would say if he was still here: "You have to keep writing, and if you feel like a beer right now, go for it, Babe!"

Sea Change

Sea change — definition: A striking change, often for the better. You have heard the words: "The only absolute is change." How true, how true. In last week's column, I mentioned the painful process of shredding dozens of my personal diaries and journals. It was time, it was necessary, and it was liberating. Since then, there have been a whole series of happy events and I hardly know how to get it all out of my head and into words. To describe how I'm feeling right now, two words come to mind — sheer joy. Instead of chronological order, I will start with five minutes ago and then work back in time.

My beloved granddaughter Autumn (finally) gave me permission to let you readers know a baby is on the way. I think of this as the circle of life. We all have loved ones who have left and new souls arriving to sop up our love. There will certainly be more details as time goes on because I will not be able to contain this amazing good news.

Last Sunday, I went to the Newport Performing Arts Center to listen with rapt pleasure as the Newport Symphony Orchestra gave the full house two hours of music from famous movies and, as a movie buff, I could barely stay seated. How fortunate we are to have such talent in this community. The day before, on the Fourth of July, I attended the annual (free to the public) patriotic concert given by the Newport Symphony. My husband Burt and I never missed it. As I mentioned in an earlier column, during the performance it is traditional that music is played for each branch of the service and veterans are asked to stand. Last year I came unglued when "Anchors Aweigh" was played and Burt was no longer beside me, standing straight and proud for having served in the Navy. I thought this year would be easier. It wasn't, but I had friends to my left and my right who all leaned in with moral support. Linda Kilbride handed me a tissue for the tears—I needed fewer than last year, so that's progress. No way can you leave that concert without feeling proud to be an American.

When I got home, I felt drained and in pain from the shoulder that will soon be fixed. Most of me wanted to crawl into bed with an ice pack, but the smart part, the intuitive part I trust said, "Get out of here and go to that barbecue." I made sure Lap Sitter was inside and safe from the noise of fireworks on the beach and headed up to the home of Janet and Al Anton, where a neighborhood party was in full swing. I had such a great time chatting with Jackie and George Stankey, Tom Sakaris, the new Seal Rock fire chief, and our weekender neighbors Betsy and John Borchardt. Get this for irony—not only is this couple the "parents" of the White Dog (who mysteriously appeared in my house last week), but both Borchardts are nurses at the hospital where I will soon be having surgery. They plan to stop by my room to make sure I'm behaving and being a patient patient. I'm so glad I followed my intuition and went to the barbecue instead of staying home.

I'm still hearing various theories about how White Dog got into my house, but the best came from readers Patricia Coats and her husband who said, "Waldo let him in." (In case you missed that column, Waldo is my robot.)

Continuing back in time this week to good news, there is now a great group of gals who will be standing by to help me through recovery from surgery. In spite of my protests, daughter

Good Grief

Rocki is coming to take care of her old mother for a few days. This column will somehow continue because there is so much good stuff ahead to share with you, like the new baby and the Great Cattle Caper. And now, since I've complained about my brain being on overload, here is a dandy day brightener that gives the best explanation.

The Explanation. (Author unknown)

Brains of older people are slow because they know so much. People do not decline mentally with age, it just takes them longer to recall facts because they have more information in their brains. (Scientists believe this, so I've decided to believe it, too). Much like a computer struggles as the hard drive gets full, so too do humans take longer to access information as their brains get full.

Researchers say this slowing down process is not the same as cognitive decline. The human brain works slower in old age, says Dr. Michael Ramscar, but only because we have stored more information over time. The brains of older people do not get weak. On the contrary, they simply know more.

Also, older people often go to another room to get something. Then they stand there wondering what they came for. This is not a memory problem. It is nature's way of making sure older people get more exercise.

This column generates a lot of mail from readers. Heaven help the fuddy-duddy who writes in suggesting a great grandmother should be sitting and knitting instead of running off to a cattle roundup with Lap Sitter's doctor!

We only live once and, if we work it right, once is enough.

And Now To Heal

As you read this, I am (hopefully) recovering from shoulder replacement surgery in a hospital two hours from home. Since there is such a thing called "deadline," this had to be written several days ago and sent to the newspaper. A part of me would love to gallop off into the sunset and avoid what is ahead, but the sensible side, the part that is sick of the pain, says, "Get it over with already." If you have gone through surgery lately, then you know the drill. It has been years and years since any doctor came at me with a scalpel, and I am astounded by all the new medical hoops one has to jump (or crawl) through.

As I write this, the washer and dryer are working overtime. Why? Because there is an incredible focus on everything being super-duper sterile, not just the surgeons and the hospital, but my own personal self as well. Here is what I have to do starting today. Nightly complicated showering using special germicidal sponges, making sure to spend an extra 5 minutes scrubbing the surgical site plus under any folds in my body (which I'm not sure exist.) Also hair washing. No shaving of anything. Use a clean towel after each shower. Then clean pajamas each night and (get this) clean sheets EVERY NIGHT. Say what? Since I have a king size bed and the use of only one arm, guess who has to swallow her pride and ask for help—and help is on the way.

Poor Lap Sitter. Can you imagine the surgeon's face if I told him my cat sleeps with me? But I know better than to do the whole sterile routine and then let an animal into my bed.

Good Grief

Here's the good news about how things work out. If you caught the recent column regarding the shredding of my journals and diaries, little did I realize that process would free me to finally venture into the garage to start what I've thought would be a sad and depressing job. I work best with peppy music, although using one arm to sort stuff slows me down. Since Lap Sitter likes to be with me, I fixed up Charley's old dog bed for her, elevated like cats prefer, and she loves it. She has fresh water, a dish of kibble, and she will be okay a few nights in the garage until I go to the hospital. You know you can survive almost anything on a short-term basis, and so can a cat. She will have a friend keeping her company while I'm gone.

Two of my friends will be delivering me to the hospital, and they insist on sticking around. I don't seem to have power over anything right now except the cat. In an attempt to prove to myself how far I have come since Burt's death, I decided to try sleeping on his side of the bed (for the first time in 45 years), thinking I could handle it now, and it would be better for my shoulder. Wrong on both counts. I lasted two nights, so tonight I'm back to where I belong and perhaps sleep will come.

Tomorrow will be the second anniversary of Burt's death and you readers have traveled the entire Grief Journey with me, through the ups and downs, the laughter, and the tears.

Everyone Needs a Humptulips

Every relationship needs a Humptulips. We didn't have an official Humptulips, i.e. a symbol for making up when things go wrong, and I'm not sure how we handled things earlier when our marriage was strained for one reason or another. We know several couples that were married by a California minister in what was called the Rose Ceremony. The minister gave the bride and groom each a rose to hold. Just before they were pronounced man and wife, the minister had them exchange roses and told them there would be times ahead when arguments and hurt feelings would preclude any real communication. When that happened, the couple was to remember the beauty of the rose and the special love that brought them to the altar—and they were to go out, get a rose, and put it in a place for the other to see. The rose would remind them that true love was still there for each other, no matter what.

About 10 years into our marriage, I had a lot of misery going on except I couldn't talk about it. Why? Because I didn't fully understand it myself. And if I tried to define my feelings, the guilt set in. It all had to do with big-city burnout and my longing to live on the ocean with some peace and privacy, which is not possible in southern California unless you're a rock star. I had grown up in Nebraska where there is not exactly a lot of ocean going on. But even by age 10, I could feel the pull of the sea.

My husband Burt had a good job with nine years to go before

Good Grief

retirement. Friends sensed my growing frustration; my husband even more so, since he had to live with me. One day when the heat, smog, and traffic congestion of Los Angeles had me particularly depressed, Burt suggested we take a short vacation, perhaps a car trip north to the U.S. border at Port Angeles, Washington, then south along the ocean back to Los Angeles. Just the two of us.

It sounded like a good idea and you'd think my spirits would have gone up. Nope. I was a miserable companion, deep in thought as we drove along, convinced we would never find a way to live on or even near the ocean. Burt put up with my gloomy mood until Port Angeles, where his patience gave out. He said I wasn't exactly a bundle of fun. (I knew that.) Did I want out of the marriage? (No.) Did I want out of the car? (No.) Would I, for heaven's sake, talk about it? (Silence.)

As we headed south on Highway 101, I noticed his white-knuckle grip on the steering wheel. I had to pull myself together and do something, but what? I remember saying a silent, desperate prayer, *Lord, I'm in trouble, my marriage is in trouble, my soul is in trouble. Help!* I glanced down at the AAA Tour Book lying on the seat and absently thumbed through to check the next town.

Humptulips, Washington.

The book listed only one thing to do in Humptulips. "The salmon hatchery, 1 1/3 miles west of U.S. 101, raises Chinook, Coho, and chum salmon. Open daily, 8 a.m. to dusk."

"Why don't we stop and visit this fish place?" I suggested, trying to sound enthusiastic. My husband gave me a surprised glance and drove toward the hatchery. The enormous parking lot was empty except for a Winnebago RV with Missouri plates. An elderly couple was about to get in it and leave.

"Anything interesting to see here?" I asked as we got out of our car.

"Nope," they said, and drove away.

We walked around and there was no one else in sight—just long rows of concrete tanks, all empty, until we came to one tank. We looked down and there was a dead fish, floating on its side in a foot of water with one glassy eyeball staring pathetically up at us. That was it. That was all there was to see.

I think it was that eyeball that did it. I felt a small grin tug at one corner of my mouth and glanced at my husband. His immediate laugh was infectious and I started to laugh. We left Humptulips holding hands, little dreaming that our lives were about to change radically when we hit the Oregon Coast. We ended up finding an affordable beach house south of Newport, bought it, took early retirement and left behind the fast lane of Los Angeles—and also quite a few shocked friends and family members.

Even after several decades of marriage, when tempers would flare—as they do in any relationship—we would only have to say the word "Humptulips." It never failed to work, as it's very hard to fight when you're laughing.

A rose would probably be more romantic, but it's just not as funny as a dead fish.

Medical Moments

There is a quotation well known to folks in Hollywood. A guy was about to wed a famous actress who had been married five times already and a reporter asked the gentleman if he was concerned about the wedding night. Here is what the prospective groom answered: "Well, I know what to do—but I'm just not sure how to make it interesting."

I am recovering from shoulder-replacement surgery and am writing this with one arm in a sling. I'm sure you have all gone through medical moments, and that I share my life experiences with you, from the awful to the sublime. Please join me as I describe the past several weeks and, like the poor guy stressing about his wedding night, I'll try to make this interesting.

First of all, I could not have gone through this without the help of several close friends plus my daughter Rocki, who arrived at the hospital post-op to take care of me for several days. This shoulder saga began with diagnosis from my primary physician, Dr. David Long, who sent me to Slocum Center for Orthopedics and Sports Medicine in Eugene. I am blessed to have close RN friends like Kath Schonau, who took me to Slocum. From the minute we walked in the door and were met by a gracious "greeter," I knew I was in for a positive experience. Everyone at Slocum is the epitome of professional efficiency. No waiting, no hassle, no confusion. I half expected to be handed a bouquet of roses.

The surgeon, Dr. Rudy Hoellrich, is well known for complete

shoulder replacements and he gave me an immediate sense of confidence. Kath made sure all my medical information was accurate. (Macular degeneration prevents me from reading regular print, but Dr. John Haines is taking good care of me). Our next trip to Eugene was for more pre-op tests, then a visit to Sacred Heart Riverbend Hospital to meet with the anesthesia people.

Now we get to the fun part called Surgery Day. Louise Waarvick and Lin Lindly drove me to the hospital, insisting on staying over to make sure I survived the surgery. How does anyone go through such an ordeal without friends? Beats me. Nurses took over, put me in a gown and warm socks, and soon I was on a gurney getting acquainted with Dr. Dan

Hagengruber is the world's friendliest anesthesiologist, not to mention he is eye candy (which I just mentioned). While Dr. Dan was prepping me for surgery, we launched into the most interesting exchange, with me asking why he chose his medical field and him asking me what I did. Here's what (I'm pretty sure) was said.

> Dr. Dan: "So what do you do?"
>
> Me: "I'm a writer, non-fiction, preferably upbeat stuff. I write a column for the Newport *News-Times* and occasional stories for *Chicken Soup for the Soul*."
>
> Dr. Dan: "Give me an example of a subject."
>
> Me: "Well, for instance, every other Christmas I write about how I hate fruitcake and that someone said a fruitcake weighs more than the oven it was cooked in."
>
> Dr. Dan: (laughing) "I hate fruitcake, too, and I personally think a fruitcake would make a good boat anchor!"

Good Grief

He had me laughing, and it wasn't because of the happy drugs. (Or maybe it was). I told him to give his card to my female friends in the waiting room just in case I write about my surgery experience. He followed through, and Dr. Dan is now a fan of this column.

The two nights and two days in the hospital meant a ton of attention from nurses, the physical therapist, and an occupational therapist. During discharge, I was given a card signed by everyone who took care of me. How cool is that?

I was anxious to get home and back to Lap Sitter, who is finally forgiving me for disrupting her life, even though Gina Nielsen showers her with TLC. I owe so many thanks to all of you who sent cards to the *News-Times* and get-well greetings to my home. Friends brought food and flowers, and when I hit a nasty bump in the road (either from the pain meds or something else) my dear nurse friend, Marylou Mate, dragged me kicking and screaming to the emergency room.

I went for my first post-op checkup with Dr. Rudy the other day, and he is as much fun as Dr. Dan. Why? Because nurse friends tipped me off that Dr. Rudy has Black Angus cattle and we got into a spirited discussion about the cattle roundup I'm going to with local favorite vet, Dr. Eric Brown. Dr. Rudy and I had such fun discussing cattle. One of us got into big trouble trying to change a bull calf into a steer, but that's all the detail you're getting. Consequently, I forgot to ask several questions about my shoulder recovery. Oh well, there is always the phone, although Dr. Rudy seemed very pleased about the progress I have made already with the help of Newport's very gifted physical therapist, Karen Smith.

That's it for today, with the hope you have found this medical report somewhat interesting, although not nearly as titillating as the poor guy being the sixth husband of a famous actress whose name I will not disclose.

With much appreciation to all of you who stepped up in one way or another to support me on this recent journey.

John Haines, M.D.
My friend and ophthalmologist

'Where My House Go, Mama?'

If you have lost everything in a disaster, you never forget it. When I watch the news of fires raging in Washington, Oregon, California, and other states, I get that old familiar painful feeling bordering on nausea. When I watch the cameras pan the faces of a family staring at the smoldering ruins of what had been their home, I want to go and hold them in my arms and tell them it's OK to cry.

A long time ago, I lived in the hills of Los Angeles with my physician husband, our little girl Rocki, three dogs, and a Siamese cat. Little did I know that on that hot, windy morning in November of 1961 my life—and the lives of hundreds of other people—was about to radically change.

At 8 a.m., I put my daughter and our new puppy into my Renault and left the house, following my husband in his car. I dropped off the pup at the vet to be wormed, and headed to our office to begin a busy day of seeing patients. Rocki literally grew up on a blanket next to my desk, playing with an assortment of toys. At 10:30, a patient came in and said, "Wow, that's quite a fire going on in Bel Air." My heart almost stopped beating. We immediately hit the freeway, breaking speed limits to get to our home. We could see balls of fire flying over the San Diego freeway, blown by the fierce Santa Ana winds from the east.

At the bottom of our hill were fire trucks and firemen who were not allowing anyone into the area. They said it was too dangerous, that the fire was out of control, that there was no water pressure to fight it anyway.

I stood by my car, clutching my daughter, feeing scared and helpless. When my ex-marine husband saw my tears, he yelled at me, "No crying!" Two days later, we were allowed to go up the hill and, of course, I was desperately praying the animals had somehow survived, perhaps rescued by people fleeing the flames. Not one house was left on our entire street, just chimneys sticking up. Other people were standing in the street, staring at their property in disbelief. I can still hear my little girl saying, "Where my house go, Mama?"

We knew right away the dogs had died, but I left a description of the cat at every animal shelter in L.A. Three weeks later, a shelter in Santa Monica said they had picked up a Siamese that had obviously been in a fire. It's funny about children. They often don't see what we see. Rocki walked right up to the cat in the cage and said, "Where you been, Ching-a-Ling?" She didn't notice how his fur was singed off and his whiskers gone. It took months to nurse Ching back to health, but for the rest of his life, he ran out of the room if someone lit a cigarette.

Here are some lessons learned when you are caught in a disaster and lose everything you own. You learn tables and chairs can be replaced, but you mourn the things that are irreplaceable, like bronzed baby shoes and pets. You learn that strong relationships grow even stronger, but shaky ones eventually fall apart, as mine did later no matter how hard I tried to hold it together. Did I ever cry? Yes, so keep reading for the rest of the story.

I eventually met and fell in love with Burt Lippman. Truthfully, Rocki loved him first and told me to grab him because I "wasn't getting any younger." The three of us, plus new dogs and cats, settled down to a very happy life. In 1977, I met a great new friend named Judy who lived in Bel Air, my old neighborhood. Judy and her family bought actor Burt Lancaster's house. The Lancasters had been neighbors of ours, their home also destroyed in that fire, but they rebuilt an even bigger place. However, like me, their marriage also fell apart. Judy, her husband and four sons had their own racquetball court and I became a regular player with Judy.

One day after a game, as I drove away from her home, my car turned right instead of left, and I found myself parked in front of where I lived before the fire. Of course, nothing looked the same, but suddenly the memories of the fire that wiped out 500 homes came flooding back. It took 16 years to release the tears, and I sat in my car sobbing until there were no more tears left. It was incredibly cathartic. I went home, sat down at my typewriter, and put it all into words on paper. Then I stuffed the story into an envelope and sent it to the *Los Angeles Times*. To my utter shock, the editor called, said they were "buying my manuscript," and I would be receiving a check, which turned out to be an amazing amount of money. To me, being paid for spilling my guts was not only a validation, but a message that finally becoming a professional writer was such a gift there was no way not to share every penny with those less fortunate—a practice I have happily continued to this day.

With so many states tinder dry, there are bound to be more fires and more heartbroken families losing their homes. The least any of us can do is to say a prayer for these people, but especially for the safety of the hundreds from all over the world who have signed on to help fight the fires.

Towanda!

Towanda—Definition: A word used to express extreme excitement while doing something crazy.

If you have lived in the same place for a long time, some people (especially women) are in tune with various household sounds, be they ever so subtle. When I was a teenager and tried to sneak up to my room after a date, my mom could tell it was me on the stairs even though I avoided the one with the annoying squeak. I could not get to my room until giving her a report of my evening. It ticked me off that this rule did not apply to my brothers. Meanwhile, Dad slept through everything.

In this column, I always make a point not to rave about a particular person, profession, or performance unless the experience is so great, or so unusual that it boggles my mind. Such an event happened recently when I was still stuck, due to shoulder surgery, wearing a sling 24/7. Trying to get a good night's sleep in that thing was a challenge, so I would often lie awake listening to the ocean and the purring of Lap Sitter curled up next to me.

I suddenly became aware that the icemaker in the kitchen fridge was not dropping ice cubes. I drink a lot of ice water, as friends can testify, and I take ice water to bed with me. Curiosity won out, and I headed for the kitchen. To my horror, the 20-year-old refrigerator had died and the freezer compartment was already dripping. It was almost midnight, and I started to panic. Both the freezer and the fridge were full of perishables,

Good Grief

much of which had been donated by friends who love to cook and know I don't.

What to do? I finally realized there were three options: (1) go back to bed; (2) call someone to help me; or (3) figure out how to transport all the perishables from the kitchen, down the steps, and across the garage to the fridge/freezer we brought with us from L.A. 10 years ago.

Options A and B were not options. I admit to being mad at Burt for not being here to help me, and I was mad at my brother Paul for living in Omaha. How irrational is that? I was also frustrated having one arm in the sling and knowing it would be really stupid to take it off. Let me describe the sling in case you are picturing an old dishtowel holding up my arm—fat chance. The sling is an engineering nightmare, full of heavy-duty Velcro straps that fit into itty-bitty little slots. When I first took it off to do my physical therapy homework, I could not figure out how to get back into it. So I called a friend who understands engineering. She was here in 10 minutes and figured out the sling in another five.

Back to that night. There is something to be said about being a stubborn Swede, and a frugal one at that. I could not stand the thought of wasting all that good food. I propped open the door leading to the garage, got a tray I could balance on my right hip with one arm, and started VERY CAREFULLY carried a few items at a time. After two-dozen trips, I quit counting, but with the very last trek, I stopped in the middle of the garage and yelled "TOWANDA!"

In case you never saw the movie *Fried Green Tomatoes*, starring Kathy Bates and Jessica Tandy, the Kathy Bates character starts out as a wimpy woman with absolutely no self-esteem or sense of her inner power. Eventually, she discovers that she does have power that she is not just a wimpy housewife, and you hear her triumphant battle cry of "Towanda!"

The point is, hindered as I was by the darn sling, I managed to schlep all the food to safety. So, that's why, in the middle of the night, in the middle of the garage, I yelled "Towanda!" Then I fell into an exhausted sleep, happy about saving all that food, but not happy about having to get a new refrigerator.

Here's a word of advice to you women with husbands who handle the major household hassles: Pay attention because one day you might have to handle things by yourself. I vaguely remembered Burt calling a local appliance company who sent someone right away to fix whatever wasn't working. Burt really liked and trusted this guy. After doing a computer search, I called a name that seemed familiar, and it did not take long for the same man to come to my rescue. While I sat on a kitchen stool watching and hoping the 20-year-old fridge was fixable, he pulled off the back panel, said the compressor was fine but a little thingy called a relay switch was all it needed. He was sure he had one in his truck. Soon the fridge was humming again and I was incredibly relieved.

I believe in giving credit where credit is due. While sitting on that stool, I could not help but think of women living alone, needing help and not knowing how safe it is (or isn't) to let somebody into your home. Hats off to Larry at Walch's Appliance in Waldport for being an efficient and honest gentleman. He probably had no idea—although he does now—how important this whole experience was to me. I would call on him again in a heartbeat, but not at midnight.

"Towanda!"

All Aboard

Jeremy deserves credit for inspiring today's subject, although I will probably never see him again. You meet people on your path through life and your time together might be a moment or last a lifetime.

Last weekend I attended a lovely wedding held at the Oregon Coast Aquarium. I have been to the Aquarium dozens of times through the years, but never for the occasion of a wedding —and what a beautiful and classy wedding it was.

After the ceremony, all the guests were seated at tables of eight for the wedding dinner. On my left was a gentleman named Jeremy. He was so unusually interesting and fun it was impossible to resist his charms. This was not the sort of dinner where you have to be quiet and sedate. Jeremy asked if I would like to know about one of his favorite things. Being of curious nature, I said, "Sure." Jeremy then scrunched up his face, and out of his mouth (and maybe also his nose) came the exact sound of a train whistle, loud and clear. When he saw my look of amazement, he repeated this talent several times. Of course he had no idea how much I love trains.

I turned on my cell phone, sent myself an email, and held the phone to his ear. His eyes went wide when the incoming mail sounded a train whistle. He was mildly impressed, but already on to other fascinating things, like how he also loves trains, had actually been on a train but not when it was going anywhere. I told him he absolutely had to take a train trip someday. I wanted to know more about him, but it was time for our table to head for the buffet line. I will never forget Jeremy. He might just be the most interesting male I have met in a long time. Oh, by the way, did I mention that Jeremy is 7 years old?

A certain day brightener has been showing up in my mail for weeks, begging to be shared with you. The first person who sent it to me was Dr. Bruce Mate, who changed it a bit by making it more personal. I hope it touches your heart as it has mine. Here is Bruce's email, word for word.

The train of life. (Author unknown).

At birth, we boarded the train and met our parents and we believe they will always travel by our side. However, at some station our parents will step down from the train, leaving us on this journey alone. As time goes by, other people will board the train; some will be significant—our siblings, friends, children, and even the love of our life. Many will step down and leave a permanent vacuum. Others will go so unnoticed that we don't realize they vacated their seats. This train ride will be full of joy, sorrow, fantasy, expectations, hellos, goodbyes, and farewells.

Success consists of having a good relationship with all passengers, requiring that we give the best of ourselves and mindfully watch for new passengers getting on board along the way.

The mystery to everyone is we do not know at which station we ourselves will step down. So we must live in the best way, love, forgive, and offer the best of who we are. It is important to do this because when the time comes for us to step down and leave our seat empty, we should leave behind beautiful memories for those who will continue to travel on the train of life.

I wish you a joyful journey on the train of life. Reap success and give lots of love. More importantly, thank God for the journey. Lastly, I thank you for being one of the passengers on my train.

By the way, I am not planning to get off the train anytime soon, but if I do, just remember I am glad you were part of my journey and that as friends we have shared love.

And now, dear readers, I hope you will pass this on to someone you care about. If Jeremy ever crosses my path again, you will certainly hear about it.

Female Fortitude

I have been pondering the differences between men and women. Well, not all of them, of course. Two thirds of my mail comes from women and the rest (well, duh) from men. I enjoy all of it, but regret not being able to send replies. My eyes get tired, and it's all I can do to get this column written. Today the focus is on females and friendship. I do know two women who either don't need or want close friendships with other women. It makes me sad because I don't understand it, and I gave up long ago trying to establish what to most women is a regular relationship.

Men, on the other hand, do things with male buddies but it seems to usually be sports related, and I doubt guys sit around discussing their most intimate feelings about hair color.

I have enjoyed female friendships all my life and have kept in touch with many—particularly the ones who are still living.

I met Teresa when we were goofy teenagers and now she sends the best jokes, like this one: Handyman wife texts husband on a cold winter morning: "Windows frozen, won't open." Husband texts back: "Pour some lukewarm water over it and gently tap edges with hammer." Wife texts back five minutes later. "Computer really messed up now."

How difficult it would have been getting through the loss of my husband, Burt, without the support of women friends. I think of them as my army of angels, and new women keep joining the ranks. How blessed is this?

A great many gals in my so-called army believe in having a

bucket list, and we often discuss various challenges or goals. It doesn't have to be a big thing, like sky diving or trekking across Africa. For 25 years, I wanted to spend one night alone at the Sylvia Beach Hotel in Nye Beach. My husband didn't quite understand it, but he was always a good sport about quirky things I wanted to do. And so I reserved the Jane Austin room, took along a good book, and loved staying in a place with no jangling phones or blaring television. I did invite Burt to join me for dinner (the food is the best-kept secret in town), and the whole experience was delightful.

And now to the main attraction of today's column.

Not long ago, a group of us spontaneously decided to take in a matinee at the local Cineplex because we are all fans of Meryl Streep. The movie turned out to be better than we expected and when we left the theater, we wanted the fun to keep on going, so we all went to dinner. It was one of those perfect summer days in Newport, and we ate outside on the patio.

Suddenly, Pat Lewis said, "I think I'm ready to go down that slide now." For those of you who live out of the area, there is a playground park with great equipment including an enclosed tube slide. Pat has been talking about that slide for over a year. She put it on her bucket list because she is claustrophobic and wanted to conquer her fear. We tried to tell her the slide is just a slide, not an MRI machine. Before she could chicken out, we quickly paid our bill and hurried to the little park, which was full of children and big people.

At this point, Pat had no choice but to go through with it, especially when Louise Waarvick and Janet Anton escorted her bodily up the hill, stuffed her into the slide, then followed her down. Those of us who stayed on the ground could hear the muffled screaming from inside the tube. Our job was to whip out cell phones and get photographic proof that Pat Lewis had indeed wiped another thing off her bucket list.

You go girl. We are all so proud of you for feeling the fear and doing it anyway. Hooray for the support of women friends! Long may we wave!

One final chuckle is from my friend Teresa: How do you get a sweet little 80-year-old lady to say a bad word? Answer: You get another sweet little 80-year-old lady to yell, "BINGO!"

Pat Lewis (center) checked an item off her bucket list when she slid down the tube at Coast Park in Newport. With Janet Anton (left) and Louise Waarvick

That Cheatin' Heart

Spousal cheating has never appeared in this column—it never occurred to me until now, and here is why this awful, but seemingly universal subject has reared its ugly head.

Last week I wrote about how women get together and throw all sorts of subjects into the ring for discussion. Most women at some time in life have had to deal with a straying male, even if it was that dude in high school who broke your heart. Right now, I know two women who decided to leave their cheating mates.

I have become emotionally strong enough to start going through boxes and boxes of photos, plus a tall stack of albums. It's not fair to leave it all to the kids. Of course, I'm setting aside the pictures I can't stand to part with, at least for now. A few women say they are going to do it, should do it, but keep putting it off. Oh well, I can only do what seems right for me.

My aging parents set an example years ago when they gathered my brothers and me into their living room. On the floor was an enormous pile of photos, most of them the old-fashioned black and white ones, mounted on cardboard—photos of long-dead relatives from the old country. My brothers and I were ordered to divvy up the pile. Our mom had lost her sight, and dad did not give a hoot about those pictures (my share is in our attic).

This brings me now to the album full of our wedding pictures. Just turning those pages floods me with memories of that joyous day Burt and I were married in an airplane. After the reception, we took off to honeymoon in Hawaii. More photos, including ones we took while lounging by the hotel pool, too lazy to walk down to the beach. I was half dozing when Burt poked me, wanting me to notice that a famous celebrity was walking our way from the beach, hand in hand with a beautiful babe.

Now the plot thickens. At the time, I was a member of a Los Angeles charity group of women, many of whom had been in show business and all of whom were married to very successful men. This group threw a lot of fancy fundraising parties and as soon as they met Burt, they wanted him to be auctioneer, master of ceremonies, or other jazzy jobs because he knew how to add bounce to a ballroom. A new member named Jane (not her real name) was recruited because she was married to a very famous TV personality. Let's call him Mike.

Meanwhile, back on that Hawaiian beach. Mike and the gorgeous gal were wearing dark shades as they walked towards us. So was I. Here is where one learns the big lesson called "never assume." As they passed by our chairs, I raised my sunglasses and merrily chirped, "Hi, Jane." Only it wasn't Jane. They both sailed on by, pretending I hadn't opened my big mouth. End of story, except a few weeks later when I attended the monthly meeting of my charity group and saw the "official" Jane. If you are thinking I should have told her about Hawaii and her unfaithful husband, no way. I felt badly for her, but grateful for a guy like Burt. Note: she eventually divorced the jerk.

Yes, it's a difficult task letting go of so many photos, but I have a heart full of happy memories and a whole lot of gratitude for having been blessed with a great marriage. And now for a day brightener that certainly fits today's subject.

A man calls home to his wife and says, "Honey, I have been

Good Grief

asked to fly to Canada with my boss and several of his friends for fishing. We'll be gone for a long weekend. This is a good opportunity for me to get that promotion I've been wanting, so could you please pack enough clothes for a three-day weekend, and also would you get out my rod and tackle box from the attic? We're leaving at 4:30 p.m. from the office, and I will swing by the house to pick my things up. Oh, and please pack my new navy blue silk pajamas."

The wife thinks this sounds a bit odd, but being the good wife, she does exactly what her husband asked. Following the long weekend, he came home a little tired, but otherwise looking good. The wife welcomes him and asks if he caught many fish. He says, "Yes, lots of walleyes, some bass and a few pike. But," he continued, "why didn't you pack my new blue silk pajamas like I asked you to do?" (You'll love the answer.) The wife replies, "I did, they're in your tackle box." Never ever try to outsmart a woman!

Somewhere in the attic is the plastic bag full of those ancient black and white photos. I figure it will take me about 20 minutes to dispatch them into the recycle bin. No pain, all gain, and daughter Rocki will owe me one.

G Strings And Other Embarrassments

I have been cleaning out my husband's files and ran across a copy of a short essay he wrote years ago. It triggered an idea for today, but as often happens, you need to know the back-story. I had totally forgotten about that essay, but it will be shared with you at the end of this column.

Last week, I wrote about a women's fancy-schmancy charity group I once belonged to in Los Angeles. Somehow Burt's essay reminded me of the time when at least a dozen members decided it might be fun to go as a group to see the famous male dancers known as The Chippendales, performing at a club in Beverly Hills. None of us had ever seen these guys who are known for their perfectly sculpted bodies and their dancing ability, which is primarily aimed at titillating a female audience.

Since I'm usually game for a new adventure, I agreed to go. Burt, being a very secure male, had no problem with this—in fact, he was working late that night and the plan was for me to carpool with some of these women and Burt would pick me up after the show. It did not occur to me to share this information with the women.

The Chippendales lived up to their reputation, danced their well-muscled legs off, and the mainly female audience screamed and giggled and had a great time. I probably should mention these guys were all about 20 years old and wore Speedos. Why? Because they could! Seems to me their youth, plus 18 hours a day in a gym, had something to do with their physiques.

Now for the unexpected. We all exited the theater and there stood Burt, waiting for me as planned. Every single woman in my group started yelling, "Oh no, there's Burt Lippman. Quick, hide!" To my amazement, some of them ran back into the theater and some hid behind pillars. That's when it dawned on me none of these women had told their husbands they were going to see The Chippendales. I found out later they were terrified their guys would disapprove, and so they made up stories—like attending a book club meeting. I reassured them that Burt would not blow their cover and tell their husbands the truth. And of course, he never did, but we laughed about this incident for years.

People who knew my husband know that he loved sharing every aspect of my life—either directly or indirectly. When the Oregon Coast Community College first opened, I was asked to teach creative writing for adults, which I had never done, but they made an offer I couldn't refuse. To me, teaching was another challenge, and the classes were loaded.

The hardest part was reading, grading, and critiquing the work handed in by students. It was truthfully overwhelming because every single person wrote two or three pages on whatever subject I threw at them. The subjects were universal, sort of, like what you read in this column. For instance, "Write about the very first kitchen you can remember." Another subject was "Your first bathroom." Everyone grew up with some kind of a kitchen and bathroom, right? I asked them to pull out all the stops using descriptive words that would make the reader (me) feel as if I had walked into their childhood kitchen or bathroom, even if it was an outhouse.

Burt was so keenly interested in my classes and the writing assignments that his right brain (the creative side) fired up, and he felt motivated to write. Although he had no interest in attending the classes, he wanted me to read his work and share my reaction. His essay about the Brooklyn bathroom he grew up with is priceless, and it appeared in the *News-Times* years ago. Perhaps it will again one of these days because it will be new to all of you new readers.

Now, as promised, this is what he came up with when I asked the class to "Write about an embarrassing moment."

The night my G-string failed me, by Burt Lippman

I had rehearsed the routine for months. Years of training and study brought me to the time when I was ready to think of exposing myself to critical review. I was dressed for the part. The music started, and I fidgeted backstage, waiting for my cue to go out and perform. Thoughts of "what if..." ran through my mind as I spent those several minutes waiting for my turn.

I was finally introduced. I walked to stage center ready to display my talent, ready to take those years of training and studying my routine and perform in public. I nearly froze as I looked out at the audience until I saw familiar faces—my mom and dad. I relaxed and began my performance. After about two minutes, it happened. My G-string snapped.

I had been instructed how to handle the situation should that happen. I calmly smiled at the audience and asked for their patience while I replaced the G-string... on my violin.

Good job, Burt. I am so grateful for finding ways to keep your wonderful memory alive.

Burt's Bucks

When I met my husband Burt in 1969, he kept a $2 bill in his wallet, which he said was for luck. Whenever he bought a new leather wallet, he kept the old one, and the $2 bill. After his death, I gave away all the wallets except the one he had in his pocket on the day he died—and I have carried that $2 bill with me, not necessarily for luck, but because it was special to Burt.

Yesterday, I was lurking around on the Internet and ran into the following hilarious story. It may or may not be true, but I found it astounding, and so will you if you are of a certain age.

The Taco Bell Story. (Author unknown)

On my way home from work, I stopped at Taco Bell for a quick bite to eat. In my billfold were a $50 bill and a $2 bill. I figure that with a $2 bill, I could get something to eat and not have to worry about anyone getting irritated at me for trying to break a $50 bill.

Me: "Hi, I'd like one seven-layer burrito, please, to go." Server: "That'll be $1.04. Eat in?" Me: "No, it's to go." At this point, I open my billfold and hand him the $2 bill. He looks at it kind of funny. Server: "Uh, hang on a sec, I'll be right back."

He goes to talk to his manager, but still within my earshot. The following conversation occurs between the two of them. Server: "Hey, you ever see a $2 bill?" Manager: "No. A what?" Server: "A $2 bill. This guy just gave it to me." Manager: "Ask for something else. There's no such thing as a $2 bill." Server: "Yeah, thought so."

He comes back to me and says, "We don't take these. Do you

have anything else?" Me: "Just this 50. You don't take $2 bills? Why?" Server: "I don't know." Me: "See here where it says legal tender?" Server: "Yeah." Me: "So, why won't you take it?" Server: "Well, hang on a sec."

He goes back to his manager who has been watching me like I'm a shoplifter and says to him, "He says I have to take it." Manager: "Doesn't he have anything else?" Server: "Yeah, a 50. I'll get it and you can open the safe and get change." Manager: "I'm not opening the safe with him in here." Server: "What should I do?" Manager: "Tell him to come back later when he has real money." Server: "I can't tell him that! You tell him." Manager: "Just tell him." Server: "No way! This is weird. I'm going in back."

The manager approaches me and says, "I'm sorry, but we don't take big bills this time of night." Me: "It's only seven o'clock! Well then, here's a $2 bill." Manager: "We don't take those, either." Me: "Why not?" Manager: "I think you know why." Me: "Not really, tell me why." Manager: "Please leave before I call mall security." Me: "Excuse me?" Manager: "Please leave before I call mall security." Me: "What on earth for?" Manager: "Please, sir." Me: "Uh, go ahead, call them." Manager: "Would you please just leave?" Me: "No." Manager: "Fine. Have it your way then." Me: "Hey, that's Burger King, isn't it?"

At this point, he backs away from me and calls mall security. I have two people staring at me from the dining area, and I begin laughing out loud, just for effect. A few minutes later, this 45-year-oldish guy comes in. Guard: "Yeah, Mike, what's up?" Manager (whispering): "This guy is trying to give me some (pause) funny money."

Guard: "No kidding! What?" Manager: "Get this... a $2 bill." Guard (incredulous): "Why would a guy fake a $2 bill?" Manager: "I don't know. He's kinda weird. He says the only other thing he has is a 50." Guard: "Oh, so the 50 is fake?" Manager: "No, the $2 bill is." Guard: "Why would he fake a $2

Good Grief

bill?" Manager: "I don't know! Can you talk to him, and get him out of here?" Guard: "Yeah."

Security guard walks over to me. Guard: "Mike here tells me you have some fake bills you're trying to use." Me: "Uh, no." Guard: "Lemme see 'em." Me: "Why?" Guard: "Do you want me to get the cops in here?"

At this point I am ready to say, "Sure, please!" but I want to eat, so I say, "I'm just trying to buy a burrito and pay for it with this $2 bill." I put the bill up near his face, and he flinches like I'm taking a swing at him.

He takes the bill, turns it over a few times in his hands, and says, Hey, Mike, what's wrong with this bill?" Manager: "It's fake." Guard: "It doesn't look fake to me." Manager: "But it's a $2 bill." Guard: "Yeah?" Manager: "Well, there's no such thing, is there?"

The security guard and I both look at him like he's an idiot, and it dawns on the guy that he has no clue. So, it turns out that my burrito was free, and he threw in a small drink and some of those cinnamon thingies, too. It made me want to get a whole stack of $2 bills just to see what happens when I try to buy stuff. If I got the right group of people, I could probably end up in jail. You get free food there, too!

Such a crazy experience is never happening to me because I have no intention of ever spending Burt's relic. I still can't believe there are young people who have never seen a $2 bill. Amazing!

A Remarkable Response

Last week, the subject of this column was an old $2 bill I found in my husband's wallet when he died, a bill he had carried with him for more than 50 years. The column included a funny account about a guy trying to buy a burrito at Taco Bell and pay for it with a $2 bill. The young servers at Taco Bell had never seen a $2 bill and accused the man of using "fake money."

Little did I know that readers all across the country would find the subject interesting until the emails started pouring in, even from New York. One reader wrote that her search turned up the fact the $2 bill was once used to pay prostitutes. Then she added, "I guess things were a lot cheaper back then."

I heard from women who found out their husbands also kept a $2 bill in their wallets for luck. I heard from readers who immediately started researching the history of the $2 bill, and the emails kept getting longer and longer until my eyeballs glazed over.

There's not enough space in this column to use all the names and information, so I've narrowed it down to a few examples, and the last one will be a surprise to you, as it certainly was to me. Here goes:

> "I grew up in Kansas and we had $2 bills, but the saying was if you kept the bill as a keepsake in your billfold or purse, it was bad luck if the bill didn't have a small corner torn off." —*Art Bradley, Otter Rock.*

"Another great column. How you make things fun and

Good Grief

poignant at the same time always amazes me. Now a $2 bill will even be more special to me. We like to get them from the bank and give them as tips. The servers are always thrilled if one is included. Almost all of them say they either save them or give them to their kids. Years ago, we used to go to Las Vegas. The MGM Grand Casino would sell them at the main cage in checkbook-like holders of 50. We'd get one there and it would last for a long time." —*Barbara and Bill McHorney, Laughlin, Nevada.*

This from Newport readers Susan and John Painter (who is a former newspaper reporter). Susan sent a photo of John's $2 bill.

"John and I howled at the Taco Bell story. The back-story about John's $2 bill is he used it as a bookmark. I happened to find it and noticed it was autographed—by Gerald Ford! Turns out, when he interviewed Ford on Air Force One in 1976, all he had for Ford to autograph—other than his reporter notebook—was that bill. So Ford autographed it. When I found it, I felt it deserved more recognition, so I had it framed—along with an autographed photo taken by then White House press photograph David Kennerly of John doing the interview. It's on our Air Force One wall in our house." —*Susan Elizabeth Reese, LLC, Trial Lawyer.*

This is the most amazing one. I have no idea who this gentleman is or where he saw the story.

"Bobbie, I just came across your article about Burt's bucks and the $2 bill he kept in his wallet. I am the producer/director of a recently completed documentary all about the $2 bill. I have learned of countless stories like Burt's, and they always fascinate me. I would also like to tell you that the Taco Bell story is completely true. I found the person it happened to, and he is in the documentary, re-telling the story. I'm sure the entire film will be of interest to you, so keep an eye out for it. You can see the preview on: www.2dollarbillmovie.com Perhaps down the road I can get you a DVD so you can watch it." —*John Bennardo*

I strongly suggest you click on the website and watch the trailer. It is beautifully done and you will learn even more interesting facts about the $2 bill. I thought there would be a different subject this week, but you know the old saying, "The best laid plans of mice and men (and women)...." This column does have a way of taking me down new and unexplored roads.

WHEN WE DANCED WITH DENNY

November is National Hospice Month, and the subject of hospice is very important to me. I got involved with the hospice movement back in the 1970s and, after 13 weeks of training, became a volunteer on a Los Angeles hospital hospice ward.

With at least eight to 10 people dying there at any given time, I was like a sponge, learning, listening, helping, and knowing I had found what I call "a work of the heart."

When we moved to the Oregon Coast, I started writing about hospice and the positive end-of-life blessing it can be for both patient and families. Before long, hospice care became available here and the local hospital asked me to write a hospice story for their publication. "Keep it upbeat and positive," they said, and "add some humor if possible." I did not use Denny's real name for that story, but I have stayed in close touch with his wife, Sally, who gave me permission to write the whole story for the *News-Times*, with no holds barred.

Were you raised, as I was, that one must always be somber around the sick and dying? I've learned from experience that people die pretty much as they have lived. If a person spent a lifetime being uptight and easily angered, they often exit the same way—mad at God and mad at the world. But if someone has always enjoyed a sense of humor, the last thing they want hovering around their deathbed is doom and gloom faces.

I'm not sure how I first met Denny and Sally, but when Denny was diagnosed with inoperable cancer, they called me for help and I handpicked a group of hospice volunteers so Sally could continue working. Denny's needs were taken care of at home, and Sally had peace of mind. During those months when his disease progressed, I spent more and more time at their home and even began going back in the evenings.

Denny had a droll sense of humor, which was infectious. Sometimes I stayed over, sleeping on a futon next to Denny's bed so Sally could get some much-needed sleep. Late one night, it was necessary to help him stand upright while Sally changed the bedding and his wet pajama bottoms. With his arms wrapped around my neck to keep his balance, he looked at me, grinned and asked, "May I have this dance?"

I often recruited my husband Burt to help with male patients, and somewhere along the line, he and Denny formed a bond. As Christmas 1988 approached, Denny asked that the house be decorated, including a tree. And he wanted us there for Christmas Eve. As I write this, it feels as if all happened yesterday. Denny was able (with help) to sit with us in their living room. Here is a direct quote from Sally in an email:

> I remember listening to Christmas music and the raucous voices of the sea lions on the docks below. Both of us treasured the view of lights on the boats in Yaquina Bay. Burt, you, Denny, and I chuckled several times during that evening together, and I remember Burt escorting Denny to the bathroom. I had covered the bathroom mirror with a beach towel so Denny couldn't see how thin he'd grown. He thanked me for doing that when he first noticed the towel. As he and Burt made their way through the narrow door, I heard Denny say something about saving this dance for Burt.

Good Grief

There are those reading this who knew Sally through the Lincoln County School District and as a Nye Beach Montessori teacher, and Denny Lund through his work with the Hatfield Marine Science Center. In Sally's email, she recalls the thorough directions Denny had written down, especially regarding the distribution of his ashes.

> Some of the ashes went to his mother's garden in Corvallis, some sprinkled on the Deschutes River by three of his best friends. Some to Sitka, Alaska, where a former fisheries student from his Aquaculture Technician Training Program at Sheldon Jackson College spread ashes in various spots along the Indian River where the salmon eggs that Denny raised in the hatchery returned each year to spawn.

Denny died January 23, 1989. He was only 41 years old. Sally and I drove north of Newport to scatter some of his ashes over the ocean, and just as we did, we were amazed to see snowflakes falling. When I think back to that Christmas Eve, I recall things Denny taught me. I truly believe the dying are our greatest teachers. One day as I was feeding him soup, he suddenly quoted Peter Pan: "Dying can be a very great adventure." Thank you Denny for what you brought to the lives of so many—and thank you Sally for giving me your blessing to write this. I will always remember when Burt and I got to "dance with Denny."

Note: Sally is now happily married to a wonderful man named Carl. They live in Anacortes, Washington, and have invited me to visit. Of course, the trip is on my bucket list, and I plan to make it happen.

Otherwise

If you are hoping for humor in today's column, there won't be any. As I face a blank computer screen, there is no way to ignore the horror of the mass shooting in France. However, I have never gone political in this column and am not starting now. Maybe you also feel there is a sad and somber blanket lying over the land, and perhaps the only constructive thing we can do is pray.

Last Friday night I attended the annual Light Up A Life hospice ceremony during which names were read of people served by our local hospice and also the names of other loved ones who are no longer here. I have been attending and supporting this event for years and never in my memory has the Light Up A Life ceremony been so special. This was the first year that it took take place in the new Samaritan Pacific Communities Hospital Center for Health Education.

As attendees joined the crowd entering the dimly lit room, we were all handed a long-stemmed rose, a program, and a votive candle (the kind you turn on with a little switch). The candle represents a loved one, and you place it with the others in a special rack at the front of the room. Someone was softly playing a flute. On a large screen, a video showed peaceful ocean scenes. I was there primarily to honor my husband Burt. While waiting for the program to begin, I kept thinking of a special piece of writing. Here it is:

Otherwise. (Author unknown)

I got out of bed on two strong legs. It might have been otherwise.

I ate cereal with milk and a sweet, ripe peach. It might have been otherwise.

I took the dog up the hill to the birch wood and all morning I did the work I love. At noon, I lay down with my mate. We ate dinner together. It might have been otherwise.

I slept in my bed and planned another day just like this day.

But one day I know it will be otherwise.

A young woman took the seat beside me. I think we both felt an instant connection as we exchanged names, and she told me she was recently widowed. We both shared our experiences that we had following the loss of our mates.

I felt comfortable telling her about Burt's love of birds, especially hummingbirds. He never let the feeder outside our kitchen window go empty, and I have continued to keep it filled. There is just something magical about those tiny birds, and the ones at our feeder stick around all winter, somehow managing to survive the coastal storms.

About two weeks after Burt's death, I remember the grief being so raw and physically painful—to be graphic, but honest, it felt as if my body had been cut in half and the other half was missing. I didn't know what to do with myself, other than walk aimlessly around the empty house while old Charley and Lap Sitter watched me with confused curiosity. I ended up standing on the front porch, crying and pleading with Burt to send me a sign to relieve the pain and let me know he wasn't far away. Suddenly, three hummingbirds showed up, circling around me twice on their tiny wings before flying away.

Only if you have dealt with terrible grief would you understand what a blessing those little birds were to me. It never happened again, and I guess it never needed to.

I told this story to my friend Linda Kilbride and it wasn't long before she called and asked to stop by, that she had something for me. It's a lovely, framed plaque of a hummingbird, with these words written in script: "Awake at dawn and give thanks for another day of living." —*Gibran*.

This morning, in heavy winds and rain, I watched three hummingbirds at the feeder outside the kitchen window. I read Linda's plaque as I often do and thought of the new friend I met at Light Up A Life. I asked for help in writing this column today.

I did get help, but it could have been otherwise.

THE WOMAN WHO COULD NOT STOP CRYING

Someone is grieving badly and most of us do not know what to say or do. Years of being involved with hospice have taught me many valuable lessons. The story that follows is almost unbelievable, but it truly happened. Since my stories have a way of circulating around the country, details have been changed to protect the family's privacy.

This story was written before Burt died. It was published in *Chicken Soup for the Soul: Grief and Recovery*. I chose to include it in this book because it is a valuable tool when helping someone deal with the loss of a loved one.

> **PART ONE.** Location: Los Angeles. Early on a Saturday morning I was on my way to run some errands. Up ahead on the street in our quiet neighborhood I could see red lights flashing and a crowd of people standing on the sidewalk. I slowed down, like most of us do, to check out the scene.
>
> To my horror, I saw a yellow tarp covering what had to be a body. Around the body were 8 or 9 scattered, broken bicycles. Having been an avid cyclist most of my life, I simply had to pull around the corner, park my car, and walk back to join the crowd of people who were quietly standing and staring.
>
> "What happened?" I asked a woman. She filled me in on what few details she knew.
>
> "There was this group of bicyclists," she said, "One of them had a flat tire, so they were all up on the sidewalk while one guy fixed the tire."

She stopped talking for a moment, then pointed at the covered body on the sidewalk. "A guy in a big truck came around the corner too fast, lost control, and plowed into all the bicyclists. Most of them have been taken away in ambulances, but that poor young man is dead."

I sat down on the curb. It seemed eerily quiet. The police were still marking the area with yellow tape and talking to the young driver of the truck. The truck itself had ended up on someone's lawn.

I never ran my errands. I could not leave and must have sat on that curb for over an hour. Eventually, I just went home, my heart aching for that young man and whoever loved him. It would be months before I would realize why I "happened" on that scene and why I could not tear myself away.

PART TWO. Location: Los Angeles, three months later. My granddaughter, Autumn, was working while in high school. One day she called me saying she had a huge favor to ask.

"You have to help," she pleaded. "I work with this woman whose son died a few months ago in some bike accident. She works for a while, then goes to the back and cries her heart out. You know how to help people and you have to do this."

Click went my brain. The bike accident. The young man under that yellow tarp. The son of a woman where Autumn worked.

I told Autumn I really had to think this through. Could I help without being intrusive? This woman did not know me and I didn't know her OR her son.

I went into what I call my "Quiet Zone," and came up with a plan, having no idea if it would work. I told Autumn to gently tell this woman that her grandma (me) did a lot of hospice stuff… and to explain hospice because this woman was from another culture and maybe didn't know all that hospice does.

Good Grief

Autumn was to give Saheema (not her real name) my phone number because maybe I could help with her grief.

I was honestly surprised when Saheema called and yes, she was crying on the phone. My intuition told me to see her on neutral ground... not my house and not her home.

I asked Saheema if she would meet me in a park. I described the park and a quiet place where we could sit at a picnic table and talk. The only time she could meet me was 7 a.m. Fine with me. Here's a tool you might use one day—I suggested Saheema bring family photo albums.

I got to the park first, with a big thermos of tea and two cups. I waited 10 minutes, thinking she wasn't going to show up. Then I saw her walking slowly and tentatively toward me, carrying several photo albums.

Yes, she was crying. I got up and helped her put all the albums on the table. Before we sat down, I opened my arms and she came to me for a hug. Neither one of us said a word for at least five minutes. I just held her, this tiny woman with a heavy accent from a far-away country, who could not stop crying. I'd brought plenty of tissues, but noticed Saheema used colorful real handkerchiefs.

We spent an hour together, drinking hot tea, and looking at pictures. As she slowly turned each page, naming the faces of her large and extended family, we lingered a long time on every picture of her son. Pictures of him as an infant, then as he grew up, school sports, college graduation. Her son was clearly the shining star in her family and particularly in her life. He was tall, dark, and movie star handsome.

By the time we closed the page of the last album, Saheema was no longer crying. She actually smiled a few times and just dabbed at her eyes. We never spoke of my hospice life, or even an "afterlife." We were just two women who knew what grief feels like, two women from different cultures whose paths just happened to cross....

I'd like to believe that Saheema began to heal that day. A lovely letter arrived from her about a week later saying, "Thank you for helping me and being interested in my family and my dear son."

I guess the best part was when Autumn told me Saheema was no longer going to the back room to cry.

I hope something in this very human story may help you to help someone who is grieving.

Death Is Nothing At All

Death is nothing at all,
I have only slipped away
into the next room.

I am I,
and you are you;
whatever we were to each other,
that, we still are.

Call me by my old familiar name,
speak to me in the easy way
which you always used,
put no difference in your tone,
wear no forced air
of solemnity or sorrow.

Laugh as we always laughed
at the little jokes we shared together.
Let my name ever be
the household word that it always was.
Let it be spoken without effect,
without the trace of a shadow on it.

Bobbie Lippman

Life means all
that it ever meant.
It is the same as it ever was.
There is unbroken continuity.

Why should I be out of mind
because I am out of sight?

I am waiting for you,
for an interval,
somewhere very near,
just around the corner.
All is well.

Henry Scott Holland
1847 - 1918

The first person who sent me this beautiful piece of writing was our dear friend Bruce Mate, who said it has given him great comfort since he lost his dad. When it kept showing up in my mail from people I know, or don't know, I printed it out to carry around and read whenever the blues set in—which continues with alarming regularity and without warning. But I've decided this has to be part of the Grief Journey.

About The Author

Bobbie Lippman has been a professional writer since 1977 when her first story sold to the *Los Angeles Times*. That story was about the pain of losing her home and dogs in a major California fire. Since then, her work appeared in numerous national newspapers, a woman's magazine in the United Kingdom, the Beijing, China, *World of English*, plus several *Chicken Soup for the Soul* volumes.

Bobbie hosted a radio show for several years called "Bobbie's Beat On The Air" for the visually impaired, starting when her mother lost her sight, and began listening to the Radio Talking-Book Network. These short human-interest programs aired in the Midwest, and then at a radio station in Portland, Oregon, serving the blind. The radio program segued into a show aired on KNPT radio in Newport, Oregon, which attracted a large audience of the blind as well as sighted people. Bobbie also taught Creative Writing at Oregon Coast Community College.

She lives in Seal Rock, Oregon, with her cat, Keeper, and Waldo her robot (Lap Sitter finally had to leave for cat heaven). Bobbie can be reached at: bobbisbeat@aol.com.

**Going Home
Burt, Bobbie, and the two miniature goats**